René Isidore Holaind

Natural Law and Legal Practice

Lectures

René Isidore Holaind

Natural Law and Legal Practice
Lectures

ISBN/EAN: 9783744653138

Printed in Europe, USA, Canada, Australia, Japan

Cover: Foto ©Andreas Hilbeck / pixelio.de

More available books at **www.hansebooks.com**

NATURAL LAW AND
LEGAL PRACTICE.

LECTURES DELIVERED AT THE LAW SCHOOL OF

GEORGETOWN UNIVERSITY

BY

RENÉ I. HOLAIND, S.J.,

*Professor of Ethics and Sociology, Woodstock College;
Lecturer on Natural and Canon Law, Georgetown University.*

NEW YORK, CINCINNATI, CHICAGO:
BENZIGER BROTHERS,
Printers to the Holy Apostolic See.
1899.

Copyright, 1899, by Benziger Brothers.

PREFACE.

In this century, political and social relations, commercial interests, and the opposite claims of Capital and Labor, of individual freedom and State authority, have grown so complex that the multiplication of legal safeguards has become a necessity of modern civilized life. We are far from the rugged conciseness of the Twelve Tables enlarged and amended by Pretorian edicts, or from the simplicity of Common Law, springing from customs, and supplemented by Parliamentary statutes: a modern jurist must be thoroughly acquainted with Constitutional Law, Law Merchant, Criminal Law, and the Law of Nations; each of these important branches of judicature is subdivided, and each subdivision requires individual treatment and special study. This complexity is bewildering, but unavoidable; for it is in keeping with the nature of the human mind, which cannot comprehend a whole subject at a glance, but must break it, as it were, into fragments, in order to master successively all its parts, and to conquer the difficulties one by one.

But if differentiation is called for, integration is no less needed: analysis presupposes principles, or needs, at least, some *postulates;* again, it remains almost barren, unless it lead to synthesis, in which all human knowledge must at last culminate. All the branches of judicature are interdependent, all assume the incompatibility of right and wrong, all rest on general principles of morality deeply rooted in human conscience, and held as certain by the common sense of mankind; and yet these familiar truths need scientific treatment in order to bear a scientific superstructure. Nowadays, nothing is granted *a priori;* no position is held as certain, unless it be clearly self-evident, or demonstrated by apodictic arguments: mere common sense, or universally received opinions, are not deemed sufficient to command our assent.

Moreover, the rise and transient popularity of such theories as Determinism, Utilitarianism, Positivism, and other similar systems, are calculated to unsettle the convictions of students, and leave their minds in an attitude of skeptical indifference with regard to the fundamental principles on which the respect for right and the permanency of the social order must ultimately depend. It is to emphasize these principles, and to demonstrate their soundness, that these lectures have been written. No attempt has been made to crowd ethics and sociology within these narrow limits; only a few points of Natural Law which are often recklessly assailed, or which bear directly on modern legislation, have been chosen from many, perhaps equally important, to be subjected to a searching analysis, and to be maintained against the attacks of subtle but pernicious errors. Should this little book serve to strengthen moral convictions, and thereby promote the interests of justice, the author would feel that his labor had been amply repaid.

In concluding these prefatory remarks, it is the author's grateful duty to acknowledge his deep obligations to Prof. R. Ross Perry, A.M., LL.D., Judge Martin F. Morris, and Mr. Thomas A. Whelan of the Baltimore Bar, who revised these lectures in whole or in part, and offered many valuable suggestions, without which the imperfections of the work would have been far greater.

CONTENTS.

FIRST LECTURE.

TELEOLOGY, OR MORAL CAUSATION.

		PAGE
1.	Man aims at Fruition—i. e., at the perfection of Activity,	17
2.	The Law of Causation,	20
3.	No Rational Being can act without a Purpose,	21
4.	The End is intended first,	23
5.	Every End is good Metaphysically, but many Ends may be bad Morally,	25
6.	What is Good considered Transcendentally,	27
7.	The concepts of Good and of End analyzed,	28
8.	The Supreme Good,	31
9.	The Supreme Good must be attainable, either in this life or in the next,	33
10.	There is but one Object that can supply the special wants of Man,	34

SECOND LECTURE.

ESSENCE, CONCRETE EXISTENCE, AND ATTRIBUTES OF NATURAL LAW.

1.	Human Legislation presupposes an ideal Standard,	37
2.	Existence and Authority of Natural Law universally admitted for many centuries,	38
3.	Equity and Natural Law must remain,	39

SEC. I. WHAT IS NATURAL LAW?

4.	Definition of Law, Moral and Physical,	41
5.	A Moral Law implies freedom of the Will; a Physical Law excludes it,	42
6.	Imputability is a consequence of Freedom,	42
7.	Moral and physical necessity,	43
8.	Common features,	45

		PAGE
9.	The Pandects agree with Blackstone,	46
10.	Definition and properties of Natural Law,	48
11.	Objective reality of Natural Law, and consequences of this reality,	50
12.	The Eternal Law defined,	51

SEC. II. POSITIVE LAW AND OTHER RULES OF CONDUCT.

13.	Various Rules of Conduct,	52
14.	Essential elements of a Moral Law,	53

SEC. III. HOBBES, BENTHAM, PUFFENDORF, AND AUSTIN.

15.	Hobbes,	55
16.	Bentham,	57
17.	Puffendorf,	58
18.	Austin,	58

SEC. IV. DIRECT PROOFS.

19.	What Natural Law is not, and what it is,	61
20.	The three axioms of Roman Law,	63
21.	Proof from experience,	63
22.	No valid objection can be drawn, either from the discovery of wild Human Beings, or from the difficulty of some Moral Deductions,	65
23.	Proof from the Existence and Attributes of God,	65

SEC. V. CONSEQUENCES OF THE REJECTION OF NATURAL LAW.

24.	Reductio ad absurdum,	67
25.	Inalienable rights,	68
26.	Conclusion,	68

THIRD LECTURE.

HUMAN ACTS AND ANIMAL MOTIONS.

SEC. I. MAN DIFFERS ESSENTIALLY FROM LOWER ANIMALS.

1.	The missing link is yet missing,	71

SEC. II. ESSENTIAL CHARACTERISTICS OF HUMAN ACTS.

2.	Powers distinctly human: Understanding, Will, Intellectual Memory,	73
3.	Free Will also is characteristic,	75
4.	Consciousness essential,	77
5.	Personality essential to Man,	78

SEC. III. MERE ANIMAL ACTS.

		PAGE
6.	The characteristics of Human Acts are not found in Animal Motions,	78
7.	Animals have no Intellect,	79
8.	Animals are not Progressive,	80
9.	Animals have no Moral Powers,	81
10.	Yet they must not be injured wantonly,	82
11.	Under what plea may Vivisection become permissible?	82

SEC. IV. MORAL CHARACTER OF HUMAN ACTIONS.

12.	Physical and Moral Liberty,	83
13.	Responsibility, Imputability, Morality,	84
14.	The End does not justify the Means,	84

SEC. V. WHEN IS MAN RESPONSIBLE?

15.	A Madman is irresponsible; a Monomaniac is often so,	86
16.	Mania wilfully brought on; Drunkenness,	87
17.	Uncontrollable Impulses and temporary Insanity,	88
18.	Want of Education is not a sufficient plea,	90
19.	Hypnotism; Doctrine of Professor Björnström,	91
20.	A man under the influence of Hypnosis may be used as a tool,	93

FOURTH LECTURE.

FREEDOM OF THE WILL.

1.	Importance of the Question,	95

SEC. I. NATURE OF FREE WILL.

2.	Freedom of Will defined. Conditions required for the exercise of Free Will,	96
3.	What Beings can be free,	99
4.	No Intellect without Will; no Will without Intellect,	99
5.	Varied Powers which influence the Will,	101

SEC. II. DEMONSTRATION OF THE EXISTENCE OF FREE WILL.

6.	Free Will proved by Consciousness,	102
7.	Consciousness may report a Power which begins to Act,	103
8.	Concept of duty. Second proof,	104
9.	Nature of Deliberation. Third proof,	105
10.	Consent of the World,	107

11. Justice supposes Freedom of the Will. . . . 108
12. Natural Order incomplete without Self-determining Beings, ... 109

SEC. III. VARIOUS FORMS OF DETERMINISM.

13. Determinism, ... 110
14. Necessity arising from the Nature of Man, . 112
15. Necessity induced by Law, or by Evolution, . . 113
16. Objection derived from the Conservation of Energy, . 114

FIFTH LECTURE.

UTILITARIANISM.

SEC. I. NATURE OF UTILITARIANISM; ITS RELATION TO OTHER THEORIES OF MORALITY.

1. Plasticity of Utilitarianism, ... 117
2. Fundamental error of Utilitarianism: Utility is not Morality, ... 118
3. A useful Good is not desired for itself, but for some other Good, ... 119
4. True Utility and Moral Goodness must meet in the end, but often follow different paths, . . 121
5. Materialism, Positivism, and Phenomenism. Mr. Huxley's lay sermon, ... 122
6. Materialism, Positivism, and Phenomenism are easily combined, but the Utilitarianism of Austin is unintelligible, ... 124

SEC. II. HEDONISM OF BENTHAM.

7. Utility as understood by Bentham, ... 127
8. Pleasure and Pain are relative; they cannot be a Moral Standard; they cannot sanction the Laws on which Social Security must rest, . . . 128

SEC. III. UTILITARIANISM OF J. S. MILL.

9. System of Mr. Mill. The End remains undefined, 130
10. The End is unattainable, ... 131
11. Four objections to Mr. Mill's main tenet, . . . 133
12. Sanctions of Moral Law according to Mr. Mill. God's pleasure or displeasure. Public opinion. Subjective sanction, ... 133
13. Is Virtue to be loved for its own sake? Evident contradictions, ... 135
14. Heroism not explained in Mr. Mill's system, . 137

Contents.

SEC. IV. UTILITARIAN EVOLUTION.

		PAGE
15.	Mr. Spencer denies the existence of Free Will, . .	140
16.	Utility a result of Evolution, ...	142
17.	Evolution is a mere Hypothesis, ...	143
18.	Evolution is not universally true, either a priori or a posteriori, ...	146
19.	Even if Man were descended from an Ape, the reasoning would be faulty, ...	148
20.	How did Moral Evolution begin ?	148
21.	A Creator and an Eternal Law must be admitted as the foundations of the Moral Order, . . .	150

SIXTH LECTURE.

JUSTICE.

SEC. I. JUSTICE AS A GENERAL VIRTUE.

1.	Meaning of the Latin word *jus* according to Ulpian, .	151
2.	Justice as a Virtue, ...	152
3.	The standard of Justice is not arbitrary, .	154
4.	Perfect and imperfect Duties, . . .	156

SEC. II. DIVISION OF JUSTICE.

5.	Commutative Justice ; equality of Value, economic or contractual, ...	158
6.	Distributive Justice ; its varied functions, .	160
7.	Legal Justice ; it requires a double equation, . .	161
8.	Vindicative Justice ; its mission is to restore Order. Threefold purpose of Vindicative Justice, .	163

SEC. III. JUSTICE, CHARITY, AND FIDELITY.

9.	Justice and Charity contrasted, . .	166
10.	Justice and Fidelity, . .	167
11.	The Contract of Shylock, ...	168
12.	Judgment of Portia, . . .	169

SEVENTH LECTURE.

THE INDIVIDUAL, THE FAMILY, THE STATE.

SEC. I. THE INDIVIDUAL.

1.	Man considered as an individual Being, in ancient and in modern Civilizations, ...	171
2.	Dignity of the human Personality a consequence of the nature of Man. Kant and Aquinas, . .	173

		PAGE
3.	Man is not the thing of the State,	174
4.	Absolute rights, according to Chancellor Kent,	174
5.	Individual and citizen ; the citizen not the whole Man ; exaggerated individualism,	175

SEC. II. THE FAMILY.

6.	Definition of society ; three complete societies ; their respective ends,	177
7.	Family, and family servants,	178
8.	Union of husband and wife ; it originates in a sacred Contract,	179
9.	Marriage did not originate either in violence or in promiscuous intercourse,	181
10.	Chief end of Matrimony ; duties resulting from the Marriage relation,	183
11.	Natural Impulse and natural Fitness of Parents to educate their Children,	186
12.	Duties of Children ; their personal Rights must be respected,	188

SEC. III. THE COMMONWEALTH.

13.	The Individual enters civil society through the Family. Why the Individual is not a perfect social Unit,	189
14.	Civil society a body politic,	190
15.	Did society originate in a compact ? Hobbes and Rousseau!	192
16.	Both Contracts inadmissible,	195
17.	Civil society originated in Human Nature,	196
18.	Authority comes originally from God, but the consent of the People determines the Ruler,	197
19.	Legislative, Executive and Judiciary Power,	199
20.	Unity and Liberty; State Atomism ; Nihilism ; State Fetichism,	200
21.	Practical rules of State polity,	201

EIGHTH LECTURE.

PROPERTY.

SEC. I. WHAT IS PROPERTY ?

1.	What is the Right of Property ? It may be limited in its exercise,	203
2.	Explanation of the definition,	204
3.	All Human Rights beget Duties,	206

SEC. II. SOURCE OF THE RIGHT OF PROPERTY.

4. Socialists and Communists. The Right of Property is founded on Natural Law, ... 207

SEC. III. DEMONSTRATION OF THE RIGHT OF PROPERTY.

5. Man is a reasonable Being, compelled to supply his daily wants, and bound to provide for the future, 210
6. Man must provide for others and support the State, . 212
7. Joint ownership presupposes Individual rights, . 213
8. Why Collective ownership cannot replace Private ownership, ... 214
9. Communistic societies, ... 215
10. Mr. Thiers' argument, drawn from personality, . . 217
11. Blind impulses and instinct show that the Law is universal, ... 218
12. Evolution of the Right of Property, . . . 219

SEC. IV. WHAT CAN WE OWN, AND HOW CAN WE BECOME OWNERS?

13. How an abstract right becomes a concrete right, . 221
14. Property in land, ... 223
15. First title, occupancy, . . 225
16. Accession or increment, ... 226

SEC. V. OBJECTIONS.

17. Appropriations of the whole world, . . . 228
18. Mr. Herbert Spencer's Cosmopolite, . . . 229

NINTH LECTURE.

ON TAXATION.

SEC. I. RIGHT OF TAXATION.

1. Nature and necessity of the taxing Power, . . . 233
2. It is neither an Evil, nor the result of a Contract or of a Partnership, ... 234
3. Taxation and Protection. Taxation and Representation, ... 235

SEC. II. EXTENT OF THE RIGHT OF TAXATION.

4. The Right of Taxation extends to all subjects and all kinds of property, ... 237
5. Is the taxing Power unlimited in its application? . 239

SEC. III. EQUITY OF TAXATION.

6. Absolute Equity is impossible. Relative Equity is obligatory, ... 240

		PAGE
7.	The diffusion of Taxation tends to equalize pressure,	242
8.	Incidence and repercussion,	243
9.	Infinitesimal system. Social dividends. Equality of ability; equality of sacrifice; equality of benefit,	246
10.	Proportional, progressive, and progressional rates,	248
11.	The three Systems contrasted,	251

SEC. IV. CANONS OF TAXATION.

12.	Canons of Taxation, according to Adam Smith,	253
13.	Canons of Sismondi, and Supplementary Rule of Mr. Atkinson,	256

SEC. V. SUBJECTS OF TAXATION.

14.	Direct and indirect Taxation. Poll tax,	258
15.	Taxes paid in labor. Taxes on property, real or personal, on profits and on rent,	259
16.	Income Tax,	261
17.	Internal revenue, Excise, duties on Imports and Exports,	262
18.	Sole tax,	263

TENTH LECTURE.

CONFLICT OF RIGHTS.

SEC. I. DIFFICULTY OF THE QUESTION: THE CONFLICT OF RIGHTS IS OVER A WIDER FIELD THAN THE CONFLICT OF LAWS.

1.	Law is the common source of Duties and of Rights; but Rights extend over a wider field than Laws,	265
2.	In cases of conflict, both authority of the Law and its connection with the Right claimed must be considered,	267

SEC. II. NATURE OF RIGHTS AND DUTIES.

3.	Definition of Right,	267
4.	Definition of Duty. Rights and Duties are interdependent,	270

SEC. III. CLASSIFICATION OF RIGHTS AND DUTIES.

5.	We owe Duties to God, to ourselves, and to our fellow-men,	272
6.	Rights natural and legal; absolute and relative,	273
7.	Rights inborn or acquired, abstract or concrete, personal or real,	274
8.	Direct and indirect Rights,	275

SEC. IV. NATURE AND CAUSES OF JURAL CONFLICTS.

		PAGE
9.	Three sources of Conflicts : uncertainty of Legislation, divided Allegiance, and incompatibility of Claims,	276
10.	Opposite Material forces are partly like and partly unlike opposite Moral forces,	278

SEC. V. SUBORDINATION OF LAWS.

11.	Divine Law and the Law of Nature. Canon Law and State Law,	280
12.	Constitutional Law supreme. Public International Law partly natural and partly conventional,	281
13.	Private International Law. Lex fori, situs, domicilii. Personal, real, and mixed Statutes,	282

SEC. VI. RULES TO DECIDE CONFLICTS.

14.	Rules of Judicature,	284

ELEVENTH LECTURE.

COMBINATIONS OF CAPITAL, AND LABOR ORGANIZATIONS.

SEC. I. THE LAW TO PROTECT TRADE AGAINST MONOPOLY.

1.	Capital and Labor are interdependent—yet Conflicts must arise. Why ?	287
2.	Text of the Act to protect Trade,	288
3.	Definition of Conspiracy,	291
4.	Ethical and Legal aspects of Conspiracies,	292

SEC. II. CONTRACTS WHICH MAY LEAD TO MONOPOLIES.

5.	Syndicates, Trusts, and Pools,	294
6.	Combinations, Corners and Lockouts,	296

SEC. III. LABOR ORGANIZATIONS.

7.	Interstate Law. Ann Arbor case,	299
8.	Ownership of man in his own labor. This ownership is not unconditioned,	302
9.	When has the State the right to make men work ?	304
10.	Nature of a Contract. Freedom essential to Contracts,	306
11.	Duties of the State with regard to Contracts,	308
12.	The right of Association; its limits. Functions of the State with regard to Associations,	310
13.	Rule XII.: Why it was objectionable,	311
14.	Strikes and Boycotts,	313

TWELFTH LECTURE.

Legal Ethics.

		PAGE
1.	In order that Justice may rule, Laws must be equitable, and they must be enforced impartially. Legislative, Executive, and Judicial functions are interdependent, ...	315

SEC. I. LEGISLATORS.

2.	Knowledge required of the Legislator, . . .	316
3.	In the framing of Laws, both Justice and Expediency must be taken into account, ...	318
4.	Beware of Laws which cannot be enforced or which must be often modified, ...	319
5.	Laws must not be multiplied without necessity. Beware of retrospective Laws, ...	320

SEC. II. JUDGES.

6.	High dignity of Judgeship, ...	322
7.	A Judge must know Equity Jurisprudence as well as Positive Law, ...	323
8.	Bribes, if received, must be refunded, . . .	325
9.	Patience necessary. Doubt, in Civil Cases and in Criminal Cases, ...	327
10.	A Judge must not act according to a mere subjective Standard; he must avoid delays, and beware of crowding the docket, ...	329

SEC. III. JURORS.

11.	Jurors must remain within their own sphere, keep free from undue influence, avoid intercourse with the parties, ...	330

SEC. IV. LAWYERS.

12.	A Lawyer need not know everything, but must be conscious of his own limitations, . . .	333
13.	A Lawyer must be truthful, respectful to the Court, obliging and peaceable, ...	334
14.	Duties of the Lawyer toward his Client. Difference between Civil Cases and Criminal Cases, . .	335

APPENDIX.

Rules for the Guidance of a Lawyer's Professional Conduct,	339

NATURAL LAW AND LEGAL PRACTICE.

FIRST LECTURE.

INTRODUCTORY.*

TELEOLOGY, OR MORAL CAUSATION.

1. Man aims at Fruition—i. e., at the perfection of Activity. BEFORE studying the laws which govern human actions, it is useful, if not necessary, to inquire into the causes from which these actions are springing. Why does man act? Why does he spurn repose? Why is absolute rest unbearable to him? We might answer that this inclination to act is an essential part of man's nature; that human faculties are perfected only by action; that, to man, immobility means death; that the present life is an unceasing process of motion and change; that man wants life, life throbbing, palpitating, and forever changing. All this is true, but it is not a solution of the problem. What we want to know is not *the fact* but *the cause* of this restlessness; we ask <u>*why* nature goads man to incessant activity</u>, and what is the goal (if there be

---

* <u>Teleology is the scientific basis of morals</u>; but students without previous philosophical training had perhaps better postpone the reading of this introduction, which is unavoidably philosophical.

any) toward which man is hurried by this irresistible impulse. It cannot be said that we move solely for the sake of moving. Motion itself soon becomes wearisome; after periods of excitement, we sigh for peace; after long-continued agitation, the need of rest becomes imperative. On the other hand, the happiest moments of our life are spent in the enjoyment of goods so pure and at the same time so pleasurable, that we forget that they are limited both in intensity and in duration. We enjoy the present and lose sight both of the past and of the future; but this delightful repose is not of long duration. A scientist who has discovered a law which had eluded the researches of his predecessors; a philosopher who has solved to his satisfaction some abstruse metaphysical or moral problem, may pass through a period of rapturous enjoyment; yet both will soon become sensible of the fact that they have explored but a very small portion of the field of science; and more than ever they will hunger and thirst for more knowledge. What human nature craves is neither movement alone, nor repose alone, but a combination of both, a sort of dynamic equilibrium: we want the kind of enjoyment which, according to Aristotle, is the complement and perfection of energy.* If we assume the existence of a good, great and perfect enough to satisfy all the cravings of the human heart, and if this good be known, its attractiveness must be felt more or less consciously throughout human life; and if this supreme good be reached at last, man must cling to it with all the energy of his nature;

* Ethica Nichomachea, Book IV., n. 46.

this is energy completed by an act of supreme enjoyment. No change can be desired, for every change would involve an irreparable loss; we have activity without mutation—that is to say, activity combined with repose, perfect activity ending in perfect enjoyment. If this hypothesis can be verified, then the *summum bonum* of philosophers ceases to be a dream, the fountain-head of moral energy is discovered, and the present continuous struggle is shown to terminate in perfect fruition—that is to say, in a kind of repose which is the complement and perfection of activity.

Man being a compound of body and soul, of matter and spirit, the causes of his activity must needs be complex; at times, material objects will exert the greatest influence in commanding action, and physical energies will predominate; on other occasions, the spiritual element will assert its proper supremacy. Again, some acts may be due to blind impulses; no deliberation may have preceded, no freedom accompanied them; others, on the contrary, are performed with full deliberation, and under the joint control of intellect and will. With the former we are not at present directly concerned; such acts are, properly speaking, neither moral nor immoral; for morality supposes responsibility, and there can be no responsibility when the agent is not *sui juris*—that is to say, when he is utterly incapable of controlling his own motions. Such acts may be performed by men, but they cannot be called, in a strict sense, *human acts,* because the two powers which are most distinctly *human,* viz., intellect and will, have not stamped them as their own. Yet all acts, whether physical or psychical, deliberate or spontaneous, are subject to the great law of causation which extends its dominion over all accidental phenomena whatsoever. Let us for the present state the law in its broadest form; later on, we shall apply it to moral phenomena, with the discrimination required by their specific nature.

2. The Law of Causation. The law of causation may be formulated as follows: *Nothing that was not can begin to be without a sufficient cause.* Schoolmen expressed it in fewer words: *Nihil fit absque ratione sufficienti.* Common people will say: No effect without a cause; and although this last formula is not free from tautology, as President Noah Porter observes, yet it conveys the idea in a clear and pointed form, if not in a philosophical and accurate manner. The learned author whom we have just mentioned holds that this principle is self-evident, and justifies his opinion by a series of arguments which may be thus condensed : *

1st. We explain the occurrence of events on the assumption of this truth.

2d. When an event has occurred which is not yet accounted for, the mind is aroused to the effort to solve and explain its occurrence by seeking the cause.

3d. The mind not only explains the past, but it relies upon the future, on the ground of its faith in causation.

4th. In these explanations and experiments the mind

---

* Noah Porter, The Human Intellect, p. 572, § 590.

is impelled by a special emotion, always present and powerful.

These reasons undoubtedly show that the law of causation is readily perceived by all; but should they fail to convince us that it is self-evident, we could go back to more elementary principles. Thus none question the old axiom, *ex nihilo nihil fit*—nothing is made out of nothing. Were the law of causation untrue, then the long-received maxim would collapse with it; for the causeless entity would come out of nothing. Whether we suppose it to be a substance, i. e., a being existing in itself, or an accident, i. e., a thing existing in and adherent to a substance, the difficulty remains the same. If it were a substance, it would have sprung from the non-existence of itself; if it were an accident, it would have proceeded from that which is not in the substance; in both cases we have a glaring absurdity which compels us to take refuge in the principle of causation. For the same reason the cause must be adequate, i. e., capable of producing the whole effect; otherwise a part, at least, of what we call effect would spring forth from nothing. Hence the truth of the law of causation: "*nothing* that was not before can begin to be without a sufficient cause," stands clearly established in its widest extent.

3. No Rational Being can act without a Purpose. With regard to inanimate beings, mechanical and chemical forces are the only direct causes of motion; in inferior animals, appetite is the controlling power, because its impulses cannot be checked by reason;

but in rational beings, intellect and will are brought into play, and may subdue the impulses of appetite; yet these superior powers have in view some object, either attractive or repulsive, which stimulates them, without compelling the will to act. In other words, no rational being can act without some end or purpose. *An end is an object which the agent tries to attain in order to satisfy a desire, and to enjoy either partial or complete repose.* A *purpose* differs from an *end* in being less distant, and consequently more within the reach of the agent. It is commonly a means to an end, and it does not necessarily imply the idea of rest, which is inseparable from the term *end,* at least when the latter is used in a strict sense. A *motive* also is an incentive to action, but it may be subjective, and it does not, like the word *end* or *purpose,* necessarily convey the idea of an objective good.

To have a comprehensive view of moral principles it is necessary to seek out the mainsprings of human actions; hence the need of teleology, or *the doctrine which treats of the ends and purposes of man;* in other words, of the causes which prompt men to act. That the theory of purposes is not useless is manifest from the rule proclaimed by the greatest of Roman lawyers; Cicero, when discussing the evidence which was to fix the guilt of intended murder either on his client Milo or on Clodius, the enemy whom Milo had destroyed, asks: *Cui profuit?* Who could have been benefited by the encounter? Clodius alone! Then Clodius attempted the murder, and lost his life in the attempt.* The great Roman orator further observes that a good man will never be led by self-interest to commit crime, but that self-interest will invariably sway a man who cares but little for justice.

4. The End is intended first. To prove that every rational being when acting has an end or purpose seems almost needless, so evident does this truth appear to common sense; and yet we have found text-books in which it was denied, and supposed to be contrary to the freedom of the will. A careful observation of the facts would have easily dispelled this illusion. Whenever a man in full possession of his faculties acts with full consciousness, if we ask him why he acts as he does, he can readily supply us with an answer; we are ourselves fully aware, when acting with full consciousness, of the reasons why we act. Nay, more, when the conduct of a man is purposeless, we conclude him to be absent-minded, distracted, or insane. On this point philosophers, widely at variance with us in most moral questions—Kant and Mr. Herbert Spencer, for instance—are of one mind with us. Then the contrary supposition involves a contradiction; for it assumes that the agent determines to accomplish something, otherwise he would remain indifferent; but to decide on accomplishing a certain effect is to have a purpose; therefore, in the hypothesis, the agent would at the same time have a purpose and be

---

* In reality, it is exceedingly probable that the meeting was accidental; but Cicero made a very strong case against Clodius. The judges, however, were not deceived by the eloquent pleadings of Milo's counsel.

purposeless, which is an evident contradiction in terms.

Lastly, a reference to the law of causation will show at once that a rational, and yet purposeless, action is unthinkable. Four different causes contribute their share to the product of our activity: the *Efficient,* the *Material,* the *Formal* and the *Final* cause. They are defined as follows by Aristotle: The Efficient cause (Ἀρχὴ κινήσεως) *is the principle of the motion or change;* in other words, the prime mover, or first active principle. The Matter, or Material cause, is the *underlying entity* (Ὕλη καὶ τὸ ὑποκείμενον), *which, left to itself, would remain formless and incapable of concrete existence.* The Formal cause, or simply *the Form* (τὸ τί ἦν εἶναι), is that which, clinging to those otherwise undetermined elements, *gives them their specific entity.* It is impossible to conceive as existent either the matter without form or the form without matter; but in a concrete being the former constitutes the passive, the latter the active element. Lastly, the Final cause *is that good the desire of which rouses the agent, or efficient cause, to activity* (τὸ οὗ ἕνεκα καὶ τἀγαθόν). "The end," says Aristotle, "is the term of every generation and every motion." No improvement, since the days of the Stagirite, has been made on this analysis of causation. Let us apply it to familiar examples, viz., to the construction of a house, to a chemical combination, to a living organism, or to a society; everywhere we will find these various causes at work. But among them there is one which is first in exercising its influence, and last in falling within the grasp of the agent. It is the final cause, or the end. This must be first in exercising its influence, because did it not possess some attraction for the agent the activity of the prime mover would remain dormant; otherwise something would come to existence without cause—namely, the determination of the agent to accomplish an act. On the other hand, before it accomplishes its purpose, the activity must exercise itself on some material, and impart to it a form; hence, the end is the last thing reached, though it is the first to be aimed at. This is what schoolmen expressed pithily by the formula: *Primum in intentione, ultimum in executione,* which I make bold to translate: first intended, last reached.*

5. Every End is good Metaphysically, but many Ends may be bad Morally.
You may have observed in the definition of the final cause by Aristotle, that the word *agathon* (good) is used as coextensive with purpose. Does this mean that all purposes are good morally? Far from it; there are wicked purposes as well as lawful ones, and a wicked purpose will vitiate any action, however harmless or even beneficial in itself. Here it is well to observe that moral righteousness requires that *every step should be lawful.* A bad end or unlawful means, a forbidden goal, or circumstances involving a moral flaw, will make the action morally bad. Thus, an alms is a very good thing in itself, but if given in order to bribe a voter, it becomes unlawful; if a man steal in

---

* Aristotle, Metaphysics, Book I., Chap. III., XLV. Also, Physics, Book II., Chap. III., *Per totum.*

order to assist the poor, the end will not excuse him, for the means is wrong, and stamps its character on the action itself. Nothing better than to open for the people parks and gardens where thousands will breathe pure air and renew their energy; but if it be accomplished with utter disregard of individual rights, or if the money of the city be squandered recklessly, or if it be done by those who are not lawfully empowered to use public money, the circumstance will vitiate the action, and the politician who may have carried out the improvement, instead of being a benefactor of the people, is a wrong-doer. Hence the old axiom of schoolmen: *Bonum ex integra causa, malum ex quocumque defectu*—good requires a faultless cause, evil results from any flaw.

Yet the definition of Aristotle is correct, for without some good, apparent or real, absolute or relative, it is impossible to rouse the will; for no power can be conceived in a state of activity without the presence, at least imaginary, of its own specific object, and the specific object of the will is good. A son may imagine that in the midst of the darkness of night he sees a faint light appear, and in that light he may think that he perceives the countenance of a loved mother growing more and more distinct, beaming forth upon him rays of solace and love; he may rush in his sleep toward the dear image and find nothing but a shadow; but the image was present in his fancy, and it is that image which conjured up all the tender memories of childhood and made him seek the delusive embrace.

One may seek in the cup, or in any unlawful pleasure,

a moment of delight which shall be atoned for with countless woes; he has been deceived by a relative good, which has ensnared his appetite to dethrone his reason. But it is not the evil that has attracted him; it is the apparent and relative good. Even those depraved men who seem to gloat over evil for the sake of evil seek the morbid satisfaction of pride, independence, or revenge; it is not evil itself, but the false pleasure which is, or seems attendant on evil, that rouses their unnatural cravings. Hence it remains true that good, apparent or real, relative or absolute, is the true final cause of every activity of the will. Proceeding from analysis to synthesis, we may argue thus: Every rational agent acts in order to satisfy a want or achieve a purpose; but, abstracting from other considerations, such as lawfulness, permanency, etc., the satisfaction of a desire or the achievement of a purpose is good, at least as far as it is the term of an activity; therefore every rational agent acts for something good.

6. What is Good considered Transcendentally. We have said that the good mentioned by Aristotle is not necessarily moral, real, or conducive to happiness and virtue: the word *good* is used here in a metaphysical sense; and good, thus understood, may be made subservient to evil; yet in this case it is not *evil as such* which attracts men: evil is essentially repulsive; it is the good, real or apparent, which accompanies evil, glosses it over, or hides it from our view.

Philosophers tell us that good considered transcendentally, that is, considered apart from individual and accidental circumstances, is coextensive with being. In other words, that it is better to be than not to be, or that being is better than nonentity. In fact, they define goodness (of course metaphysical or transcendental) as *the fitness of a thing to afford repose by satisfying a want.* In this broad and very abstract formula we do not consider whether the wants are actual or potential, whether there are powers to be satiated, whether those powers are intellectual or material. It is evident that all that *is* may become the object of an act, even if that act is but perceptive. All we consider is the fitness to terminate some activity by supplying it with an object, and that fitness is found wherever there is being. On the other hand, it is impossible to conceive nonentity as terminating an operation; it is only thinkable by referring to what *is*. Nothingness is but an absence, a privation, a negative sign. Since good is found wherever being can be discovered, and excluded whenever we have only a negation, we see the justification of the old maxim: *Good and Being are convertible terms.*

7. The concepts of Good and of End analyzed. In our attempts to use a definition of good broad enough to meet any generalization, we may have been transcendental to excess. Let us now select for ordinary use more intelligible formulas. St. Thomas defines good: "That in whose possession desire finds repose." Plainer yet are the words of Aristotle: "Good is what all desire." It needs hardly to be said that good may be material or spiritual, concrete or abstract, physical, temporal or eternal, etc. In that immense storehouse of entity, every power, every form of energy, seeks what is fitted to its wants and capacity. No doubt grievous errors are committed when the light of reason is dim, but all seek something which is supposed to be good and to meet their wants. As the result of the preceding analysis, three conclusions stand out in bold relief:

1st. Every activity, every energy, aims at an end.—Aristotle.

2d. Every agent aims at some good.—St. Thomas.

3d. Among causes, the end is intended first and reached last.—Schoolmen generally.

If you will bear in mind these three laws and fully realize their meaning, you will find in them the solution of many an intricate moral or physical problem.

Before answering the various questions which spring spontaneously from the doctrine which we have tried to explain, it is necessary to complete the analysis of the terms *End* and *Good*.

We have said that the end is the good which an agent, or any faculty of that agent, tries to reach in order to find repose. Now, this repose may be partial and momentary, or perfect and immutable; the end may be either provisional and partial, or complete and final. Between the last end and the most direct and immediate purpose, that is to say, the means next at hand, there may be a chain of almost countless links. Thus, you all want to be happy, but the means, in your opinion, is to achieve distinction in the profession which you have chosen. Sometimes you think of the distinction only, and pay no attention to the sequel; for you take it for granted that happiness will necessarily follow distinction at the bar or on the bench. But to rise to eminence, hard study is necessary. You may or you may not love study for its own sake. If you like it for its own sake, it becomes a partial end; if you do not, but undertake it cheerfully to arrive at the object of your legitimate ambition, it is to you only a means. If your ambition soars, as doubtless it does, beyond the limits of a temporal happiness, then the object of your earthly desire is a partial end, but it is subordinated to a higher one, which is the last, and to that complete felicity it bears the relation of a means. A means is not desired for itself, but only for the end; an immediate or subordinate end is sought in a measure for its own advantages, but chiefly for the superior purpose which a person has in view; the last end is desired for itself, and for itself alone.

Again, when you strive to obtain an end, several considerations present themselves. For whose benefit do you wish the good which you strive to obtain? Not always for yourselves; far from it. Many parents labor very hard to acquire wealth. Is it for their own sake? Very often it is solely for their children; were they bereft of their family, the struggle would end at once. Hence, the person for whom we want a certain good is one of the factors which influence activity. The excellence of the object desired is another. Lastly, the object itself may be of great excellence, but the enjoyment of it, not the object itself, may be what we desire. Thus the sybarite cared nothing for the exquisite beauty of roses upon which he reclined, but loved the softness of the couch and the scent of the leaves. In analyzing the influence of final causes, we must bear in mind these three factors—the person for whom we act, the object itself, the enjoyment of that object. This distinction is essential in ethics. We must observe also that good may be either honorable, useful, or pleasurable. If it be honorable, it is desirable for its own sake, because the object aimed at is lovable; such is virtue. If it be merely useful, it does not challenge our love for its own intrinsic value, but derives all its worth from a higher and nobler object. If it be merely pleasurable, it will afford a partial and transient satisfaction, but often at the expense of utility.

We are now supplied with the necessary data to answer several important ethical questions: 1st. Is the end of man one or manifold? 2d. Is it attainable? 3d. What object is great and good enough to meet all the wants which are essential to human nature?

8. The Supreme Good. The first question, viz., Is the end of man one or manifold? can be solved by analysis if we can find a general intent or want underlying all human desires; for if there be such a want or purpose, all other purposes, whatever their diversity, are reducible to that one, and bear to it the relation of means to end. Observation shows that there is such a general intent. Amid the countless motives which bring into play human energies, a common, universal, all-permeating desire is clearly discernible—that of obtaining for all the human powers that particular object which specifies their several tendencies; in other words, an intense craving for happiness; since perfect happiness, according to the definition of Boethius, is *a state made perfect by the accession of all goods*—that is, of all things desirable, all things that can satiate the longings of the human heart. Yes, this is the innate desire of human nature. Men are made to be happy; they hunger and thirst for true happiness; and this intense and universal craving survives all their trials, all their thwarted hopes, and all their woes. The great philosophers of antiquity, and, we may say, all the wise men of modern times, with very few exceptions, have come to the conclusion that the one universal want permeating and giving the prime impulse to all others is the want of happiness. Widely as they differ with regard to the object or being that can satisfy that longing, they agree on one point—that the desire of happiness is the prime mover of human activity; hence their pursuit, often baffled, ever renewed, of that *summum bonum* which could give rest to wearied humanity. To prove the oneness of the human end, St. Thomas has a deductive argument, as well as an analytical proof, equivalent to what I have given above. The deduction is perfectly valid, but too abstract for those who are not thoroughly trained in metaphysics. I mention it without dwelling upon it. It is substantially as follows:

The tendency of nature is toward unity. This was considered at the time as an axiom. It rested on the fact that, in every species, nature works out one type; in every living being it subordinates all the parts of the organism to the functions of the living principle; and, lastly, that unity is the perfection of being. But that which tends toward *one* thing cannot have two different and independent purposes, for this would be a contradiction; therefore nature has but one end. I will not insist upon this argument, because the analytical proof is enough for us.

We have found by analysis that in every action we look for happiness, and that happiness is the satisfaction of all the powers that are *specifically* human. On the other hand, the human being is one, hence all its specifical tendencies must converge in the direction of *one* object. Therefore this object, and this object alone, is the *summum bonum*.

9. The Supreme Good must be attainable, either in this life or in the next. But is perfect felicity obtainable? In this world, we say emphatically, no. What man ever had all his intellectual and moral wants satisfied in this world, to say nothing of the wants of his sensitive powers? Besides, felicity cannot be complete when it is not permanent, when at any moment it may be suddenly terminated. A relative happiness we may enjoy in this life; but if there were no hereafter, that abiding, all-pervading craving for the full satisfaction and the full development of our activities would remain without an adequate object—an abortive, ill-directed tendency. We should be driven to the conclusion that man's creation is a failure, a conclusion which is inadmissible. On the strength of that natural craving, Kant postulates both the existence of God and the immortality of the soul. Let us remember the law of causation and the functions of the end or final cause. The Author of our nature must have had before His all-seeing intellect the full type of this nature, with all its powers and cravings; for otherwise He could not have been its efficient cause, no agent being able to realize what He has not conceived. If He has fully perceived the essence and the potentiality of His own work (and the contrary is unthinkable), and yet has left it imperfect and unfinished, then either His wisdom or His power must have failed Him; for perfect wisdom always adapts the means to the end, and perfect power always carries to completion the work which has been both conceived and decreed. Where we speak of the first cause, a deficiency either in wisdom or power is utterly inadmissible; therefore, if the testimony of human reason is worth anything, we must admit as a necessary conclusion the existence and attainableness of perfect bliss. *Natura nil facit frustra,* said the ancient philosopher; and we say in turn, it is not in vain that all our desires and all our energies turn toward felicity, as flowers bend toward the sun to drink in its warmth and its light.

10. There is but one Object that can supply the special wants of Man. But if man is made for bliss, what object is fit to supply his want? The answer is at hand: There are two powers in man which belong to him essentially, and mark the specific difference between man and the lower creation. Those powers are Intellect and Will; the former has truth for its object, the latter seeks after good; both are universal in their tendency, and no individual and finite object can satisfy either. Nothing, then, short of infinite truth and infinite goodness can meet their wants and give them repose. This is the *summum bonum* which the philosophers sought. When we leave the shadowy realm of abstraction, and seek substantial reality, we find but one Being which answers the description; and that Being is God.

But to this conclusion an objection arises: Are we not both selfish and wanting in reverence, do we not degrade our Maker by reducing Him to a mere means toward our happiness, thus inverting the order of reason, and making of the end a means, and of the means an end? This difficulty disappears if we bear in mind the distinction already made between the object of happiness and the enjoyment of it. Were enjoyment the prime mover of our will, or the last term of its activity, the objection would obtain; but the *summum bonum* is not what it is because we can enjoy it, but we can enjoy it because it is the *summum bonum*. In other words, its own intrinsic goodness is the cause, not the effect, of enjoyment. If, then, we have a rational tendency, which needs must seek the first principle, it cannot stop at the effect, but must rise higher to find the cause. Enjoyment is, indeed, both a necessary condition and a necessary effect of this higher tendency, but it is neither its final object nor the prime mover of its energy.

This is the philosophical as well as the Christian solution of the most important problem of teleology. Plato had anticipated it; witness the following passage, and many others which might be quoted if time permitted:

"Poets have wisely said, when making known the essence of friendship, that it is *the God* that makes friends and binds them together—He, then, is the true friend for us, in whom all friendships have their consummation. All other friends owe to Him their friendship; but He must be *the friend* who is the cause of all friendship." *

---

* Plato, Lysis, Chap. X., CXVII.

SECOND LECTURE.

ESSENCE, CONCRETE EXISTENCE, AND ATTRIBUTES OF NATURAL LAW.

1. Human Legislation presupposes an ideal Standard. BEFORE the existence of civil society, before constitutions were framed and human laws were enacted, there must have been some rules of conduct, already possessing a binding force. The dependence of man on his Maker must have existed as soon as man drew the breath of life; the mutual relations of husband and wife, of parents and offspring, must be coeval with the existence of the family circle. Was Abel right when he offered the firstlings of his flock? Was Cain wrong when he shed his brother's blood? If so, there must have been a standard of right based on nature itself, and anterior to all human legislation. Again, when legislators devise a system of rules to prevent the clashing of rights and the conflict of interests, they must have before their minds an ideal of justice anterior to human rules and binding on the human will: this ideal cannot be derived from the laws which they are just then engaged in framing, for the effect cannot exist before the cause, and *an imitation presupposes* *a model.* Lastly, when unjust or pernicious laws have been enacted, and the people wish them to be repealed and replaced by just and beneficial laws, whence do the citizens derive their ideal of what a law ought to be? Certainly not from the existing legislation, since the modification or reversal of this legislation is demanded; then the people must appeal to a higher standard, which existed before the passing of the obnoxious laws, and which has remained unchanged despite *the sins of legislators.**

2. Existence and Authority of Natural Law universally admitted for many centuries. For many centuries the existence and authority of this high standard was acknowledged by legists, by philosophers, and by the whole civilized world. The Greek poet merely voiced a universally accepted belief when he said:

" Be it my lot ever to bear with me the holy and spotless purity of words and deeds. Their laws dwell on high, heaven-born, ethereal, by Olympus begotten. Mortal man did not beget them, and never shall oblivion shroud them; for in them abideth the great God, who knoweth not the decline of years." †

Such was the belief of mankind until Hobbes, Bentham, Austin and their followers boldly characterized it as *a great superstition, an exploded fallacy, a chimera of abstract ethics.*

" What with very mild defenders and vigorous enemies," says Prof. Taylor, " the venerable doctrine is almost out of court. And really, when one reminds himself that for

---

* Title of an essay by Mr. Herbert Spencer.
† Sophocles, Œdipus Tyrannus, vv. 363-371.

nearly twenty-two centuries this doctrine had practically universal acceptance, that it was the creed of Plato, Aristotle, Cicero, Marcus Aurelius, Gaius, Augustine, Aquinas, Grotius, Hooker, Locke, and Kant, its present forlorn state is certainly somewhat noteworthy. The simple fact is that there is a most astonishing acquiescence in the denunciation of the doctrine here considered. . . . Is this acquiescence warranted? Is natural law a myth? an exploded fallacy? The conviction of the writer is that consent to this proposition has been somewhat too hasty; that in fact, even if we chose to discard the name, still all that is essential in the doctrine remains, and must remain." *

3. Equity and Natural Law must remain. We thoroughly agree with Prof. Taylor, *the doctrine must remain.* In all questions of equity,† and in all constitutional cases,‡ whenever new legislation is to be framed, or existing laws must be interpreted, a reference to that high standard of morality is absolutely indispensable. No legislator or body of legislators can foresee all the cases that may arise; with the elements of which human life is

---

* Prof. F. M. Taylor, University of Michigan, The Law of Nature, 1891, pp. 1, 2.

† "In many branches of this most complicated system, composed as it is partly of the principles of natural law, and partly of artificial modifications of those principles, the ramifications are almost infinitely diversified, and the sources as well as the extent of these branches are often obscure and ill-defined." —Judge Story, preface to his Equity Jurisprudence.

‡ E. g., in the case of Chisolm *vs.* Georgia (2d Dallas, p. 419 and seq.) the decisions rendered *seriatim* by the judges are based almost entirely on natural law. In the case *In re Debs* (U. S. Reports, 158, p. 564) Mr. Justice Brewer, after discussing both the legal and the constitutional side of the case, adds: "We do not care to place our decision upon this ground alone."

made up an indefinite number of combinations is possible. Whenever an unforeseen combination occurs, a recourse to natural law becomes necessary. It is true that, as the years of a nation's life are multiplying, laws are becoming more numerous; an effort is made to provide for all contingencies, and to replace equity by positive legislation; but it would take an infinite number of laws to meet all possible cases. Hence equity jurisprudence must remain, and with it must remain the old doctrine on which it is founded. Natural law may have been neglected, but it has not ceased to be necessary. A *pettifogger* may, perhaps, do very well with positive law alone, so long as he confines himself to legal technicalities; but a *constitutional lawyer* is often obliged to refer to those high maxims of individual and social morality which are axioms of natural law, or evident deductions from these axioms; a judge, especially a judge possessing equity jurisdiction, must be as well acquainted with natural law as with precedents and statutes.

In order to avoid the misconceptions which have caused the present forlorn state of the old doctrine, we shall, first, explain the definitions of law in general, and especially of natural law; our explanations will be nothing more than a commentary on Blackstone's introduction; in section 2d, we shall contrast it with other rules of conduct; in the 3d section, opposite doctrines shall be stated and refuted; in the 4th, we shall prove directly the existence of natural law; and lastly, we shall show the consequences of blotting out natural law, and replacing it by positive legislation.

SEC. I. WHAT IS NATURAL LAW?

4. Definition of Law, Moral and Physical. Sir William Blackstone opens the second section of his introduction to the study of the laws of England with the following words:

"Law, in its most general and comprehensive sense, signifies a rule of action, and is applied indiscriminately to all kinds of actions, whether animate or inanimate, rational or irrational. Thus we say, the law of motion, of gravitation, of optics, or mechanics, as well as the law of nature and of nations. And it is that rule of action which is prescribed by some superior, and which the inferior is bound to obey."

In order to make his definition sufficiently universal, Blackstone has used the words *action, prescribed, obey,* to denote irrational as well as rational activities; the indiscriminate use of these terms has led modern writers to conclude that physical laws and moral rules are of the same nature, and that both are equally inflexible in practice. Nothing could be further from the mind of Blackstone, and from truth. Let us briefly point out the differences between a physical and a moral rule of action.

1st. A moral law is imposed upon reasonable beings; a physical law does not suppose intellect in its subject; nay, if it be not *physical* only, but *material* also (that is, ruling material forces only), it formally excludes the use of reason on the part of the beings which it governs. Thus the great Gospel maxim, *love thy neighbor as thyself,* requires in men both understanding and will; but the law of chemical affinity excludes both. Man must know who is his neighbor, and what is charity, in order to carry out the behest of Christ: an atom of sulphur does not know what oxygen is, or in what manner chemical elements combine, but absolute incapacity to think does not prevent sulphur from combining with oxygen according to definite proportions. A moral law must be known in order to be binding; ignorance of a physical law does not impair its efficiency.

5. A Moral Law implies freedom of the Will; a Physical Law excludes it. 2d. A moral law implies freedom of will, for it would be absurd to *command* if the precept could not be either obeyed or disregarded by him who has to carry it out. Kant says very justly: "The word 'ought,' when we consider merely the course of nature, has neither application nor meaning." The reason is plain: the word "ought" supposes the word "can;" when possibility is replaced by absolute necessity, then the word "ought" and the word "duty" become meaningless. Nobody orders a flower to bloom, throw out its petals, or make room for the fruit; the command would be supremely absurd; but a father may, by his precepts, direct his son to acquire those intellectual and moral developments which go to make the perfect man.

6. Imputability is a consequence of Freedom. 3d. The actions performed in pursuance of, or in opposition to, a moral law are imputable to the agent; for being free to give or to refuse compliance, his determination is truly his own. The agent is *sui juris,* and therefore accountable for what he does or refuses to do. Not so with regard to physical laws, even when they affect reasonable beings. A man may study or not, do good, remain idle, or do evil, but he cannot add one inch to his stature, or delay death by one single moment. All he can do with regard to physical law is to use his knowledge of physical forces to place himself in the best possible conditions to be beneficially affected by their influence: *directly,* he is unable to control their energy. An engineer may see a train rushing to destruction; if he has not at his disposal a force equal and contrary to the momentum of the ill-fated train, all his will power will be of no avail to avert the disaster. Again, you cannot say that the locomotive does right or does wrong, for it has no control whatever on the force which drives it forward; look, however, upon man, apparently carried away by the passing madness of anger; perhaps he has already his hand on a death-dealing weapon, but he recollects the command: *Thou shalt not kill:* his will makes a powerful effort to control the frenzy of passion; a brief thought, a brief struggle, and reason has conquered; the weapon falls harmless from his hand. The locomotive cannot check its impulse; man can control his passion. Hence the locomotive is not accountable for its work, which is not really its own; but man is responsible for his action, since he shapes it himself.

7. Moral and physical necessity. 4th. Both moral and physical laws impose a necessity. But that necessity is moral in the one case, and physical in the other. A physical necessity is the inevitable sequence of cause and effect in the material world. If two locomotives are sped toward each other on the same track, then unless forces equal and contrary to their respective momenta be applied in time, it is a physical necessity that they should crash into each other. Moral necessity is the impossibility of *rightfully* committing an unlawful act, or of making unlawful an act in every respect lawful; in other words, it is the incompatibility of lawfulness and unlawfulness as predicated of the same act under the same aspect. A sane man may abstain from lying, stealing, or committing murder, but these criminal acts once perpetrated, he cannot alter their character in the least. It will be forever true that on a certain day he became a liar, a thief, or a murderer. W. S. Lilly expresses this truth with great clearness in the following words:

"Physical law says, 'Given such and such antecedents, and such consequences follow.' Moral law declares, 'In such circumstances, such action *ought* to follow.' Physical law declares, 'This is how things are.' Moral law says, 'This is how things *ought* to be.' You cannot get that 'ought' from a universe of observed facts, from an infinite series of experiences. The word 'ought,' Kant observes, in a well-known passage of his *Critique of Pure Reason*, expresses a species of necessity which nature does not and cannot present to the mind of man. The understanding knows nothing in nature but that which is, or has been, or will be. It would be absurd to say that anything in nature *ought* to be other than it is, in the relation in which it stands. Indeed, the word 'ought,' when we consider the work of nature, has neither application nor meaning. . . . Whatever number of motives nature may present to my will, whatever sensuous impulses, it is beyond their power to pronounce the word *ought*." *

Thus, moral and physical law differ with regard to the beings to which they apply; the former requiring in its subject intelligence and free will, the latter demanding no intelligence, and excluding free will on the part of the subject. Actions performed in obedience or in opposition to moral law are imputable to the agent; under the sway of physical law, the agent is not responsible.

8. Common features. While the differences between moral and physical law are profound and well defined, there are some features common to both. They are both rules or patterns, and both suppose a lawgiver. The distinctions which we have just mentioned, far from being overlooked by Blackstone, are clearly stated in the following text of the great jurist:

" Thus, when the Supreme Being formed the universe and created matter out of nothing, He impressed certain principles upon that matter, from which it cannot depart, and without which it would cease to be. When He put that matter into motion, He established certain laws of motion, to which all movable bodies must conform. . . . If we farther advance, from mere inactive matter to vegetable and animal life, we shall find them still governed by laws, more numerous indeed, but equally fixed and invariable. . . . This, then, is the general signification of law, a rule of action dictated by some superior being: and in those creatures that have neither the power to think nor to will, such laws must be invariably obeyed,

---

* Right and Wrong, p. 52.

so long as the creature itself subsists, for its existence depends on that obedience. But laws, in their more confined sense, and in which it is our present business to consider them, denote the rules, not of action in general, but of human action or conduct. . . .

"As man depends absolutely upon his Maker for everything, it is necessary that he should, in all points, conform to his Maker's will.

"This will of his Maker is called the law of nature. For as God, when He created matter, and endued it with a principle of mobility, established certain rules for the perpetual direction of that motion; so, when He created man, and endued him with free will to conduct himself in all parts of life, He laid down certain immutable laws of human nature, whereby that free will is in some degree regulated and restrained, and gave him also the faculty of reason to discover the purport of those laws." *

9. The Pandects agree with Blackstone. The following passage of the Pandects, Book I., Tit. 2, has been often misunderstood and travestied; yet it means substantially the same thing as the text of Blackstone:

"Natural law is what nature has taught all living beings, for it is not the exclusive property of man, but extends its sway over animals, whether born in the air, on the earth, or in the depths of the sea. . . . Civil law must be distinguished from the law of nations, for each civilized nation uses partly the laws common to all, and partly those that each commonwealth has instituted for its own benefit; and these laws, devised by each people for its welfare, constitute the civil right, i. e., the individual right

---

* Introduction, § 2, n. 39.

of the city. But what the rational nature has established among all men is equally in force everywhere, and is called the right of nations, because it is observed by all nations. . . . Natural laws, which are observed alike among all nations, are due to a divine providence; they remain in full force and are immutable; but the laws which are enacted by individual commonwealths are wont to be often changed, either by the tacit consent of the people or by new legislation."

That the jurisconsult does not mean that animals are amenable to law in the same sense as man, is evident from what is said in Book IX., Tit. 1. *Si quadrupes;* there it is stated that animals cannot be sued for damages, because they have not the use of reason; but their masters or keepers may be sued for damages inflicted by their four-footed subjects. The true meaning is this: When a purpose is to be obtained universally, such, for instance, as the preservation of species, nature gives animals an instinct which makes up for the absence of reason; or, as St. Thomas has it, some faint reflection of the divine reason pervades the whole universe. The law which is exclusively human, and at the same time universal, is what Justinian calls *jus gentium,* and is what we understand by natural law or natural right.

Cicero, in his oration *pro Milone,* describes it as follows:

" There is a law, Judges, not written, but born with us, which we have not learned or received by tradition, or read, but which we have sucked in and imbibed from nature itself, which we were not trained in, but which is ingrained in us."

And elsewhere:

"No nation can overthrow or annul it, neither a Senate nor a whole people can relieve us from its injunctions."

10. Definition and properties of Natural Law. Whether this unwritten law be a noumenon only, or a phenomenon also; be it ideal merely, or real as well, we can now realize what those great legists understood by natural law; let us try to embody the concept in a short and scientific definition: *Natural law is a body of moral principles which reason itself teaches, and which are binding on all men.* The properties are easily derived from the definition. Natural law must be universal, perpetual, immutable, and easily known, at least with regard to its first principles. It must be universal, since it binds all men and comes directly from nature, which is the same in all men. Just as in the physical order, assuming that the law of gravitation rules all material bodies, we must conclude that it is universal in the realm of matter. It must be *perpetual,* because coextensive with nature, and nature, considered ideally, or as a noumenon, is eternal; in its concrete existence it is, so far as we know, perpetual. It must be *immutable,* as universal truths are immutable. Of course, its applications may change. Thus the law of gravitation remains the same, although it causes a balloon to rise and a stone to fall; its application is modified by the specific gravity of bodies and by the presence of other forces. Natural law must be *easily known,* at least with regard to its first principles; otherwise it would not be a fit rule of conduct to direct mankind. It may be, of course, better known and better applied by some than by others, for reason is not equally developed in all men. We have a parallel case in theoretical knowledge. The axioms and postulates of geometry are so evident that any rational being to whom the terms are properly explained sees at once the truth of the position. Some theorems are so closely connected with those principles that it is difficult to know whether the theorems are not as self-evident as the axioms themselves; a sort of impatience is clearly perceived on the countenances of the disciples when the master goes through a demonstration which to his pupils appears unnecessary; the first postulates are understood by all; subsequent deductions may require greater mental powers, while the most distant conclusions may be reached only by superior intellects. If there be such a thing as natural law, a similar progression must be observable. Some rules will be self-evident for all men who can understand their meaning; immediate conclusions will be accepted almost as readily as the first principles; remote conclusions may tax to the utmost the minds of philosophers, legislators, and judges. If it be asked why moral conclusions are not, in fact, accepted as readily as mere mathematical truths, I will answer that the former involve consequences which are not always acceptable to self-love, and that, moreover, elementary mathematical laws take hold of the senses as well as of the mind, and with the combined energy of both imperatively demand the assent of the intellect.

11. Objective reality of Natural Law, and consequences of this reality.

Since the essential properties of natural law are universality, perpetuity, immutability, intelligibility, where shall we find its origin, or, if you will allow me this metaphor, the first and standard text of this law? Not in beings that surround us, for they have none of the properties which are essential to it. Not in our intellect, for the intellect perceives but does not *create* the objects which it perceives; a proposition must be true before the intellect sees that it is true; moreover, as these truths are practical and imperative, they suppose an authority capable of commanding the obedience of man. No wonder, then, that Kant said that two things struck him with awe—the expanse of the heavens and human conscience. Both point unmistakably to a real being which this world cannot encompass. The German philosopher had attempted to build the whole edifice of philosophy on a mere subjective basis; and behold, there appears an objective reality which marks its impress on this world with such overwhelming power that it is impossible to mistake it for the footprint of man. Kant does not close his eyes to the evidence thus thrust upon him; he admits that this fact involves both the immortality of the soul and the existence of God, and he postulates both. Weaker minds, obscured by a subjective theory, would have failed to acknowledge the cogency of the deduction:

"Happiness is the condition of the rational being in whose whole existence everything goes according to wish and will. . . . As practical reason demands the conjunction of moral perfection and felicity, it is to be found in a being who is author at once of nature and of the moral law, and this is God." (Kant, as quoted in Bain's *Moral Law*, p. 323.)

But the same reasoning compels us to advance one step further and accept the statement of Aquinas (as St. Thomas is called by modern philosophers): " The natural law is but a participation of the eternal law mirrored in a created intellect." (Sec. 1, 2d Ed., p. 91, Art. 2.)

12. The Eternal Law defined. What then is the eternal law? St. Augustine answers the question:

" It is the reason, or the will of God, commanding the observance of the natural order, and forbidding its violations."

One may be perplexed at first by seeing apparently two sources assigned to human obligation, but a little reflection shows that both spring from the same fountain-head. If we trace to its source the idea of *obligation* alone, then we stop at the will of the Superior Being, who has the right to command; but if we seek the *reason* of the obligation, then we must go to the intellect which has conceived the existing order. It is this order eternally perceived by God, and decreed by His will, which is the *ultima ratio* of the law of nature. Its genesis involves the following series: Order perceived by the divine intellect, decreed by the divine will, mirrored in created intellects, binding on created wills. Strange to say, this very doctrine is strongly advocated by Cicero in his treatise *de Legibus*. One short quotation will suffice:

" This law did not begin to exist when it was written, but when it was *born,* and it was born at the same time with the divine intellect. Wherefore, the true law, the primary law, the law which can fully command and forbid, is the ever true mind of the supreme being, Jupiter. . . . If the supreme law is the divine intellect, when introduced in man, it dwells in the mind of the wise." *

SEC. II. POSITIVE LAW AND OTHER RULES OF CONDUCT.

13. Various Rules of Conduct. This explanation of natural law would remain incomplete if we did not compare the law of nature with positive law and with other rules of conduct, connected with either or with both.

Natural law is that which originates in nature itself— that is, in the intellect and will of the Author of nature, and which is imperfectly reproduced in the human intellect.

Positive law is that which has its source in the wisdom and free will of men.

Equity is a part or an application of natural law. Legality, properly so called, is the body of existing positive laws.

Natural and revealed law come directly from our Maker; the former is " born with us," to use the words of Cicero, the latter is manifested by supernatural means. The very same precept may be both natural and revealed. For instance, " Thou shalt not steal " is both a rule of natural law and a precept revealed on Mount Sinai.

---

* Cicero, de Legibus, Lib. 11, Chap. IV.-V.

Human positive law derives its binding force directly from the authority of the State; indirectly from the divine power, some share of which is communicated to the State.

"This law of nature," says Blackstone, "being coeval with mankind and dictated by God Himself, is, of course, superior in obligation to any other. It is binding all over the globe, in all countries, and at all times: no human laws are of any validity if contrary to this; and such of them as are valid derive all their force and all their authority, mediately or immediately, from this original. . . .

"Providence . . . in compassion to the frailty, the imperfection, and the blindness of human reason, hath been pleased, at sundry times and in divers manners, to discover and enforce its laws by an immediate and direct revelation. . . .

"Upon these two foundations, the law of nature and the law of revelation, depend all human laws; that is to say, no human laws should be suffered to contradict these."

14. Essential elements of a Moral Law. Every orthodox ethical writer, nay, every sound theologian, will endorse the words of Blackstone. Let us now give a definition broad enough to embrace all the rules of good conduct. A moral law may be defined thus: *A permanent rule of conduct, laid down by a lawful power, for the good of the community, duly promulgated, and protected by a sufficient sanction.* We say *permanent* to distinguish a law from a command issued to meet particular circumstances; thus, when a general sends a regiment to charge a battery, he issues an order, but does not enact a law. A law must be laid down by the lawful power, otherwise it is null and void. Thus the President alone, the Senate alone, or the House of Representatives without the concurrence of the Senate, cannot enact laws properly so called, though they can make regulations for their own conduct. *A fortiori,* if a successful general should unlawfully seize the supreme power, he could not enact or sanction laws, and his efforts to enforce his behests would be so many treasonable attempts. A law must be for the good of the community. For if it were absolutely evident that it is contrary to the good of the people, or in opposition to the Constitution, it would have no binding force. Observe, however, that the mischievous tendency must be perfectly evident, and that every individual citizen is not judge of that evidence. In this country, if a law be decidedly mischievous, it is likely to be also unconstitutional, and the Supreme Court is the ultimate judge of its constitutionality. But if we suppose that it is mischievous, yet constitutional, then Congress is the judge; and the people have in the ballot-box a means to compel legislators to rescind it. No subject can, on the strength of his own private opinion, bid defiance to the law; all the subject can do is to judge that the law does not bind him in the secret recesses of his conscience; and even in that *forum internum* he must have complete evidence; as soon as there is a doubt the axiom holds good: *In dubio standum est pro superiore*—in doubt, we must stand on the side of authority.

Promulgation is essential for the validity of law, because, in order to be binding, it must reach the subject and bear the stamp of authority, and both conditions are fulfilled by the official declaration called *promulgation.* Sanction does not add to law any moral binding force, but it is necessary for its permanence and protection; it does not belong to the essence, but to the integrity; not to the *esse,* but to the *bene esse* of the law.

Wherever laws properly so called do exist, we must be able to find: 1st, a rule of conduct; 2d, a lawgiver having sufficient authority; 3d, a public good to be obtained; 4th, a clear promulgation of the law; 5th, a sanction to maintain its stability.

SEC. III.   HOBBES, BENTHAM, PUFFENDORF, AND AUSTIN.

15. Hobbes.   Among those who denied the existence of natural law, none had so great an influence over modern thought as John Austin. As a mere legist, we do not question his merit; as a philosopher he is below mediocrity. His system is an incoherent compound of the doctrines of Hobbes, Bentham, and Puffendorf. A brief notice of the respective systems of those three writers will give us a clear view of the errors which have confused a mind which otherwise might have had a truer conception of the basis upon which human legislation must rest. According to Hobbes, the natural condition of man is that of " war of every man against every other man." "Men have no pleasure, but, on the contrary, a great deal of grief, in keeping company where there is no power able to overawe them all." * There is no escape from that chaotic state

---

* Leviathan, Chap. XIII., p. 112.

but a complete surrender of all individual rights to a sovereign power, which he appropriately calls *Leviathan*, the monster of the deep whom none can resist. In that supreme power lies the origin of all morality; here we must quote *verbatim:*

"No rule of good and evil (is) to be taken from the nature of the objects themselves, but from the person of the man, where there is no commonwealth; or in a commonwealth, from the person who representeth it, or from an arbitrator or judge whom men disagreeing shall by consent set, and make his consent the rule thereof."

"Free will is a thing that was never mentioned among Christians. . . . But some years past, the doctors of the Roman Church have exempted from this dominion of God's will the will of man."

The world did not know that Roman Catholics had invented free will; but let us pass on.

"The standard of men living in society is the law of the State. . . . Before the names of just and unjust can have place, there must be some coercive power to compel men equally to the performance of their covenants by the terror of some punishment greater than the benefit they expect by the breach of their covenant." *

Whereupon Mr. Spencer exclaims:

"Grant that justice is the performance of a covenant. Now, suppose it is to be performed voluntarily: there is justice. In such case, however, there is justice in the absence of coercion: which is contrary to the hypothesis. The only conceivable rejoinder is an absurd one: voluntary performance of a contract is impossible. Assert this, and

---

* Leviathan, Chap. XV., p. 131.

the doctrine that right and wrong come into existence with the establishment of sovereignty is defensible. Decline to assert it, and the doctrine vanishes." (*Data of Ethics,* Chap. IV., n. 18.)

We need not discuss this horrible system, which would justify any excess of despotism. Presented in its nudity, it can have no attraction whatever.

16. Bentham. Let us pass on to Bentham: "Pleasure and pain govern the world," so he tells us. "It is for those sovereign masters alone to point out what we *ought* to do as well as to determine what we *shall* do." (Introduction, Chap. I.)

The rest of the theory we must merely sum up. Happiness is the preponderance of pleasure over pain. In pleasure we must consider: 1st, intensity; 2d, duration; 3d, certainty; 4th, proximity; 5th, fecundity; 6th, purity —i. e., its being unmixed with pain; 7th, comprehensiveness—i. e., number of persons benefited.

The standard of morals is utility—i. e., the tendency of an action to promote happiness and to prevent misery.

The renunciation of pleasure for any other motive than to procure a greater pleasure, or to avoid a greater pain, Bentham sneeringly terms *Asceticism.*

We will not stop to refute this system.* It is enough to observe that it follows *logically* from its teachings that every successful rascality must be perfectly moral; and every deed of heroism which involves sacrifice of pleasure

---

* We shall return to this subject when treating of the various forms of Utilitarianism.

or self-interest is contrary to the standard of morality set up to guide mankind. A scoundrel who is led to the gallows is only foolish; he has lost the advantages which good conduct might perhaps have secured to him, and incurred the anger of society, which he might have avoided. A Damien who for many years courts death under its most loathsome aspect, without even knowing whether the world at large will gain anything by his long martyrdom, is not a hero, but a lunatic.

17. Puffendorf. Puffendorf's theory is immeasurably nobler than Utilitarianism: he seeks the standard of morality in the free will of God, but he is guilty of the following absurdity: "All the motions and actions of men, upon setting aside all law, both divine and human, are perfectly indifferent." (*Law of Nature,* Chap. II., Book I., n. 6.) Indeed, even blasphemy, murder, and lying! Puffendorf imagined that his opponents admitted the existence of some principle coeval with God and superior to Him; such a thing was never thought of by those who asserted that morality did not originate in a free decree of the divine will. But as the divine intellect is the fountain from which flows every truth, we compare human actions with the divine ideal, which, in its perfection, is realized in God alone. No exterior principle can lay God under obligation, but He cannot be inconsistent with Himself, and His might cannot be at war with His wisdom or His justice.

18. Austin. Austin attempted to combine all these systems together. With Hobbes he held that morality originated in positive law; with Bentham, that utility was the rule of moral excellence; with Puffendorf, that the positive will of God was the test of moral righteousness. God's will, according to him, always coincides with utility. It is unnecessary to distinguish natural from positive law. Utility always coincides with the free will of God, and positive law is the expression both of the will of God and of utility. Of course, his system abounds in contradictions.

"The distinction of law and morality," says he, "into natural and positive is a needless and futile subtility; but still the distinction is founded on a real and manifest difference." *

Here is a distinction, not without a difference, but based on a *manifest* difference, which, according to him, is a useless subtility. Elsewhere he declares that the distinction is important. Thus, there is an *important distinction,* based on a *manifest difference,* which is a *useless subtility.* This extraordinary logician calls the majestic language of Blackstone *jargon,* and the nervous language of Hooker *fustian.*† He finds fault with Blackstone for saying that a human law which conflicts with the law of God has no validity, and in the same breath he says that "such a law ought not to be imposed . . . for a human law which conflicts with that *ultimate test* (utility) and a human law which conflicts with the law of God, are one and the same

---

* The Province of Jurisprudence Determined, London (1861), pp. 163, 164.
† Ibidem, pp. 234, 235.

thing denoted by different words. And so utility and the law of God are one and the same thing."

Immediately after he adds: "But to say that a human law which conflicts with the law of God is, therefore, not binding is stark nonsense."

And then he adds that: "Numberless laws adverse to utility have been and are enforced in every age and nation; and yet that such human laws conflict with the law of God is known through the very exponent adopted by Blackstone."

And thus there is a command contrary to God's will, contrary to utility (the very standard set up by Austin), which is binding on human conscience. And in order to prove this absurdity, he appeals to the hangman, and assures us that if he (Austin) objects: "The tribunal demonstrates the unsoundness of my objection by hanging me up in pursuance of the law which I impugn."

A strong argument indeed, but is it a *jurist* that makes use of it?

Austin does not deny free will as Hobbes does, but, like him, he gives Leviathan unlimited power: "Now, it follows from the essential difference of a positive law, and from the nature of sovereignty and independent political society, that the power of a monarch properly so called, or the power of a sovereign number in its collegiate capacity, is incapable of legal limitation."

Here we must part company with Austin: he has supplied us with a good demonstration *ex absurdis;* we must now turn our attention to the direct proofs, which establish beyond the possibility of a doubt the real and concrete existence of natural law.

SEC. IV. DIRECT PROOFS.

19. What Natural Law is not, and what it is. We have briefly noticed the opponents of Blackstone who have retained some hold on public opinion; let us now prove directly the main thesis. But first let the question be clearly defined. When we say that natural law is *inborn, engraven* by nature itself in the heart of man, we do not pretend that every man is born with a tablet containing the ten commandments printed in bold, legible type. No, the question is whether there are some moral truths which hold in the moral order that place which the axioms and postulates of any science hold in the intellectual order; whether the three fundamental axioms of Roman law, " Live honestly—harm nobody—give every one his due," are as clear in the moral order as the axioms: " One thing cannot at the same time be and not be. The whole is greater than the part. A straight line is the shortest distance between two points." We do not hold that either set of axioms is intuitively known by man the very moment he comes into this world, but we maintain that as soon as these propositions are duly explained to a man who is not mentally blind, they are at once accepted as evidently true. Such is the sense of the following passage of Blackstone:

" As He (the Creator) is a Being of infinite wisdom, He has laid down only such laws as were founded in those relations of justice that existed in the nature of things antecedent to any positive precept. These are the eternal, immutable laws of good and evil, to which the Creator Himself in all His dispensations conforms, and which He has enabled reason to discover, so far as they are necessary for the conduct of human actions. Such among others are these principles: that we should live honestly, should hurt nobody, and should render to every one his due; to which three general precepts Justinian has reduced the whole doctrine of law."

Observe that it is not necessary that every man should accept them; there are insane persons who will deny evident moral truths, just as there are intellectual lunatics who will deny the clearest axioms of science; the former may call good *evil,* as Proudhon actually did; the latter may go on looking for the squaring of the circle; it is enough that every well-disposed man of sound mind should feel compelled to admit the three rules of Justinian, without requiring a demonstration. Nay, the idea of duty, more or less clearly defined, exists in all reasonable men. If the " ought " of Kant is found to be the common property of all mankind, the fact is sufficient to prove the existence of natural law. For the concept of duty contains the idea of permanent obligation; it argues the existence of a superior being; it is unquestionably for the good of the human race; it is known better than any human law; and if any one should attempt to throw off every moral obligation, he would soon find out that the law is abundantly sanctioned. We have here the essential elements of a law. It is not *written,* except metaphorically; but it is so well promulgated that it abides in the conscience of every reasonable man.

20. The three axioms of Roman Law. But we are not reduced to the monosyllable "ought." Are not the three axioms selected by the Roman jurists and by Blackstone as clearly known to the whole human race as the concept of duty? In Austin's *Province of Jurisprudence* we find a proof the strength of which escapes his mind, and for which he has no rebuttal whatever. It is drawn from the Roman jurists:

"Besides such portions of positive law as are respectively peculiar to particular nations or states, there are rules of positive law which obtain in all nations. And since these moral rules are observed by all mankind, they may be called the *jus omnium gentium,* or *commune omnium hominum jus.* Now, these rules being universal cannot be purely or simply of human invention and position. They rather are made by man on laws coming from God, or from the intelligent and rational nature which is the soul and guide of the universe." *

Very true; but if there are such rules binding on the whole world, and coextensive with human nature, are not such rules natural laws, or laws of the human nature? Thus Austin himself supplies us with a fact which proves the existence of natural law, the very thing he so loudly denies. After giving us a proof *ab absurdo,* he kindly supplies us with a direct one.

21. Proof from experience. But we need not call all nations to bear witness to the truth of axioms which are based on the eternal fitness of things and on the

---
* The Province of Jurisprudence, Author's Preface, p. XLIIII.

rational nature of man; let us consult our own consciousness and our own experience. Since we first enjoyed the use of reason, was there ever a time when we did not believe that man must live honestly, harm nobody, and give every one his due? Did we need reasoning to prove that to us? If, as far as we can recollect, those principles were always clear to our mind, then at the very dawn of reason we were in possession of some evident rules of conduct. The possession of those universal first principles, which are not acquired by a toilsome effort of the mind, but seem inborn because the mind is naturally disposed to assimilate them, is what St. Thomas Aquinas calls a participation of the divine reason, whose light permeates the whole world.

Passing from ourselves to others, have we ever found persons who refused to accept these axioms? *And if we found such persons, had they not before accepted them as self-evident?* Were not the causes of this waning of that natural light clearly traceable to moral deteriorations? What man by a legitimate use of his intellect ever came to the conclusion that he need not live honestly, nor refrain from harming his neighbor, and that he may with impunity defraud others of their just dues? If, however, it be asserted that such cases are more common in the moral than in the speculative order, we will answer that there is no motive for a man to deny that the three angles of a plane triangle are equal to two right angles. Yet if one of those men of ill-balanced mind who are occasionally met with in this world should find that this simple theorem runs counter to a pet hobby, he would soon amuse us or bore us with his attempts to upset it. A man who would deny a first principle, such as *the whole is greater than the part,* would unquestionably be considered as insane; and it may very well be doubted whether a man could succeed in sincerely denying the three moral principles mentioned by Blackstone, without first dethroning his reason.

22. No valid objection can be drawn, either from the discovery of wild Human Beings, or from the difficulty of some Moral Deductions.
From the beginning we have stated that when we spoke of moral law, we considered it as applying to reasonable beings, not to irresponsible agents. For this reason, the objection drawn from wild children discovered in the woods is totally irrelevant: such beings are human indeed, but cannot exercise the powers distinctly human. Deductions from the first principles of natural law are subject to the same difficulties that surround other scientific reasonings; with this addition, that passions and self-interest conspire against reason. Nobody would question the ten commandments if they had not to be put into practice.

23. Proof from the Existence and Attributes of God.
The existence of natural law can also be proven from the existence and attributes of God, unless we have, with Kant, deduced the existence of God only from the noumenon and phenomenon of natural law; for, if we have followed this course, the deduction would involve a vicious circle. However, as the demonstration of the divine existence is chiefly based on the necessity of a first cause and

of a prime mover, we are perfectly justified in assuming as demonstrated the conclusions of theodicy * when we discuss ethical doctrines. Supposing, then, that God exists, that He is infinitely wise and infinitely just, we are compelled to admit that He must have made known to man through his natural reason the first principles of human conduct; otherwise man would have been placed in this world without the necessary means to attain the end for which he was created. Such a supposition is inconsistent both with wisdom and with justice; with wisdom, because there would be a want of adaptation of means to end; with justice, because God would have required of man the performance of acts to which, in the hypothesis, man would be bound without being aware of his obligation. Thus man would, at the same time, be bound and not bound morally; he would be bound, because on his conduct would depend his reaching the end for which he was created; he would not be bound, because the dependence would remain unknown to him. A contradiction would become unavoidable, and a contradiction as the term of divine activity is simply unthinkable. Thus we have an *a priori* as well as *a posteriori* proof of the existence of natural law, and it is impossible to deny it without ignoring evident facts and rejecting the divine existence. In fact, even those who consider God as a shadowy sort of unknowable entity admit some kind of natural law. Their contention is not that it

---

* Theodicy is the knowledge of God based on human reasoning. Theology is the knowledge of God derived from revelation.

does not exist, but that it may be traced to utility, evolution, or some other similar cause, as vague as the reality of an impersonal God. The existence of laws anterior and superior to man remains for them, as for us, unquestionably true.

SEC. V. CONSEQUENCES OF THE REJECTION OF NATURAL LAW.

24. Reductio ad absurdum. We can give but little time to the consideration of consequences which follow from the rejection of natural law, but we believe that common sense alone is quite equal to the task of drawing them and perceiving their absurdity. These consequences will form another demonstration *ex absurdis.*

1st. If morality and legality are the same thing, then laws may make any offence against what we call *morals* perfectly lawful. Should oppression, murder, wholesale robbery be commanded by law, they would become praiseworthy deeds. Does not common sense rebel against such a theory? Moreover, legality and morality in such case are in complete antagonism, and yet, according to the theory, they are one and the same thing. Here is a contradiction, evident enough to put all logicians to flight. "But," says Mr. Austin, "such laws *ought* not to be passed." Why, unless they are at variance with a higher standard of right? If so, there must be rules more imperative than legality, and we come back again to some sort of natural law from which we can judge whether the law ought to be passed, or ought not to be passed. Legality is and is not at the same time the highest standard.

2d. Legality itself falls to the ground and all jurisprudence with it. For why should we obey the law? Apparently on account of the general principle that a citizen must obey the laws of his country. But this principle does not belong to positive but to natural law. Therefore it cannot derive its validity from positive law, since the validity of the latter is derived from it. Unless we admit the existence of natural law, we run in a vicious circle from which there is no escape whatever.

25. Inalienable rights. 3d. If legality is supreme, there can be no inalienable right, no right that the majority is bound to respect. Austin does not shrink from this consequence. He tells us seriously: "A sacred or inalienable right is truly and indeed invaluable; for seeing that it means nothing, there is nothing with which it can be measured." *

What then becomes of the Declaration of Independence?

"We hold these truths to be self-evident: that all men are created equal; that they are endowed by their Creator with certain inalienable rights; that among these are life, liberty, and the pursuit of happiness."

Why are the existence and sacredness of natural rights so solemnly asserted? Because the Constitution of the United States, and the constitutions of the several States, are all based on natural law.

26. Conclusion. 4th. If the doctrine of Hobbes and Austin be true, any act of tyranny may become lawful, for

* Province of Jurisprudence, p. 48.

both tell us in almost the same words that the power of the sovereign, from its very nature, is incapable of legal limitation; and as no other can be found in the absence of natural law, the power of the sovereign is strictly unlimited. Thus, granting that Herod was the legal sovereign of the Jews, he had the right to order the massacre of the little babes of Bethlehem, and the soldiers were bound to carry out his infamous order. This illustration is not ours; it is supplied by Austin himself. We are not yet ready to prostrate ourselves at the feet of Hobbes' *Leviathan;* but let us also beware of sporting with theories which, if carried into practice, would destroy every liberty, and give up the whole world to absolute despotism.

THIRD LECTURE.

HUMAN ACTS AND ANIMAL MOTIONS.

SEC. I. MAN DIFFERS ESSENTIALLY FROM LOWER ANIMALS.

1. The missing link is yet missing. AMONG a few scientific men and a large number of would-be scientists may be observed a twofold tendency, as shocking to common sense as it is derogatory to the dignity of human nature. While some try to lower man to the rank of an improved monkey, others do their best to raise animals to membership in the human family. Happily, the missing link is yet missing—so at least says Dr. Virchow of Berlin, one of the most illustrious scientists of the present time.*

" Practical anthropology begins only with the quaternary or diluvial epoch, from which parts of skulls and skeletons are preserved. . . . But what do these remains teach us? Do they show us man in a lower stage of bodily development elsewhere unknown? . . . Fanatics themselves were contented when they could approximate these skulls to the type of the Australians or Fuegians, or even of the *Batavus genuinus,* i. e., of an old Frieslander.

" The distance of this position from what has been

---
* Wiesbaden, Sept. 24th, 1887.

expected is very great indeed. An Australian may have many defects or excess-formations, which give him a somewhat brutal appearance. Formerly this property was called bestial; recently it has been deemed better, in the interest of the theory of descent, to call it pithecoid. But, bestial and pithecoid though he be, the Australian is neither a monkey nor a pro-anthropos. On the contrary, he is a true man; and if our ancestors, perhaps, were once like him—which, by the way, is doubtful—all the same this would be irrelevant to the theory of descent. Fuegians have of late come among us, and we have had a chance to study their case. Brains of this tribe have been examined with all conceivable care, and the result is that our present methods are not sufficient to ascertain any fundamental difference between their brains and the brains of Europeans.

"The organization of diluvial man, as far as we know anything about him, was not below that of the savages of the present day. . . . It is now out of question to consider any savage tribe of to-day as an intermediate link between man and brute.

"Hence I declared several years ago, in the Anthropological Congress, that practical material has not yet been found for an inquiry into the pro-anthropos, and the possible pithecoid intermediate links." *

According to Prof. Virchow, there is nothing whatever to prove that our ancestors were arboreal in their

---

* Since this was written, Prof. Dubois has discovered a few scattered bones which some supposed to have belonged to a pro-anthropos. Their contention has not been made good. Krause, Virchow, Rosenberg hold that the bones do not belong to the same species; and Kropotkin, although himself an evolutionist, says that the *pithecanthropus* must be placed a *long way off from man.*—Nineteenth Century, March, 1896, p. 442.

habits, and we may yet trace our pedigree to Adam and Eve; but it is my purpose to show that between man and beast, besides the difference in *skulls*, there are mental and moral chasms which evolutionists cannot bridge. Let us first consider the nature of a human action, then the energies at work in mere animal activity. We shall next determine the properties which make human actions amenable both to natural and to positive law, and lastly touch upon the conditions which may exempt human acts from the sanctions of positive law, and free man himself from responsibility.

SEC. II. ESSENTIAL CHARACTERISTICS OF HUMAN ACTS.

2. Powers distinctly human: Understanding, Will, Intellectual Memory.
In order that the acts of man may truly be called *human,* they must bear the mark of the powers which belong to man alone, and which divide him from the lower orders of creation. These powers are the understanding, the will, and intellectual memory. We say *intellectual memory* because the recollection of phenomena does not necessarily involve intellectual power, while the remembrance of ideas, judgments, and reasonings is a consequence of mental activity. The common characteristic of these essentially human powers is the *universality* of their objects. When the eyes of the body see a plane triangular figure, the mind discerns what constitutes a plane triangle, and the concept thus acquired is applicable not only to the particular geometrical figure

mirrored on the retina, but to all plane figures limited by three straight lines forming three angles. As the same type can be reproduced indefinitely, the object is universal —that is to say it comprises all possible plane triangles. Thus also when our senses receive the impress of the human form; or, to speak more plainly, when we see a man, the mind knows that it is a being composed of body and soul, or a soul united with a body and forming with it a person. This is a concept which is universal, because it can be applied to all the men that were, that are, and that can ever be. Such universality is absolutely indispensable in order that the mind may compare different objects, discover what they have in common, and what belongs to the one and is wanting in the other. Hence those varied and complex processes which belong to the domain of reason, and enable it to step from known to unknown truths. Thus, considering several men, and eliminating the peculiar qualities and features which belong to them individually, it arrives at a concept of man in general, and determines the type of the human species.

General ideas are the specific operations of the human intellect. Its object is universal truth. Just as the human intellect goes beyond the physical perception to reach the general idea, so the human will goes beyond the present good to seek good itself. It may discard a present pleasure, however enticing it may be, to seek a good which is more substantial and more useful. It may also despise present pain for the sake of a good which is yet unseen. Why? Because no individual and limited good can fill the capacity of the human heart. Hence, when an individual and limited good solicits the acceptance of the will, the volitive power may pause, see how far the promised satisfaction falls short of the perfect bliss which is its goal, and discard this satisfaction for some other joy, less intense, perhaps, but which may bring it nearer to the possession of the infinite good, the *summum bonum,* which alone can satisfy its cravings.

As universal truth is the specific object of the intellect, so universal good, the *summum bonum* of the ancients, is the specific object of the human will.

Without universality, no comparison; without comparison, no deliberation; without deliberation, no free will. In a paper on *Darwinism and Politics,* Prof. David Ritchie accidentally lets fall from his pen the following sentence, which conveys more meaning than he seems aware of: " The capacity for thinking constitutes man's freedom. It is by thinking alone that he can rise above the position of nature's slave."

The capacity for thinking is not freedom itself, but it is unquestionably the foundation of free will. Were man unable to think, to compare, to deliberate, he would be captivated by any and every fleeting allurement; he would be the slave of his appetite; he would, like the lower animals, be led into captivity by every attractive object.

3. Free Will also is characteristic. Free will is another characteristic of human actions, and it follows naturally from the trend of the intellectual and volitive powers toward universal objects. As during this life an infinite good is never fully attained by man, his will is never attracted by an object coextensive with its capacity. What is wanted in attractive energy on the part of the object must be supplemented by the inward energy of the soul. The soul has that energy; it is too great to be mastered by any object which is not coextensive with its perceptive and volitive powers. It is attracted, but not carried away without its consent. The determination of its acts remains with it. The acts belong really to the will, or rather to the man who owns both the reason which has turned its light on the object, and the will which has either rejected or accepted it. We cannot here stop to prove the existence of free will; we shall devote the next lecture to this momentous question; for the present we shall assume the existence of free will as *one of those primary truths which cannot be discarded for any other truth which may seem to conflict with it.* Such is the stand taken by Wharton in his able work on Criminal Law.

" To responsibility (imputability) there are, we must remember, two constituents: capacity of intellectual discrimination, and freedom of the will. If there be either incapacity to distinguish between right and wrong as to the particular act, or delusion as to the act, or inability to do or refrain from doing the act, then there is no responsibility. The difficulty is practical. No matter what may be our speculative views as to the existence of conscience, or of freedom of action, we are obliged, when we determine responsibility, to affirm both." *

---

* Wharton, Criminal Law, Chap. III., p. 53. " This view (Determinism) takes not only from jurisprudence, but from

4. Consciousness essential. Thus, actions, in order to be truly and perfectly human, must be done with knowledge, with deliberation; they must be the result of a free determination of the will; they must be truly traceable to the agent, and therefore imputable to him. Such are the only actions which deserve either praise or censure, reward or punishment. Such are the only actions whose moral righteousness or moral obliquity is to be discussed by lawyers and determined by judges.

Human actions must be *conscious;* that is, they must be known to the agent. They must be accomplished for some end or purpose, for otherwise they could not exist; since no rational being can act without a purpose. In fact, the last condition involves all the others. A man who acts with the view to obtain a certain end acts with some degree of deliberation; he exercises his understanding, for without understanding no deliberation is possible. Hence we might briefly define a human act: " That which is freely accomplished by man with a view to an end."

It follows from this definition that if a man moves about without any aim at all, if he be idiotic, insane, asleep, or in a trance, his act is not fully *human;* in other words, it is not such as the powers *distinctly human* would make it were they brought into play. Let a philosopher, in a fit of abstraction, put on an unseemly garment, or a man walk in his sleep on the ridge of a high building, or a maniac insist on being recognized as the king of the Sandwich

---

life, its moral dignity, making the former a mere marshalling of mechanisms, and the latter a mere mechanism of necessities."

Islands; such acts are performed by men, but they do not reflect the fulness of human nature.

5. Personality essential to Man. Man being conscious of his own acts, and being the cause or principle of his own acts, is what we call a *person*. A person, according to Boethius, is a *reasonable nature subsisting individually;* that is to say, a certain type of being endowed with reason, having the essentials of the kind to which it belongs, but enjoying a distinct existence of its own, which persists throughout the minor changes which may affect the body or the spirit.

As a person, man can say, I, *Ego,* referring to his own self, whatever happens to his compound being. Man, as Kant says, is an end-in-self; that is, he has a certain felicity to attain, and that felicity belongs to him and is the goal of his own desires. He can have rights and duties, and can be called to account for his acts, for it is his own will that determines whether they shall be in accordance with moral law or at variance with it. This independence constitutes his dignity, but also his responsibility. Not so with the lower animals.

SEC. III. MERE ANIMAL ACTS.

6. The characteristics of Human Acts are not found in Animal Motions. The brute has no universal perception; it is, therefore, incapable of reasoning, deliberation, or free will. It is incapable of rising to a reflex consciousness of its own existence, of its pains, and of its pleasurable sensations. It cannot utter the *Ego* which is characteristic of man. It is not a person, but simply an individual irrational being. Hence it can feel pleasure or pain, but it is not, in a strict sense, happy or unhappy; because happiness and misfortune properly so called require conscious knowledge and appreciation of the facts which go to make up the lot in life of the being which is said to be happy or unhappy. The keen and witty author of *The Tribes on Our Borders* remarks that animals have no imagination, and that in this life imagination is one of the chief sources of what is commonly called happiness or unhappiness.*

7. Animals have no Intellect. But how do we prove that animals have no intellect, but instinct only—in other words, that they perceive individual objects, but cannot reach the essential idea, the nature, the general type, which is reproduced in every individual? By a proof which is negative indeed, but which is nevertheless convincing. We must start from the principle that a supposed cause which has no effect at all, even under the conditions best calculated to bring out its activity, were that activity real, cannot have a real existence. Now, in the action of animals, no trace of a universal idea

---

* The anonymous writer of this charming book is said to be an officer in the British Army. His assertions must be qualified: animals have no power of combining images, so as to make up new fanciful devices—in other words, they have no *fancy;* but they may receive images which leave a more or less permanent impression on the brain. That they have *imagination* of the latter kind is proved by the fact that they can *dream.* During his sleep a dog will bark or growl at an imaginary intruder, or fawn on a master who has no real existence. These impressions, however, are not referred by the animal to his individuality: the personal *Ego* is wanting.

can be detected; connected impressions are indeed clearly discernible, but no reasoning is manifested. A scientist who took up the cause of animals, after trying to prove that animals have not instinct only, but intelligence also, admits in a note that they are incapable of universal ideas, of conceiving time, space, of knowing spiritual objects, of accomplishing any progress by their own effort. How did that author fail to see that he was giving up his own thesis?

8. Animals are not Progressive. In fact, animals are not progressive; they perform their instinctive acts without the advantages of education. A bee shapes the cell as well at the beginning as at the end of its existence. No improvement has marked the shaping of the honeycomb since the beginning of the world. None were needed, for under the direction of instinct, as if governed necessarily by a master mind, they have always done their work perfectly, although without deliberation. Evidently their Maker has so framed their tiny organism that the right impulse comes just at the right moment, and is entirely independent of reflection. On the other hand, the simplest acts of reflection are absolutely wanting when circumstances would certainly conjure them up were the reflecting power present. Thus a dog will sit by a fire when the flame flickers and the embers are dying out. The poor beast may yelp to call its master, but it will not take up a stick of wood to replenish the hearth. A horse will shy at a piece of white paper, although repeated experiences have shown that wind-tossed paper is perfectly harmless.

Animals may indeed be trained, but by the skill of man, who compels them to repeat mechanically a series of acts until repetition produces connected impressions in their organism. This training, animals do not as a rule transmit to their young, and man has to begin the work again with each new offspring. As soon as the influence of human reason is withdrawn, the brute sinks again to its own level. Moreover, there is the strongest contrast between the perfection of natural instinctive acts and the bungling manner in which animals imitate man, or perform the tricks which man has taught them. Impressions connected naturally or artificially make up the whole fabric of the so-called animal intelligence.

Having no power of deliberation, animals cannot be free; they follow mechanically the predominant impression, and the skill of the trainer consists in developing and connecting those impressions which will make the animal subservient to his will.

9. Animals have no Moral Powers. Having no free will, animals can have no rights, properly so called. For right is a moral power, enabling a rational being to act or to abstain from acting, and requiring of others to perform certain acts, or abstain from them. Rights must reside in persons, and persons are, as we have seen, reasonable natures subsisting individually. Animals have no personal end, but their end is that of the species to which they belong; and they are put in this world to subserve the purposes of men.

10. Yet they must not be injured wantonly. But does this justify man in ill-treating animals or killing them wantonly? Not at all, for man is placed on earth not to mar but to maintain order. To introduce suffering where suffering is not useful is unquestionably to mar the beauty of God's work; it is to bring evil where good should have existed.

The State may enact laws for the prevention of cruelty to animals; not in order to maintain animal rights which have no real existence, but to prevent the deterioration of the species, or to save men from the brutalizing influence of wanton torture inflicted on their dumb subjects.

11. Under what plea may Vivisection become permissible? What about vivisection? If it be indispensable in order to acquire a knowledge of some organic laws, which, if better understood, may enable us to benefit the human race, vivisection is permissible, just as it is allowable to kill animals in order to support our own life. Animals have no end of their own; they are created for the sake of man. No more suffering than is strictly necessary should be inflicted on animals. In maiming or killing animals, man reaches the extreme limit of his dominion over them, and nothing but an urgent need can justify him in using his power to such an extent as to make it destructive. Let us avoid both extremes; we must not inflict torture or shed the blood of a brute needlessly, but neither should we, on the other hand, bestow on animals the prerogatives of man.

12. Physical and Moral Liberty. We have seen that without free will, actions cannot be morally attributed to the agent; for he that cannot act or abstain from acting and choose between different modes of action does not himself determine the character of his action; that character cannot, therefore, be attributed to him. The definitions of the terms which we use in connection with this important truth will help to form an accurate idea of the doctrine itself.

Liberty is the power to act or not to act, and to choose between several courses of action. It may be physical or moral. Physical liberty is freedom from violence or physical coercion; moral liberty is the absence of any prohibition. We are all physically free to violate the laws of the country, at least as long as we are not held in duress, but we are not free to do so morally, for we cannot do so without committing a wrong.

Coercion is the use of physical force to compel man to do or not to do a certain act. The will in its own inward domain cannot be coerced. You can force a man to swallow a bitter draught, but you cannot compel his will to consent to your violence. When a physical act is obtained by coercion, it is not to be morally attributed to the agent who does not wilfully yield to coercion. Nay more, if you resort to excessive fear to secure compliance, you diminish notably and sometimes take away liberty. Even when liberty is not altogether gone, the use of excessive fear as a means to force compliance will annul the consequences of an act. Thus a man who, pistol in hand, or a bag of dynamite close by, compels you to sign a check, has no right to the payment of this check, because your compliance was merely compulsory. This holds good especially in contracts. Yet violence must be proven, and the burden of the proof lies with him who seeks relief from the contract.

13. Responsibility, Imputability, Morality. A man who is free to act or not is said to be responsible. Responsibility is *the condition of a man* who, having sufficient knowledge, and being free from coercion, can act or not as he chooses, and is, therefore, accountable for his determination. Imputability is *the character of an act* which is freely performed, so that the good or evil of it is attributable to him who performs it. The morality or immorality of an act is its *conformity* or *non-conformity* with natural law. The case supposed by Austin of an act contrary to natural law, but right from the standpoint of positive law —such, for instance, as the massacre of the innocents—is simply absurd. No positive law has any validity if contrary to natural law. This principle of Blackstone may seem to Austin *stark nonsense,* but he is himself guilty of a most glaring contradiction by making the same act both right and wrong, just and unjust at the same time.

14. The End does not justify the Means. In order that an act may be morally good, every essential element, the object, the end, and the circumstances, must be good. The end is what the agent intends; the object is what is to be accomplished by the act; the circumstances are the conditions under which the act is accomplished. The object of an alms is to relieve suffering; that object is good in itself, yet if an alms be given with a view to bribe an elector the action is bad. A lie may be told in order to shelter a guiltless man from the consequences of an unwilful breach of the law; the end, that is, the saving of the man who in his conscience is really not guilty, that end, I say, is very good, but the object, that is, the perversion of truth, is wrong; the act bears the stamp of that wrong. It is a very good thing, nay, it is a sacred duty, for a son to help his father out of danger; yet, in war time, should the son abandon his post when the safety of the army depends on his vigilance in order to do what, under other circumstances, would be a sacred duty, that son would commit a wrong. Hence the old axiom of schoolmen: *Good requires a perfect cause, evil comes from any flaw.* The main reason is this. An action, in order to be right, must agree with the rule or standard of righteousness or justice; if it fail to agree with that standard in anything, it so far takes the character of evil. It can never be said of that action that it is just, that is, coincides with the rule or pattern by which it must be tested. This principle is fundamental in ethics.*

---

* When the means are morally indifferent, then the morality of the act depends on the object or on the end.

SEC. V. WHEN IS MAN RESPONSIBLE?

15. A Madman is irresponsible; a Monomaniac is often so.
After establishing the essential conditions of human responsibility, and considering the requirements of moral law, let us see how man loses his responsibility; that is to say, under what conditions may human justice consider a man as irresponsible.

To be responsible, man must be free; to be free, he must be able to deliberate; to be able to deliberate, he must know several objects, compare them, see how they differ, and what they have in common: in one word, he must have the full use of reason, be *compos mentis;* that is to say, able to control himself, his faculties, and his own actions. Now, what states or conditions make it impossible for man to enjoy this mastery over himself? In the legislation of nearly every State we find that the great test of responsibility is the capability of knowing the difference between right and wrong. This requires some explanation. It is perfectly evident that when a man has ceased to see any difference between right and wrong, he is completely bereft of reason, he is no more *sui compos,* and consequently he is not responsible for the moral character of his acts. The moral law for him is a blank. But is it equally evident that any one who does know right from wrong is also *sui compos* or *compos mentis?* We think that some qualification must be added to the affirmative. I do not believe that two out of one hundred insane persons are ignorant of the difference between right and wrong, and I have had varied opportunities to form an opinion; but a monomaniac may ignore the distinction with regard to a certain class of facts. What then? If a kleptomaniac commit murder, must he be hanged as any other murderer? I think not; for whenever there is a serious and deep-seated disturbance in the brain, it is next to impossible to know whether the criminal act has been committed under a hallucination or not, and the culprit must always have the benefit of the doubt. Whenever conscientious experts declare that the man is insane, take it for granted that he is insane, whether or not you can elicit from him by cross-questioning answers which betray a knowledge of right and wrong. This does not mean that the dangerous maniac must be let loose on the community.

16. Mania wilfully brought on; Drunkenness. What if the mania has been brought on by criminally yielding to passions which were known to be morally wrong? Here, I think, legality and ethics give a somewhat different answer, because ethics considers conscience only, while legality must take into account social order, and the safety of all the citizens. Ethics tells us that almost every passion indulged without restraint may culminate in insanity. The criminal may not be responsible at the very moment when he commits the crime, but he is fully responsible for creating an excitement which, he knows, must eventuate in crime. I believe the horrible murder committed by Guiteau to be a case in point. The jury felt that he was guilty, yet the proofs of insanity were unmistakable. Guiteau certainly knew that right differs from wrong, yet it is far from certain that, at the precise moment of the murder, he was responsible. However, he was responsible when he indulged self-love to the extent of making himself a maniac. Such is the answer of ethics.

Law does not consider *how* a man has become insane; if at the time of the crime he *was* insane, law considers him as irresponsible.

There is an exception to this rule; before the law, the criminal is held responsible for the crime committed when drunk, on the ground that he wilfully drank to excess, and that he must have foreseen the consequences of his criminal indulgence. Ethics holds that when he became conscious that intoxication was imminent and yet continued to drink, *at that moment* he became guilty of the crime of intoxication, and of all the consequences which he foresaw. When once intoxicated, if he did not know what he was doing, he could commit no moral crime. The guilt preceded the loss of reason.

17. Uncontrollable Impulses and temporary Insanity. Is temporary insanity possible? Is an uncontrollable impulse possible? Unquestionably. Passions may rise so suddenly and so madly that reason may, for a time at least, completely lose its sway: but as long as reason holds its own, man is responsible. "Irresistible impulse," says Wharton, "is not moral insanity, supposing moral insanity to consist of insanity of the moral system coexisting with mental sanity. Moral insanity thus defined has no support either in psychology or in law." *

---

* Wharton, Criminal Law, § 43; Ibid., § 47.

Law cannot search the recesses of the human heart; it must judge of human intents by the outward manifestations of such intents. Hence it may happen that acts ethically excusable, because deliberation and responsibility were wanting, are justly punished by law, because no outward sign of insanity was perceptible. Such errors are purely accidental, and may be unavoidable: " Supremacy of reason over passion," says the eminent jurist already quoted, " on the part of all persons possessing such reason, is essential to the safety of the State; and the State is bound to educate its subjects to the exercise of their reason to that extent." *

But if it is often difficult to know whether a man was responsible when he performed a certain act, does the presumption stand on the side of sanity or on the side of insanity? Here we must distinguish. In civil cases, *every man is presumed to be sane . . . until the contrary be proved.*† In criminal cases, the culprit must always have the benefit of the doubt; such is the rule, according both to Natural Law and to Canon Law. In Common Law, the practice has not always been uniform. The fifteen English judges whose concurrent opinion was quoted before the House of Lords in 1843 held that *the defect* of reason, from *disease of the mind,* must be *clearly proved* to the satisfaction of the jurors. A milder construction of the law has prevailed in this country. " In

---

* See Hansard, Parliamentary Debates, 3d series, vol. 67, pp. 288-353. It contains a full discussion of the question from the standpoint of English jurists.

† Greenleaf on Evidence, p. 124, note 1.

criminal cases," says Greenleaf, "there are two widely different views. In Massachusetts, it is held that the burden of the proof of the prisoner's sanity is upon the Government, and that this fact must be made out to the satisfaction of the jury beyond a reasonable doubt, before they can convict the prisoner of the crime with which he is charged. In Pennsylvania and other States, it is held that insanity must be proved by the prisoner by a preponderance of evidence, and it is not sufficient for him to raise a doubt."

The rule adopted by the Massachusetts jurists is more humane, and should prevail everywhere. However, in order that the prisoner may claim the benefit of the doubt, the doubt must be reasonable.

18. Want of Education is not a sufficient plea. Can criminals be acquitted on the ground that they have been raised among the worst offscourings of society, in the slums of a big metropolis? Not if the man be sane; we have never found a case where the moral sense was entirely wanting in a sane man. Yet the fact that such criminals are partly the victims of their environments calls for compassion and clemency on the part of the judge. If possible, some chance of receiving a moral education must be afforded such criminals; this is a duty on the part of society; for penal legislation must be, as far as possible, remedial as well as vindictive.

It need not be said that acts committed during sleep, or in the state of somnabulism, are not imputable to the sleeper or somnambulist; but the sleep must be proved; presumption is against it.

19. Hypnotism; doctrine of Prof. Björnström. Before concluding these remarks, we must say a few words about hypnotism. It has become a very serious question in France, in Italy, and in Germany, and the mischief is spreading. It is not within the range of this paper to treat hypnotism scientifically; all I wish to do is to draw your attention to the legal aspect of that so-called science; and as I find that Dr. Björnström of Stockholm, an experienced professor of psychiatry, sums up the data of the highest authorities in this department of medical jurisprudence, I shall merely give an abstract of the 11th chapter of his work on Hypnotism, the caption of the chapter being "Hypnotism and the Law." After making this acknowledgment, I shall dispense with the quotation marks, and merely state that by making a free use of the text I do not mean to endorse every proposition contained in the book. Every one knows that there are several different and opposite schools, and that the so-called science of hypnotism is far from having reached a consistent body of fundamental axioms. The questions which must receive at least tentative answers are the following:

1st. Can the hypnotized be physically or mentally injured by hypnotism? 2d. Can the hypnotized fall victim to crime? 3d. Can the hypnotized be used in the service of crime as a ready tool without a will? 4th. Are the hypnotized responsible? 5th. Should hypnotism be prohibited?

I believe that the first question is answered affirmatively by nearly all the authorities on the subject. " By hypnotism, a natural, normal sleep is *not produced* in a person." This is *verbatim* from Dr. Björnström. The hypnotic condition is essentially a morbid one. Cases of insanity, hysteria, catalepsy, caused by hypnotism are innumerable. Nay, worse than all the rest, unnatural lust and hideous passions have often resulted from its use. It is true that hypnotism provides some remedies for the mischief that it brings about; but, as a rule, the cure is incomplete. Hence I fully endorse the rule given by Björnström—*Investigate, but do not experiment.* Fearful evils and very little good can come from experimenting; but when a case comes before the bar of human justice, it is evident that careful investigation is indispensable.

The second question, can the hypnotized fall victim to crime? admits also one answer only. He can; and if he allows himself to be hypnotized by unscientific and unscrupulous men, he is responsible for the consequences. But this supposes another question: Can a man be hypnotized without his consent? Berheim says no; Björnström says yes. We believe that both opinions must be qualified. A strong man who carefully avoids placing himself in conditions prejudicial to his nervous soundness, and who is determined to resist the influence of the magnetizer, may bid defiance to all the hypnotizers in the world; but a person with weak nerves, or even a strong man who assists at one of these séances, where everything is calculated to excite the nerves, may not be able to resist the wiles of a skilled charlatan like Donato. Moreover, it is comparatively difficult to hypnotize a man for the first time, especially against his will, but every succeeding séance weakens his will power, until he can be cast into the lethargic sleep with the utmost facility, and even from a distance.

Children and weak persons can easily be magnetized and become the victims of the most dastardly crimes. Hypnotism has been resorted to in India to kidnap children; the men who made it a practice were called thugs or cheels.

20. A man under the influence of Hypnosis may be used as a tool. Can the hypnotized person be used as a tool in the commission of crime? Certainly, but the will power is not always entirely neutralized: in many cases on record the hypnotized person has resisted the will of the hypnotizer, when the act required was absolutely repulsive. Yet the resistance was extremely painful and sometimes overcome by repeated and peremptory orders. In such cases it is evident that the crime is to be imputed to the man who suggests it rather than to his tool.

Are the hypnotized responsible? When they allow themselves to be hypnotized they incur a serious responsibility; but once in the hypnotic trance the guilt must attach to the man who suggests the crime. Donato and others pretend that even then the victims may resist, but this is extremely doubtful.

Should hypnotism be prohibited? It has been severely prohibited in France, Italy, and other countries. An exception has been made in favor of physicians duly qualified by their knowledge in the art of healing, and by special studies in neurology. Laws should not be multiplied without necessity; but should hypnotism spread in this country, and cause as much evil as it has caused elsewhere, we certainly would favor the enactment of repressive laws.

In Milan and Turin many of those present at the séances grew sick, and contracted headache and insomnia. The physicians of Turin found a decided change for the worse in their nervous patients who had attended either as subjects or as spectators. Like *sequelæ* were also reported in Paris and Breslau. We conclude that hypnotism should be treated as any other dangerous poison, and that those who trifle with it should be held responsible for the consequences; but that the hypnotizer is far more responsible than the person subjected to his influence—in many cases, the hypnotizer alone is guilty.

FOURTH LECTURE.

Freedom of the Will.

1. Importance of the Question. No one will question the importance of the doctrine maintained in the present lecture. If man be free, then he is accountable for his actions; be they good or evil, they are his; praise or blame, reward or punishment, which follow in their wake, are deserved, when those who render the verdict follow the dictates of justice. Were man constrained by necessity, were his action the fatal results of his environment, then he would be rewarded or punished for what he could not help; and laws, either divine or human, would be nothing more than additional forces, which would combine their strain with the pressure of surrounding circumstances. Such a theory saps the very foundations of morality, at least of that which is now called morality by civilized mankind. Utterly reckless of consequences, Materialists, Fatalists, Determinists, and for the most part Evolutionists, assail human freedom. Confident that they can substitute another principle to account for the variability and responsibility of human conduct, they bring down the house about our ears, trusting that they can rear for us another resting-place more solid, more scientific, than the former. Already they have made several attempts at rebuilding. With what success, we shall see later on.

The freedom of the will is rather a psychological than an ethical question, and we might have borrowed the answer from psychology, as we have taken from it the immortality of the soul, and from theodicy the existence of God; but the heat of the contest and the important bearings of the issue on every department of ethics compel us to discuss the claims as fully as space allows.

For the sake of distinctness and perspicuity, this lecture shall be divided into three parts. In the first we shall define free will, describe the circumstances which are necessary for its exercise, and briefly mention the powers which it brings into play; the second part will be devoted to the statement and demonstration of our thesis; in the third, the claims of other systems will be investigated.

SEC. I. NATURE OF FREE WILL.

2. Freedom of Will defined. Conditions required for the exercise of Free Will. By freedom of the will, we mean the power to act or not to act, to choose an act or volition in preference to another act or volition, whenever the conditions required for self-determination are present. Now, what conditions are required in order that the will may determine itself?

1st. The object to be obtained must be known. Thus a hunter would not buy a breech-loader if he were totally ignorant of the existence of such weapons. Hence the old axiom: *Nil volitum quin prae-cognitum*—nothing unknown can be wished for.

2d. An end or purpose is necessary. If a man had no good in view, not even comfort or a momentary pleasure, his volition would be causeless. Our hunter must have pleasure or profit in view, else he would not buy a weapon. It has been objected that if a motive be necessary, when the motive is actually present liberty is at an end. It would be so were the object so attractive as to overcome reason, or exhaust all the will power of the person under its spell, but it is not with regard to such cases that we assert human freedom. A motive may be necessary without imposing a necessity on the will.

3d. In order to act freely, man must be able to compare, for without comparison there can be no choice, and without choice no liberty. Our Nimrod must prefer the excitement or the probable success of the chase before the allurements of the *dolce far niente*. The choice may be instantaneous, almost instinctive, but it must be a choice; and a choice involves comparison and the use of reason. Without the exercise of reason there can be no liberty. If you suppose a being entirely destitute of the power of comparing or of forming general concepts, the actions of such a being will be merely animal; they will be determined by the surroundings, and liberty cannot exist. If you take a man acting with only one idea, or obeying a blind impulse (*motus primo primus*) before reason has had time to speak, such a man will be *for the time irresponsible*. It may be difficult, perhaps impossible, to prove to a jury that he was momentarily insane; presumption is against his insanity; nevertheless, if he was the victim of an irresistible impulse, reason had nothing to do with the act, and the agent was irresponsible.

4th. The will must be undetermined; or, as schoolmen say, *passively or actively indifferent.* It is *passively* indifferent when the will is yet unsolicited, because no object is presented to it; the will becomes *actively* indifferent when it begins to be conscious of rising activity, and of its own power to choose.

Lastly, freedom supposes immunity both from coercion and from necessity. The former, indeed, interferes with the exterior act only, for a coerced volition would be at the same time a volition and its exclusion, or a circle not a circle, a square circle. But necessity reaches volition itself. It is conceivable in two different ways. First, the necessity may come from the object if it be present and fully satisfy every craving of the soul, for in such a case there could be no reason not to will, the whole tendency of the soul would be absorbed, the act would yet be voluntary, but it would cease to be free. No object of the kind is thinkable except the *summum bonum actually possessed.* If not fully and actually possessed, it leaves a gap, and a part of the will power remains unoccupied and free. This goes to show that every voluntary act is not necessarily a free act. *An act is voluntary when elicited by the will; it is free when the will is not determined by necessity.*

3. What Beings can be free. So far we have merely analyzed the concept of freedom, without asking the question: *If such a power exists, in what sort of being can it be vested?* This shall be the subject of our next investigation. It is evident that such a being must have both intellect and will and must be a person. It must have intellect, because it must be able to compare; it must have a will, because it must move toward its object and cling to it. These faculties must be defined by referring to their formal object. *Intellect is the faculty which has for its object Truth, not only individual but universal*—i. e., it does not perceive only an individual man, say Socrates or Plato, but it discerns in that individual man the type of humanity; it can frame the proposition: *this is a man.*

What *Truth* is to the intellect *Good* is to the will. We shall therefore define the latter: *That power which has for its object good, not only individual but also universal.* We must add that while intellect aims at the contemplation of truth, will aims at the possession of good, for truth is *knowable*, good is *desirable*. Hence schoolmen called the will *appetitus rationalis*—rational appetite. Will evidently depends on the intellect to apprehend its object, and in turn it reacts on the intellect by applying it to the consideration of the good toward which attraction or repulsion is experienced.

4. No Intellect without Will; no Will without Intellect. President Porter, in *Moral Science,* Chapter III., Sec. 23, has revived incidentally the old scholastic question, whether a mere intellect could subsist without will, but with sensibility. We cannot pause to solve this curious problem, but two things are evident: First, severed from the intellect, the will is unthinkable, for without intellect the will is blind, no power exhibiting to it its specific object; second, an intellect with sensibility alone would be a monstrosity, for while it could discover the universal good, *summum bonum,* there would be no corresponding power to approach it. We have already shown that without both powers no rational explanation of liberty is possible; where both exist in one substance, then consciousness and personality must be present. By consciousness we mean *an inward perception of our being and of our own operations.* This is not a distinct power, for it is impossible to conceive an understanding ignorant of its own perception. In fact, since we know objects through our perceptions, if consciousness did not exist, we should know and ignore the same object at the same time, which is an absurdity. We must also forbear to discuss the identity or non-identity of intellectual memory with the intellect itself. We are in possession of the fact that men have both consciousness and memory; this is taught by constant experience, and the certainty of the fact is all that we need for the present; the explanation belongs entirely to psychology. Yet there is one point to which I must draw your attention. In human consciousness, and in the consciousness of every being endowed with intelligence, there is *introspection,* which produces the famous *Io ego;* that is, an assertion of our own existence and activity. It is exemplified in the dictum of Descartes, " I think, therefore I am." We prescind now from the logical value of that much-quoted assertion; we simply use it as a means to illustrate what St. Thomas calls the complete circuit or evolution of intellectual substances; in exercising their activity, they reach out for the object, return to the activity itself, and terminate their act in the substance from which it emanated. This evolution is inseparable from human personality, and without personality no being can determine its own motions, and truly claim its acts as belonging to itself; these acts are the results of appetites which are depending on the organism, and are modified by the environments.

5. Varied Powers which influence the Will. We have seen that in order to predicate freedom of a being we must suppose it endowed with reason, will, consciousness, and personality. In man we have other factors which influence the determinations of the will. *We have sensibility, or the power to receive impressions from outward or physical objects.* Man is provided with five senses to bring to the soul a variety of impressions which the mind may afterward analyze, and which may be used by the intellect as a matter to abstract from. Thus a rose may offer to the eyes the beauty of its shape and the wealth of its hues; to the sense of smell, the sweetness of its perfume; to the touch, the softness of its tissue together with the sting of its thorns; and out of these and many other sensations the mind will elaborate the type or model of countless other flowers of the same kind and variety; nay, by comparison with others, departing more or less from the pattern first observed, it will find out what is common to all the members of the Rosaceæ family, what is special to this or that variety. *We have passions,* i. e., *those emotions of the soul which go out to their respective objects* with a blind impulse, unless they be checked by reason. *We have imagination,* which reproduces past impressions and combines them into fantastic shapes, scarcely less vivid than real objects. All these varied forces influence the will; sometimes help, at other times oppose, reason; and often get the mastery over the higher powers that should control them.

SEC. II. DEMONSTRATION OF THE EXISTENCE OF FREE WILL.

6. Free Will proved by Consciousness. Such is man of whom we aver that he is free; not free from duty, or moral obligation, but free from necessity, and, as far as will is concerned, free from coercion in the depths of his inward self. It is now our duty to make good our assertion.

The first and, in my opinion, the strongest proof is drawn from consciousness. Consciousness, when speaking distinctly and unequivocally, is a criterion of truth; in fact, its testimony must be admitted before any argument whatever can be accepted as valid. But consciousness unequivocally asserts that when acting we do so in consequence of a wish which could have been withheld, and that between several courses of action we can choose whatever one we please. Therefore we must, on the testimony of consciousness, admit human freedom. Dr. McCosh of

Princeton, quoted and endorsed by Prof. Gregory, expresses nearly the same thought as follows: "This truth is revealed to us by immediate consciousness, and is not to be set aside by any other truth whatever. It is a first truth, equal to the highest, to no one of which will it ever yield. It cannot be set aside by any other truth, not even by any other first truth, and certainly by no derived truth. Whatever other proposition is true, this is true also— that man's will is free. If there be any other truth apparently inconsistent with it, care must be taken so to express it that it may not be contradictory." * In this passage Dr. McCosh considers the freedom of the will as one of those primary, self-evident truths from which others are derived; such, for instance, as the postulates of geometry. Against this argument a subtle objection is raised: "Be it so," say our opponents, "the testimony of consciousness is admissible, but only when the thing attested is within the objective range of consciousness. Now, consciousness does not report powers or possibilities, but only interior phenomena; therefore when we act it cannot report that we might have acted otherwise, but only that we acted as we did." We answer:

7. Consciousness may report a Power which begins to Act. Consciousness does not report powers which have no activity at all, it does not bear witness to mere potentialities, we admit. But to say that we are never conscious of a power whose energy we actually feel, is contrary to our daily experience. It is, therefore, a false con-

---

* Christian Ethics, by D. S. Gregory, D.D., p. 141.

clusion to say that it cannot attest that an act is free, for we can be conscious while acting that we act by choice, or that we are self-determining. Such a power is, according to schoolmen, *in actu primo proximo*—in the first period of activity. Besides, consciousness has certainly reported the deliberation, however short, which has preceded the act, and during which the force which you would call a mere potentiality was exerted to suspend the action, if but for a moment; for when we speak of free acts we denote deliberate resolves, consequent upon a choice. Now, during that moment the negative power, far from being a mere potentiality, sufficed to counterbalance all the opposite forces. Surely consciousness can report the fact and its consequences; therefore it is falsely asserted that the power to act otherwise than the agent has acted could not be reported by consciousness. Our argument retains all its cogency.

8. Concept of Duty. Second proof. We come now to the argument of Kant, which is new only in its form. As it is spread over a vast amount of very abstract speculation, we strip it of its terminology and reduce it to its simplest terms. In the critique of pure reason, i. e., in examining the synthetic principles which are found in speculative or *a priori* knowledge, we discover a categoric imperative—namely, the concept of duty. In subjecting to the same analysis our practical reason, we are struck at once with the " ought," which is the application of the categorical imperative and makes it for us a rule of action. We have, therefore, both a concept and a fact, a noumenon and a phenomenon, which are inconceivable without the freedom of will; for a precept or a duty cannot be imposed on a being on whom the action does not depend. We are, therefore, justified in assuming as a self-evident truth, or postulate, the freedom of the human will. The argument, though somewhat involved and connected with a great deal of questionable speculation, is valid in itself; for it starts from a concept and passes from the ideal world to the actual by means of a fact that any one can verify by self-examination. It might possibly be made clearer by being reduced to the following syllogism: When by introspection we find both a universal concept and an actual practical rule, we must admit as a reality what both involve; but such is the case with regard to human freedom; therefore it must be admitted as a reality.

9. Nature of Deliberation. Third proof. It is a fact that when man shows in a most striking manner the attributes which distinguish him from the lower animals, he pauses before acting and deliberates. In deliberation, wisdom, counsel, prudence become conspicuous; we have a rational being at its best. Mr. Spencer, who wrote a whole work, *The Data of Ethics,* to prove that man was ruled by necessary laws, and led by rational utilitarianism, agrees with us in considering deliberation as of high ethical value. After describing in its early stages the process by which acts are fitted to ends, he exclaims eloquently: " At last arise those long deliberations during which the probabilities of various consequences are estimated and the prompting of the correlative feelings balanced, constituting calm judgment. That under either of its aspects the later forms of this mental process are the higher, ethically considered, as well as otherwise considered, will be readily seen."

Very well; but if man is not free, if he cannot choose the means which he prefers, what is the use of deliberating? Nobody deliberates to do what he cannot help. It may be said that he is the victim of an illusion; he thinks he deliberates when he is merely obeying a law that brings a series of thoughts to his mind to drive him to a necessary result. Such, in fact, is Spencer's assumption: "Man," he tells us, "is led into the error of supposing that it was not the impulse alone which determined the action." (*Principles of Psychology*, Sections 218-219.) If so, then nature deceives him throughout the entire process; he thinks that he deliberates, but really he does nothing of the kind, for to deliberate is to consider several courses of action with a view to making a choice. In reality he has no choice to make, for all springs from a necessity which he obeys unconsciously. His deliberation is wise and unwise at the same time. It is wise, since it has a *high ethical value;* unwise, since it is intended to achieve a result which cannot be helped. Such a fraud on the part of nature would be simply inconceivable; it is contrary to all the facts of experience; it puts nature in contradiction with herself, and, if true, would recoil on the first cause from which the deceit must have originated. The opposite alternative is the only one that reason can admit—that deliberation of high ethical value was a *bona fide* one, the outcome of it was a real choice, and consequently the agent was free.

10. Consent of the World. We, and the whole world with us, praise a Washington for saving his country, and censure an Arnold for betraying it. If their actions were not really *theirs,* if those actions were the product of necessary laws and blind forces, the blame, as well as the praise, were senseless. We might as well praise oxygen, hydrogen, nitrogen, and carbon for sustaining the bodies of men, and condemn the microbes for attacking and ultimately destroying them.

No, mankind is not mistaken in thinking that good and bad actions are imputable to those who accomplish them; that those actions belong to the agents, and that on their own deeds such agents must stand their moral trial. Mankind is not wrong in holding firmly the doctrine of imputability; but imputability necessarily involves freedom; both come to us borne up by songs of the poets, the eloquence of the wisest men, and the consent of all civilized races. No source of error can be found to account for this universal consent. I may well say universal, for the few men who deny freedom in theory constantly suppose it in practice. It is a moral intention; consequently the illusions of the senses have nothing to do with it. It is a check on the passions of men; therefore passions have not inspired men with this belief. Nothing remains but to take it as one of those primary truths, which may be sometimes obscured by sophistry, but which, in spite of all sophisms, win and retain the assent of mankind.

11. Justice supposes Freedom of the Will. Lastly, if the world at large is deceived with regard to freedom, imputability, and responsibility, then society is guilty of a great wrong, for it has instituted tribunals with the mission to defend justice and punish iniquity. Judges and juries have taken it for granted that they had to punish criminals according to their ascertained guilt; that if men were proved to be irresponsible, then punishment was to be withheld, unless they had wilfully made themselves irresponsible by seeking temporary madness in the cup; that they had to make a difference between a man who had shed blood directly and with malice prepense, and one who had dealt a fatal blow unintentionally, under provocation, and when excitement precluded deliberation. Now, if there be no such thing as freedom, all this is wrong. All that society can do is to modify the environments of criminals. They are not really guilty, they are driven by a relentless necessity; nature is responsible, not the unfortunate murderer, however deliberate his crime may have been. What was the use of finding out whether Guiteau was insane? Insane or not, he was irresponsible. For the same reason, a nice grading of penalty is quite superfluous—all are equally innocent and equally guilty. Can any one admit such strange conclusions? Yet they flow from the premise that man is not free, and therefore that he is not accountable for his acts, but that he is the sport of laws which he can neither control nor modify. Let, therefore, these consequences stand as a *reductio ad absurdum*.

No, society is right; the judges are right; it is only the sophists who are wrong.

12. Natural Order incomplete without Self-determining Beings. In concluding these series of proofs, I beg leave to sum up some considerations of St. Thomas, which open the way to broad generalizations. In the scale of beings we find one who does not depend on pre-existing matter and is perfectly free from necessity; others that are both dependent on pre-existing matter and bound by necessity. The mean term consists of those that depend on pre-existing matter, but are free from necessity.

Again, among the beings which are both passive and active, some receive motion from outside, but have active properties; such, for instance, are the beings which have weight. They cannot be free, for they are not the cause of their own operation. Others have within them a principle of action; but of these some are led by reason; such are men, for they deliberate on the course of action to be chosen; animals, on the contrary, are led by the impulse of natural instinct, and this is made manifest by the uniformity of their operations, which, under the same circumstances, are always the same.

Thus, according to the greatest philosopher of the Middle Ages, God alone has freedom in its fulness, because independent even of pre-existing matter; man is free, yet dependent on pre-existing matter; animals are not, because they have no reason, but instinct only.

13. Determinism. We must now make a brief examination of the systems which conflict with the doctrine of free will. After the explanations of the first part, and the demonstrations of the second, it is hoped that a few remarks will suffice. All those systems may be comprised under the modern name of *Determinism,* a system which asserts that man does not himself determine his own volition, but that it is determined for him by other causes. That determination may be attributed to the First Cause; it may come from a necessity founded on the nature of man; from a law which man obeys unconsciously but necessarily; or, lastly, from evolution. Fatalism teaches that all the actions of man are pre-ordained, so that, do what he may, he cannot alter the sequence of events. Two arguments are advanced in defence of this proposition: First, God's foreknowledge is inconsistent with any mutation whatever; second, the First Cause ceases to be what it was when man becomes the true cause of his own volition.

The first objection starts from a wrong hypothesis; it supposes a time preceding volition, during which God sees beforehand the action of man. Now, God does not live in time, but in eternity; to Him every definite duration is present. In other words, an infinite existence is forever fully present; past and future are terms which may be applied to transient and contingent beings, but not to the Eternal Being. Secondly, foreknowledge is a perception or vision; but vision does not alter the phenomenon which is perceived; therefore it is impossible that the divine vision should necessitate an act which otherwise would be free.

The second objection is more plausible; if God is the First Cause, then all effects must be attributed to Him; but if man determined his own volition, something would be attributed to man and not to God; therefore man cannot determine his own volition. This sophism starts from the false assumption that the same effect cannot be attributed entirely to different causes under different aspects. The contrary is evident. For instance, the existence of a body is entirely attributable to the efficient cause, to the material cause, to the formal cause, and to the final cause; each one of these causes extends its influence to the whole effect, but in a different manner.

The First Cause reaches the whole being, which it creates and sustains, with all the forces and activities which belong to that being; in turn these activities and forces have their full effect. Human volition must be attributed to God alone, inasmuch as He alone gives the human will its being and activity; but to man alone, in so far as he uses the energy which he has received from the First Cause. Nay, we would destroy the concept of First Cause were we to aver that it cannot create a self-determining being.

We need not consider the peculiar form of fatalism adopted by Spinoza; it must stand or fall with pantheism, on which it is founded. It is liable to all the objections of other forms of fatalism, and to all those which shatter pantheistic tenets.

14. Necessity arising from the Nature of Man. We come next to the necessity arising from the nature of man—we might call it intrinsic necessity. We will express it almost in the words of Mr. Mill: "There is nothing in causation but invariable, certain, and unconditional sequence. A man's actions are the invariable, certain, and unconditioned results or consequences of his motives and his character. Volitions are *voluntary* acts, but not *free* acts."

We are as badly off as ever; for whether man be inwardly necessitated by a superior power, or by circumstances over which he has no control, his volition is determined for him, not by him. This error is connected with another, also advocated by Mr. Mill; in common with Spinoza, he eliminates *efficient* causation: "There is no thing produced, no event happening, in the known universe which is not connected by uniformity or invariable sequence with some one or more of the phenomena that preceded it. The state of the whole universe at any instant we believe to be the consequence of its state at the previous instant."

Well, then, let us go at once to the first instant; *who* or *what* caused the world's existence? That being, at least, must be an efficient cause. Spinoza boldly asserts that the universe is eternal and is one substance with God. Mr. Mill does not go so far, but is less consistent. Let us suppose, for the sake of argument, that there is no creative power; will it be true that there is no efficient cause? Not at all; an efficient cause, according to Aristotle, is *arche kineseos*. Mr. Mill admits that the will is a principle of motion, for he says: " Volitions are not known to produce anything directly except nervous action." (*System of Logic*, 3d ed., Vol. I., pp. 370-72.) If so, it is a principle of action, and therefore an efficient cause; hence the fundamental assertion that " in causation there is nothing but invariable and unconditioned sequence " is simply indefensible.

15. Necessity induced by Law, or by Evolution. Let us come to the necessity said to be induced by law. The argument may be summed up in the following syllogism: Everything is governed by law, even the will of men; but what is governed by law is not free; therefore the will is not free. Now, this syllogism is a beautiful instance of the sophism which consists in supposing in the premises the very thing which is to be proved. By laws do they mean *physical* and *necessary* laws? Then they assume in the major that the will is not free. Do they mean also *moral* laws? Then they suppose in the second premise that moral laws necessitate the will, the very thing to be proved. In both cases they throw themselves out of court.

The necessity supposed to arise from evolution rests on a yet worse foundation, because it assumes not only that all laws are of the same nature, which is utterly unwarrantable, but it also supposes—first, that evolution, such as Mr. Darwin or his disciples have understood it, is self-evident, or strictly demonstrated; secondly, that the same sort of evolution extends its sway over the moral as well as over the physical world. In fact, the very word "evolution" is misleading. Nobody questions the fact that the organism evolves itself according to fixed laws, but many do not admit that men had *arboreal progenitors.* With regard to the moral world, it is true that mind and will develop themselves, and that morals may become more perfectly known; but that it is by a necessary and unavoidable evolution of character, our consciousness absolutely negatives. I may be permitted to say more: When we take the data of ethics which are found in Aristotle, Plato, St. Thomas, and Suarez (I purposely abstain from mentioning sacred names), and compare them with those theories which destroy the dignity of our nature by making of men dumb cattle, "driven by an inexorable master, Fate," but luckily unconscious of their own bondage and of their awful destiny, we cannot escape the conclusion that we have before us well-defined cases of *in*volution and *retrogression.*

16. Objection derived from the Conservation of Energy.
We must meet a last objection which is just as irrelevant as that derived from evolution, but which claims to be drawn from advanced scientific theories. It may be stated as follows: If will is self-determining, it may bring new energies into the world; but this would be at variance with the universally accepted theory of the conservation of energy; hence it must be rejected as contrary to modern science. We may first observe that the so-called law of the conservation of energy is in accordance with the data of modern physics, but that it is not yet proved to be

universally true; it is an extremely probable hypothesis and nothing more, and no scientist should discard a moral truth for a physical hypothesis, however probable the latter may appear. But let us suppose that the conservation of energy is not only an hypothesis but a verified law, does it negative the existence of free will? Let us see how this law is stated by Clerk Maxwell, an authority which is paramount in this matter: "The total energy of any body or system of bodies is a quantity which can neither be increased nor diminished by *any mutual action of those bodies,* though it may be transformed into any one of the forms of which energy is susceptible." *

Such is the law. Now, is the action of the intellect or of the will an action of those bodies which are comprised within our present cosmic system? Not at all, unless we hold that nothing exists but matter. Moreover, is it asserted that spiritual forces create new material forces? Not in the least. It only supposes that spiritual substances may determine already existing material forces to act, a fact which happens at every moment in the human life. The soul is not supposed to introduce new physical forces, but to avail itself of forces already existing. At most, it might be said to transform latent forces into kinetic forces; but the possibility of transformation is explicitly admitted in the very statement of the law; therefore the freedom of the will is in perfect accordance with the law of the conservation of energy.

---

* Clerk Maxwell, quoted by William Garnett, Ency. Brit., art. Energy.

FIFTH LECTURE.

Utilitarianism.

SEC. I. NATURE OF UTILITARIANISM, ITS RELATION TO OTHER THEORIES OF MORALITY.

1. Plasticity of Utilitarianism. Many attempts have been made to reject natural law as the moral standard of human actions. That all these attempts have failed with the great bulk of civilized mankind is due to the strong and steady protests of common sense, which could never be either compelled or persuaded to recognize a law without a lawgiver, to deny the freedom of the will which is attested by consciousness, or to bow before a power which claims no higher origin than the whim of rulers. Yet there is one system which seems to survive all other moral heresies, because it is capable, like Proteus of old, of assuming any shape in order to elude the grasp of logic, and because it has a wonderful plasticity which enables it to combine with any other theory that does not admit an eternal and objective standard of right and wrong. That such a delusive, shifty, and pervading error is extremely dangerous needs no demonstration; yet utilitarianism must lose most of its power for evil, if its nature be clearly defined, its central and crucial tenet be thoroughly tested, and if the various combinations into which it enters be submitted to a searching analysis. In order to show clearly the unsoundness of this pretended rule of conduct, let us first point out the fundamental error which is common to all the forms of utilitarianism; then we shall examine successively the utilitarianism of Bentham, or *egoism*, the utilitarianism of John Stuart Mill, or *altruism*, and, lastly, the utilitarianism of Mr. Herbert Spencer, which is based on the theory of evolution.

2. Fundamental error of Utilitarianism: Utility is not Morality. The principle which is common to all the forms of utilitarianism may be formulated as follows: *Utility is the true standard of morality; if you wish to know whether an action is good or bad morally, find out whether it is useful or not. If useful, it is good; if hurtful, it is bad. Virtue, no doubt, is an excellent thing in its way, but it is excellent because it gives the greatest amount, and the highest order of pleasure.*

Here is the whole system, stripped of its accessories and of its sentimental dress. For the thoroughgoing utilitarian there is no difference between utility and morality—they are convertible terms. The first question suggested by the theory is this: As a fact, is it true that utility and morality mean the same thing? When a man says that such an action is morally good, does he mean that it is useful? And when he says that another act is morally wrong, does he mean that it is hurtful? The answer must evidently be negative, and the two concepts are different. When we say that to help the needy is morally good, we mean that it is in accordance with a standard of right which our own mind accepts as absolutely true, whether or not the action be useful to ourselves or to others. Our help may be misapplied by the recipient, and involve on our part a sacrifice, without bringing as a compensation the good of our neighbor; but, if so, it is the fault of the recipient, not ours; if our gift has been dictated by charity and regulated by prudence, we feel that the action is truly good, its accidental sequence having nothing to do with its intrinsic worth. Again, when we say that to secure a competence for our old age is useful, we do not consider *how* the competence is secured. It may be by means which are in themselves wrong, and consequently the act of saving or accumulating may have been tainted with moral obliquity; yet the act of securing what will be needed at a future period remains useful to us, perhaps even to others. No doubt in the long run utility and morality must coincide, at least if we admit a final judgment by which each one will be rewarded or punished according to his deeds, but in the meantime utility and morality may walk different paths, to meet only when utility is final, and has reached the supreme good (*summum bonum*).

3. A useful Good is not desired for itself, but for some other Good. This brings us to the second question, which is even more important than the first: What is the good which utility strives to attain? It is evident that utility, considered in itself, cannot be a standard of excellence, for that is useful which leads to the attainment of a purpose or end. To convey the idea of utility as pagan and Christian philosophers alike have conceived it, we must say that honorable good, or virtue, is desirable for its own sake, but useful good is desirable for something else to which it leads, as a means leads to an end. An instrument is useful when it enables us to accomplish our task; exercise is useful to the extent that it conduces to the acquirement or preservation of health; food is useful because it supports life; study is useful because it leads to knowledge, and knowledge is power. If, then, the excellence of utility depends on the good which it enables us to reach, its goodness, like the splendor of a satellite, is derived or borrowed, and it depends on the brightness of the centre toward which it gravitates. Then it is this centre of attraction, not utility itself, that is the standard of morality. Hence we must ask the utilitarian: What is the aim or goal of those actions which you call moral because they are useful? Or, to put the question on a higher plane, what is the end of the moral man? What is the good which utility must bring within our reach, and which is the end and aim of the human life? As long as you have not answered this question, you have not made one step toward the solution of the moral problem. Moreover, we must know whether that good is to be attained in this world or in the next, for until this is determined, we are unsettled as to the nature of your utility, and consequently we have no real standard to ascertain or measure the goodness of human actions.

4. True Utility and Moral Goodness must meet in the end, but often follow different paths.

But we have said that in the end, true utility and moral goodness must meet; yes, because the same object which is attained by virtue is also the term of true utility. But utility and morality meet without confusion. Two orders terminate in the same object, but under different aspects. In the supreme good the order of duty (*ordo deontologicus*) rests as in its final termination. Man is bound to aim at his highest perfection, and in the union with the supreme good this final perfection is attained. In the possession of the same supreme good the tendency to happiness also finds a resting-place, and true utility its final end--this is the last term of the order of happiness (*ordo eudaemonicus*). As Kant has truly shown, in the attainment of their final object both orders must necessarily coincide, because both postulate a perfect good; but the one aims at perfect justice, the other at perfect happiness, and both are found in a supreme or perfect good, the *summum bonum,* which Aristotle and Plato have sought so persistently.

We have seen that the fundamental doctrine of utilitarianism is based on a confusion of two different concepts, utility and morality; that utility considered in its essence cannot be a standard at all, because whatever goodness it may possess is necessarily derived, and consequently referable, to its source as a standard; that it is indefinite, we might say meaningless, as long as it does not tell us what good is to be attained by useful actions. We must now briefly mention the various systems with which utilitarianism most readily combines to form various and worthless alloys.

5. Materialism, Positivism, and Phenomenism. Mr. Huxley's lay sermon. We must beg leave to put together materialism, positivism, and phenomenism, for, however bitterly their respective advocates may wrangle, these three systems spring from the same root. All agree in putting aside everything that the senses cannot verify, and in reducing everything to matter governed by mechanical and chemical forces. Materialism is the most brutal; it boldly states that beyond matter and material forces there is nothing whatever: " Is this egg (from which the human being springs) matter? I hold it to be so, as much as the seed of a fern or of an oak. Nine months go to the making of it into a man. Are the additions made during this period of gestation drawn from matter? I think so, undoubtedly. If there be anything besides matter in the egg, or in the infant subsequently slumbering in the womb, what is it? . . . Matter I define as the mysterious thing by which all this is accomplished."* I know that the learned gentleman who said this spoke differently elsewhere (consistency is a rare jewel), but I am free to use these words of his as the embodiment of the rankest materialism.

Phenomenists deny every doctrine that is not made knowable by a sensible fact, or that cannot be verified by an experiment. Broussais denied the existence of the soul, because he had never found a soul in the corpses

---

* Tyndall, quoted by Mallock, New Paul and Virginy, p. 136.

which he had dissected. One cannot help wondering at the strange aberration of a man who looked for a soul in a dead body. This is phenomenism run mad.

Positivism agrees substantially with phenomenism, but it gives us a great consolation; for it asserts that we shall live forever, not in our own present mortal tenement, but in the person or persons of our descendants, or of those who shall succeed us on this planet. Prof. Harrison tells us that this is *inexpressibly solemn;* yes, it is very solemn. Moreover, he consoles us for the loss of an unknowable God, for he tells us to worship humanity. Unfortunately there are people who do not care to worship humanity *in general,* because it is a mere abstraction; and who positively object to concrete humanity, which they declare to be a fetich. Mr. W. S. Lilly says of Prof. Harrison: " His creed may be summed up, it would appear, in the simple symbol, ' I believe in the brain, the viscera, and the reproductive apparatus.' " Mr. Lilly does him injustice, for Mr. Harrison believes also in humanity and in a vicarious future life, too shadowy indeed for common mortals, but very comfortable and very solemn for him: " As we *live for others* in life, so we live in others after death. . . . How deeply does such a belief as this bring home to each moment of life the mysterious perpetuity of ourselves." All this is entirely too solemn for Mr. Huxley; he might accept phenomenism, but he does not care a rap for vicarious existence.

" I must respectfully, but steadfastly decline to give any one who cares for my opinion the slightest excuse for supposing that I give my assent to a single doctrine which is the peculiar property of positivism old or new. I prefer frank atheism to the acknowledgment, in any shape or way, of a human ' Grand Etre Supreme.' I really do not care one straw for ' subjective immortality,' nor desire any place in the minds of coming generations, beyond that which may be kept warm for me by those whom I love and who love me. Most strongly do I object to have anything to do with the attempt to persuade simple people that the position of a pallid shadow in the shades of futurity is, in any sense, an equivalent for the vivid and palpitating individual deathlessness of old and new theological faiths." *

For once, Mr. Huxley preaches a good lay sermon, and every one will be tempted to say with him that the condition of a pallid shadow wandering in the shades of futurity is too unsubstantial to satisfy human ambition.

6. Materialism, Positivism, and Phenomenism are easily combined, but the Utilitarianism of Austin is unintelligible.

It is not difficult to understand how utilitarianism combines with materialism, phenomenism, or positivism. If all is matter, and mechanical or chemical force, if there is no God but a human " Grand Etre Supreme," if all ends in the grave, *all,* but a pallid shadow wandering in the darksome realms of futurity, then it is perfectly evident that *utility* of the grossest, most selfish, and most material kind must be the only rule of conduct. Only one may well ask the question, Is life worth living? and, we fear, the answer must be negative.

But if the combination of all these crude systems is in-

---

* Fortnightly, Nov., 1892.

telligible, the peculiar mixture concocted by Austin seems to defy analysis. Austin has three standards of morality. With Puffendorf, he admits that morality has its source in the will of God; not in that eternal and necessary will which is one with the Godhead, and which is determined by infinite holiness and always in perfect harmony with divine attributes;—to trace morality to such a fountain-head would be to admit the existence of a natural law (and a natural law Austin will not accept on any terms);—but in the free will of God which moulds every created thing as it listeth. Secondly, with Hobbes, Austin holds that legality, i. e., the sovereign will of Leviathan, is the source of all morality. Thirdly, with Bentham, he maintains that utility is the great, the only, test of right and wrong. How does he combine these incongruous elements, and reduce to one these three conflicting standards? The process is apparently very simple. He states that utility always coincides with the will of God; as for legality, it may be at variance both with the will of God and with utility, but we must obey it notwithstanding, because—well, because if we don't they will hang us—certainly a convincing argument, to which no answer whatever is possible.

This theory is not free from difficulty; nay, it involves some palpable contradictions. If it were true, then God could turn a very heinous action, say a lie, a murder, an adultery, into a very moral and even pious work; and, conversely, He could make of praying, assisting the needy, and paying honest debts, as many criminal offences; just as well could He make a square circle, contradict Himself, and belie His own attributes. Moreover, the same actions could be both moral and immoral at the same time, for they could be at the same time in agreement with utility, or with the will of God, but at variance with the human law; the author himself asserting that there are a thousand such laws which are absolutely contrary both to utility and to the will of God. Thus, to take the example suggested by Austin himself, the soldiers of Herod did the right thing in killing the innocents in cold blood, because Herod commanded it; yet very few will pretend that such an infamous butchery was in accordance either with utility or with the will of God. Those soldiers must have been both right and wrong at the same time. These are appalling difficulties for a philosopher; but we have said elsewhere that Austin was not a philosopher, but only a legist, and these glaring contradictions do not seem to have given him the least misgiving with regard to the soundness of his doctrine.

We have mentioned some of the systems with which utilitarianism has a decided affinity; let us now consider the principal shapes that it has assumed or retained in this the nineteenth century. Of course these shapes are many, for we have said that utilitarianism is protean in its transformation, yet it seems to me that these flitting forms can be reduced to three, the hedonism of Bentham, the altruism of John Stuart Mill, and the combination of utility and evolution excogitated by Mr. Herbert Spencer.

SEC. II.   HEDONISM OF BENTHAM.

7. Utility as understood by Bentham. The hedonism of Jeremy Bentham consists in the doctrine that the chief good of man lies in the pursuit of pleasure, and that pleasure and pain are the standards of right and wrong.

" The principle of utility," says Bentham, " is the foundation of the present work; it will be proper at the outset to give an explicit and determinate account of what is meant by it. By the principle of utility is meant that principle which approves or disapproves of every action whatsoever, according to the tendency which it appears to have to augment or diminish the happiness of the party whose interest is in question; or what is the same in other words, to promote or oppose that happiness. I say of every action whatsoever, and therefore not only of every action of a private individual, but of every measure of government. By utility is meant that property in every object whereby it tends to produce benefit, advantage, pleasure; good or happiness in the present case comes to the same thing. To a person considered by himself the value of pleasure or of pain will be greater or less owing to the four following circumstances: First, its intensity; secondly, its duration; thirdly, its continuity; fourthly, its propinquity." (Collection of his works, 1st Essay, 1st Chap.) " Pleasure and pain govern the world; it is for these two sovereign masters alone to point out what we ought to do, as well as to determine what we shall do."

8. Pleasure and Pain are relative; they cannot be a Moral Standard; they cannot sanction the laws on which Social Security must rest.

It is evident that this system, held long ago by Aristippus and Epicurus, and revived by Bentham, is liable to all the objections which are fatal to utilitarianism in general; moreover, it has some of its own. Pleasure and pain being forever changing and being dependent on the character, condition, and temper of each individual, it follows that there is no fixed standard of right and wrong, and, consequently, that it is impossible to say whether an action is good or evil, unless we know whether it has afforded pleasure or pain to its author. The concept of duty is simply annihilated, for duty, as understood by men, is often at variance with pleasure, and pleasure and pain are the standards, and must govern the world, according to Bentham.

Then, it becomes impossible to maintain, and *a fortiori* to sanction, those moral principles on which society is founded. Take, for instance, the good old precept, "Thou shalt not steal." I urge this injunction upon a young man who has a fair chance to run away with $100,000, or to a politician who is offered a share of State money in so discreet a manner that no trace of the transaction shall remain to fix the guilt on the perpetrators of the crime. He replies reasonably enough: "Why should I not steal?" "Because it is for the general interest, which is in truth your own interest, that you should not. Don't you see? Some day when you feel secure in the possession of your wealth a gang of robbers may conspire against you, rob you of all your money, perhaps kill you." " May—yes; but I shall take good care that they do not. Moreover, the danger is so remote that I am willing to take the risk. Meanwhile I'll fill my pockets and go to foreign parts; it is not every day that a fellow gets a chance to capture $100,000; hypocrites (whom you call honest people) never get such chances, or do not know how to avail themselves of them, and they have to drudge and live from hand to mouth. Serves them right—honesty when conflicting with utility is thoroughly immoral." " But this is contrary to the greatest happiness of the greatest number." " I don't know; this money does not do much good here, and I intend to use it well. Besides, why should I sacrifice my own interest to the happiness of men whom I do not know, who perhaps are yet unborn? Is not pleasure the sovereign master? I find great pleasure in laying my hands on this little bundle of papers, hence it is supremely moral to take them. Once more, good-bye; if you get a chance of benefiting yourself or others, don't indulge in foolish scruples."

Is it true, as often claimed, that our own interest is always in accordance with that of humanity? From the utilitarian standpoint, and taking pleasure and pain as the standard of goodness, we must say emphatically, no! Moreover, if we seek the good of others because it affords to us a sort of refined pleasure, we have merely combined egoism with hedonism, we have not succeeded in setting up a standard of morality. " If agreeable feeling be the sanction of ethics," says W. S. Lilly, " be assured an immediate and certain agreeable feeling will be found a stronger sanction than a future and contingent agreeable feeling." *

SEC. III. UTILITARIANISM OF J. S MILL.

9. System of Mr. Mill. The End remains undefined. The utilitarianism of Mr. Mill appears at first just as grovelling as that of Bentham, but the explanations of the author make it somewhat nobler and more rational: " The creed which accepts as the foundation of morals, utility, or the Greatest Happiness principle, holds that actions are right in proportion as they tend to promote happiness; wrong, as they tend to produce the reverse of happiness. By happiness is intended pleasure and the absence of pain; by unhappiness, pain and the privation of pleasure. To give a clear view of the moral standard set up by the theory, much more requires to be said; in particular, what things it includes in the idea of pain and pleasure, and to what extent, this is left an open matter. But these supplementary explanations do not affect the theory of life on which this theory of morality is grounded—namely, that pleasure and freedom from pain are the only things desirable as ends." † But it does affect it, and very substantially! We are told that the theory of life is that " pleasure and freedom from pain are the only things desirable as ends; " in other words, that all our actions, in order to be *moral,* must aim at pleasure or the

---
* Right and Wrong, p. 51.
† Utilitarianism, p. 9.

absence of pain, and we want to know what sort of pleasure must be the goal of our ambition;—is it the possession of wealth, the enjoyment of leisure, or the command of power? Is it to last forever, or is it a fleeting delectation, vanishing like a dissolving view? It is evident that the value of the end of morality will determine the worth of morality, and the amount of effort which may be justified by morality in striving to win the prize. You might as well say the performance of *Hamlet* would not be affected by doing away with such a supplementary article of property as a ghost. We want to know what we have to hope for, and whether we can secure what we are told to hope for. Otherwise the whole of our life might be a desperate struggle without an object to struggle for; a most dreary and unsubstantial sort of morality.

10. The End is unattainable. Turning over a few pages, we find some sort of an answer, but how vague, how unsatisfactory it is! "The main constituents of a satisfied life appear to be two, either of which by itself is often found sufficient for the purpose—tranquillity and excitement. . . . Great numbers of mankind have been satisfied with much less."* And so our actions will be good morally on condition that they aim at tranquillity or excitement, for this is the necessary conclusion. We are told that pleasure and the exemption from pain are the only standards of morality; then that happiness resulting from pleasure or from the absence of pain consists in tranquillity, excitement, or both. Then the end of morality, what forms its

---

* Ibid., p. 15.

real standard, is tranquillity, excitement, or both; such objects are the only things desirable as ends. Is not such a statement gravely uttered by a philosopher a libel on the common sense of mankind? But that poor boon, wretched as it is, are we sure to obtain it if we spend our life in toiling for it? The answer is truly dismal. Mr. Mill replies to those who put to him the following questions: "What right hast thou to be happy? What right, a short time ago, hadst thou even to be? Cannot man do without happiness?"

In answer, he says: "If happiness is not to be had at all by human beings, the attainment of it cannot be the end of morality. . . . If by happiness be meant a continuity of high pleasurable excitements, it is evident enough that this is impossible. . . . Unquestionably it is possible to do without happiness; it is done involuntarily by *nineteen-twentieths of mankind,* even in those parts of our present world which are least deep in barbarism." This is, indeed, a bright outlook. Men must be moral, of course; now, morality consists in seeking happiness—i. e., tranquillity, excitement, or, better yet, an alternation of both. Strive for that end, but have no illusion about the matter; you will have but a few moments of real happiness, the rest of your life will be only an approach to it. Moreover, we must suppose that you will be counted among the privileged few; for nineteen-twentieths manage to do without happiness; and if you are wise, although happiness is the term and end of morality, you had better prepare yourself to do without it.

11. Four objections to Mr. Mill's main tenet. To this theory of the end of human actions we object: first, that the concept of duty and the concept of utility, considered as the preponderance of pleasure over pain, are different and cannot be expressed in terms of each other. Secondly, that when applied as standards to the same action they often lead to contrary decisions. Thirdly, an object which is not always attainable, nay, which in nineteen cases out of twenty cannot be attained, which we may do well to consider as unnecessary, cannot be a rational motive of human conduct, much less a standard of right and wrong. Fourthly, such a law as that of utility—i. e., pleasure or the absence of pain—is without sanction.

12. Sanctions of Moral Law according to Mr. Mill. God's pleasure or displeasure. Public opinion. Subjective sanction. Mr. Mill tells us that it has sanction enough, viz., The pleasure or displeasure of the Ruler of the universe. But, if that pleasure is dependent on utility, you make of the will of the Supreme Being a stepping-stone to utility; that is to say, the means is greater and nobler than the end; if you refer utility to the will of God, then the will of God, not utility, is the standard of morality. The second sanction mentioned is the displeasure of our fellow-men; in other words, public opinion. A very uncertain sanction this is, and many make light of it: "Kneel before a thing which always lies at the feet of triumphant might," says Quinet, " crawl before that creeping myriapod! This is no faith of mine. What care I for that manner of God? What queer sort of fetich! I have seen too much of it." But, you will say, I care only for the approbation of sages. Alas! even the praise of the wise often attends successful hypocrisy. What! do not utility and justice meet in the long run? Not always in this world, which worships success.

Mr. Mill continues: " The ultimate sanction of all morality (external motives apart) being a subjective feeling in our minds, I see nothing embarrassing to those whose standard is utility, in the question, what is the sanction of that particular standard?" So says Mr. Mill; but other men see particular difficulties. In the first place, what can the criminal tax himself with? What can utilitarians lay at his door? They can say that the criminal has been foolish, rash, imprudent, for he has thrown away the advantages of a better conduct; but how can they say that he is wicked? A man is not wicked because he throws away his chances. He is foolish, that is all. He can feel *regret,* but not *remorse.* Besides, this sanction is wanting where it is most needed; for a hardened rascal, by the frequent repetition of the most criminal acts, will stifle the voice of conscience, while a good man for every peccadillo will have to bear the reproaches of that watchful monitor. Neither the verdicts of conscience nor those of public opinion, not even the displeasure of a God made subservient to the standard of utility, surround its dictates with sufficient sanctions. Utilitarianism holds out to us a prize which we are almost certain to miss, and which is not worth winning; it mixes two concepts different in their nature, and disagreeing in their applications; it is not provided with adequate sanctions; it is incapable of setting up a standard of morality, and of impressing the human heart with the love of right and the hate of wrong.

13. Is Virtue to be loved for its own sake? Evident contradictions.
We have said that the utilitarianism of Mr. Mill was nobler than that of Bentham; and so it is, but at the expense of consistency. Mr. Mill admits that virtue must be loved for its own sake, and that self-sacrifice deserves admiration: " Does the utilitarian doctrine deny that people desire virtue, or maintain that virtue is not a thing to be desired? The very reverse. It maintains not only that virtue is to be desired, but that it is to be desired disinterestedly, for itself. Whatever may be the opinion of utilitarian moralists as to the original conditions by which virtue is made virtue; however they may believe (as they do) that actions and dispositions are only virtuous *because they promote another end than virtue;* yet this being granted, and it having been decided, from considerations of that description, what is virtuous, they not only place virtue at the very head of the things which are good as means to the ultimate end, but they also recognize as a psychological fact the possibility of its being, to the individual, a good in itself, without looking to any end beyond that."

This is pure moral legerdemain. Can virtue be truly a good in itself to that individual man? Is he deceived? Either he is deceived or he is not. If he is deceived, and if virtue is only an end insomuch as it is a psychical illusion, then, in truth, it is a mere fiction of the brain. If it is truly lovable for its own sake, how is it a mere physical fact, and how is it an end for the individual only? Either it is a true end, or it is not a true end; in the first case, it must be an end for everybody; in the second, it cannot be an end for the individual; it is and must be a deception.

Next, you say that utilitarians believe that virtuous actions and virtuous dispositions are only virtuous because they promote another end than virtue. Then virtue is virtue on account of something else; its quality of virtue comes to it from something different from it. Is it desirable for itself or for something else? If it is desirable for itself, how can you say that actions are virtuous only because they promote another end? If it is not desirable for itself, *why must it be desired disinterestedly for itself?* If it is to be desired for itself, how can you say, in stating the principles of utilitarianism: " Pleasure and freedom from pain are the only things desirable as ends. . . . All desirable things are desirable either for the pleasure inherent in themselves, or as the means to the promotion of pleasure and the prevention of pain" (p. 10). If virtue is only desirable for the pleasure it contains, or as a means to the promotion of pleasure and the prevention of pain, why tell us at the beginning of the paragraph that virtue is to be desired disinterestedly and for itself? Is it to cheer up the honest simpletons who, as a psychological fact, take it to be a good in itself, without looking to any end beyond it? (p. 27). It would seem so. In the meantime the question of Mr. Carlyle and others, " What right hast thou to be happy? What right, a short time ago, hadst thou even to be?" has received from Mr. Mill no satisfactory answer. Orthodox moralists would have replied: "Of course, before we were in existence we had no right, for nothing can have no right; but when the Creator had caused us to be, and endowed us with personality, He owed it to Himself to give us the rights which accompany personality. Those rights we derived from Him; but once received, they become our own; they have a higher source than ourselves, but they abide in us. The principal one is to reap the benefit of our good deeds, and to be happy either in this world or in the next. In this world we have a right to so much happiness as may be required to work out our destiny in accordance with the order of nature, made known by natural law." This answer is clear and consistent. It involves, it is true, the immortality of the soul and the existence of God, but any other solution makes the work of nature *purposeless,* and therefore *causeless.* Then let us postulate both, and virtue becomes at once an end in itself, because it is a participation in the *summum bonum,* which is the supreme end of our life.

14. Heroism not explained in Mr. Mill's system. Despite his doctrine of utility, which holds out to us no better reward than tranquillity and excitement, Mr. Mill admires heroism; and there he uses glowing words that bespeak not only sincerity, but enthusiasm: " Unquestionably it is possible to do without happiness; it is done involuntarily by nineteen-twentieths of mankind, even in those parts of our present world which are least deep in barbarism; and it often has to be done voluntarily by the hero and the martyr, for the sake of something which he prizes more than his individual happiness. But this something, what is it, unless the happiness of others, or some of the requisites of happiness?" Well, if the hero gives up happiness, and stops at some of its requisites, he gives up the end to stop at the means; this is very unwise, to say the least. He gives up the standard of morality to let others reach it. The actions of others may be moral, for they may reach the standard, but his own are divided from it by an unknown quantity, the uncertain determinations of others. As far as the act is in *him*, its morality is imperfect. This consequence is strange, but it follows from the premise that an action is good inasmuch as it has a tendency to give pleasure or to remove pain. Mr. Mill seems to have some misgivings on the subject, for he adds: "He" (the hero) "may be an inspiriting proof of what men *can* do, but assuredly not an example of what they *should* do." With regard to the hero, it is clear that the sanction of utility is all wrong; he deserves happiness, and he reaps misery. Surely this is not what justice and reason require. "I fully acknowledge," continues Mr. Mill, "that the readiness to make such a sacrifice is the highest virtue which can be found in man. I will add, that in this condition of the world (the present condition), paradoxical as the assertion may be, the conscious ability to do without happiness gives the best prospect of realizing happiness." This is undoubtedly paradoxical, too much so to be inspiring. When a poor soldier dies on the battle-field, or a martyr dies on the rack or on the cross, how can that consciousness give the best prospect of realizing happiness? Not in this world, which for both passes away in darkness and blood. Is it to be realized in the next? Then the highest sanction is not an earthly mixture of tranquillity and excitement. Take away every sanction but earthly pains and earthly pleasures, and the self-sacrifice of the hero is simply absurd. It is very well to say: " All honor to those who can abnegate for themselves the personal enjoyment of life, when by such renunciation they contribute worthily to increase the happiness of the world." This is a noble enthusiasm, but let us refer the question to sober reason. On utilitarian principles, why should a man sacrifice his own happiness to increase the happiness of the world? He should not; that is, he is not bound to do so, says Mr. Mill, but if he choose to do so he will make a sacrifice which is an example of the highest virtue in man. But why will it be virtue at all? Because it promotes the highest happiness of the greatest number. But why is it a virtue to promote the highest happiness of the greatest number at the expense of one's own happiness? Is it a law? No, you answer; men who do so give an inspiring proof of what men *can* do, but assuredly not an example of what they *should* do. Is it, then, a counsel? No, again, for if every man acted on altruistic motives, nobody would reap the benefit of utility. If you come to me in the name of God and tell me, *If you give your life for your fellow-men, He shall be your reward exceeding great,* I see that I have a reasonable motive to sacrifice my temporal interest for the sake of my neighbor. But if you came as representing a doctrine which holds that pleasure and freedom from pain are the *summum bonum,* and tell me to give up all self-interest, even life itself, for others, I can but answer: "My good fellow, take your own medicine; as for me, nature tells me that I must first take care of my own person, then do what I can for others; and this is the rule I intend to follow." In the light of Christianity, the conduct of a Damien who courts a long martyrdom ending in a loathsome death, and all to do good to some poor lepers—that conduct, I say, is both wise and heroic; considered from the standpoint of utility, with pleasure as the standard of right, and pain as the embodiment of wrong, it is simply insane.

We have called the system of Mr. Mill, altruism, for such is the name commonly given to all the theories which make the happiness of others (*alter*) the standard of morality. Judged from the standpoint of true utilitarian premises, it is nothing more or less than refined and sentimental egoism—*vulgo,* selfishness.

SEC. IV.   UTILITARIAN EVOLUTION.

15. Mr. Spencer denies the existence of Free Will. Mr. Herbert Spencer, in the eleventh chapter of his *Data of Ethics,* shows with a clearness of reasoning and a vividness of style which have seldom been surpassed, how untenable are the assertions of altruism, and how suicidal is altruism severed from egoism. But he falls into an error which is even more fatal to morality than the chivalrous nonsense of altruistic philosophers. For him, morality is nothing but the necessary offshoot of evolution. All other systems, according to him, ignore the rule of causation. Of course, a self-moving, self-determining cause is no cause at all; a free will is a contradiction in terms: " Freedom of will would be at variance with the beneficent necessity displayed in the evolution of correspondence between the organism and the environment." (*Principles of Psychology,* Sec. 220.) " Psychical changes either conform to law or they do not. If they do not conform to law, this work, in common with all the works on the subject, is sheer nonsense; no science of psychology is possible. If they do conform to law, there cannot be any such thing as free will." This is yet more emphatic than the statement of Mr. Mill: " Men imagined what they called the freedom of the will; fancying that they could not justly punish a man whose will is in a thoroughly distasteful state, unless it be supposed to have come into that state through no influence of external circumstances " (p. 50).

It is a fact that judges, legislators, and nearly all the moralists think that a man should not be punished for acts which he could not help doing; but when did men invent free will? Who caught the idea first? The inventor should certainly have the honor of the discovery duly awarded to him.

Hobbes has already answered the question, but his answer is not likely to be accepted: " Free will," says the author of *Leviathan,* " is a thing that was never mentioned among Christians. . . . St. Paul never useth the term free will; but some years past, the doctors of the Roman Church have exempted from the dominion of God's will the will of man." (Chap. VI.) Honestly, we did not know that we had invented, or even rediscovered free will. Aristotle has so strongly proved its existence that we thought that the question had already been settled in pagan times.

16. Utility a result of Evolution. But utility does not depend on free will, according to Mr. Spencer; it is the necessary result of evolution. If so, it seems a very useless work to write for us a treatise on ethics, for evolution will have its way, whether we will or not. To thwart the necessary laws of evolution would be a miracle, and Mr. Spencer does not believe in miracles. It is difficult to understand how the English philosopher could undertake such a thankless job. He tells us seriously that "either free will is a fiction, or his own work on psychology is sheer nonsense." We do not see how we can avoid the latter alternative and we feel compelled to apply it to his *Data of Ethics*.

The fact is that the really subtle intellect of Mr. Spencer has been warped by a controlling idea, that of evolution. Evolution in its narrowest sense, that is, considered as the increasing complexity of results from elementary changes, or, as he expressly tells us, " a redistribution of matter and motion " (*Ethics*, Sec. 29), is forever haunting his mind, and must be found everywhere, even in the spiritual world. We quote from his *Ethics:* " Here, then, we have to enter on the consideration of moral phenomena as phenomena of evolution, being forced to do this by finding that they form a part of the aggregate of phenomena, which evolution has wrought out. If the entire visible universe has been evolved; if the solar system as a whole, the earth as a part of it, the life in general which the earth bears, as well as that of each individual organism; if the mental phenomena displayed by all creatures, up to the highest, in common with the phenomena presented by aggregates of these highest; if one and all conform to the laws of evolution—then the necessary implication is that those phenomena of conduct in these highest creatures with which morality is concerned also conform " (n. 23).

This is doubtless a bulky and ponderous enumeration. Let us see what it amounts to: First, the entire visible world has been evolved; second, man also has been evolved; third, conduct therefore must be a result of evolution.

17. Evolution is a mere Hypothesis. We do not deny that there has been evolution going on in the world; but what of that? When you say that the highest creature, *man,* has been evolved, I ask what you mean. Do you wish to imply that man is only an improved pithecoid, descending from simian ancestors? Then I say you build your new moral philosophy on an assertion which is neither self-evident nor demonstrated. That it is not self-evident every one will admit; that it is not demonstrated, the very defenders of the system will tell us. The most uncompromising upholder of the doctrine of descent, Ernst Haeckel, chides unsparingly his old master, Dr. Virchow, who had said as the conclusion of his study of skulls: " It is, therefore, self-evident that man can never by any progressive development have originated from the apes." Worse yet, Dr. Virchow had shown that the doctrine of descent was an unproved hypothesis; Haeckel, of course, abuses him roundly:

"Virchow has no suspicion even of all these immeasurable strides in morphology, for this department always lay out of his ken." Again: "Inasmuch as Virchow persists in treating the theory of descent as an unproved hypothesis; inasmuch as he ignores all the forcible evidences of that hypothesis, he deprives himself of the right of speaking a decisive word in this the most important dispute of the present day. Virchow is, in fact, simply incompetent in the great question of evolution." Herr Haeckel disposes in the same way of Von Baer: "He is an old man, and it is wrong to make capital of the harmless talk of the old Von Baer" (p. 18).* Du Bois-Reymond is shallow, and unacquainted with comparative and genetic psychology (p. 47). Bastian finds no more favor—"he is *un enfant terrible,* the acting privy counsellor of the board of confusion" (p. 12). Yet after this wholesale slaughter, we are startled to find the following wrathful admission: " Semper and others of my opponents assert that I teach my specific genealogies as infallible dogmas; it is simply false. I have, on the contrary, pointed out on all occasions that I regard them only as heuristic or provisional hypotheses" (p. 24). "Now, it is clear that this theory (the theory of descent) never will be 'proved,' if the proofs that

---

* Freedom in Science.

already lie before us are not sufficient. How often has it been repeated that the scientific certainty of the hypothesis of descent is not grounded in this or that isolated experiment, but in the collective sum of biologic phenomena, in the causal nexus of evolution" (p. 13). Again: "This demand that the doctrine of descent should be grounded on experiment is so perverse and shows such an ignorance of our theory that from the lips of Virchow it has positively astounded us." Unfortunately we belong to that ignorant crowd who want a good proof before they accept a startling theory, which, if true, would revolutionize morality. Mr. Huxley, probably the most prominent defender of evolution among the scientists, in a prefatory note which he kindly contributed to Herr Haeckel's factum, speaks as follows: "Now, I cannot find that Prof. Virchow anywhere distinctly repudiates the doctrine; all he distinctly says is that it is not proven, and that things which are not proven should not be authoritatively instilled into the minds of young people. If Prof. Virchow will agree to make this excellent rule absolute and applicable to all subjects that are taught in schools, I should be disposed heartily to concur with him." It is true that Mr. Huxley says, a little later, that he does not want evolution taught in the schools, not because the evidence is insufficient, but because the problems it evolves are too difficult; yet the whole drift of the preceding paragraph shows that he does not believe the theory to be strictly proven, but to have as much probability as the history of the deluge, or the linguistic accomplishments of Balaam's ass, which, in his own opinion, are not capable of demonstration, and which, however, are taught in schools. Observe that such thinkers as Virchow, Von Baer, Du Bois-Reymond, and Bastian have tried the theory and found it wanting; that outside of the English-speaking countries it meets now with scant support; that mankind at large has never accepted it; in presence of such a *not-provenness,* to use the very word of Mr. Huxley, it is clear that the fundamental principle should have been clearly demonstrated to become able to bear the weight of the superstructure which Mr. Spencer built upon it.

18. Evolution is not universally true, either a *priori* or *a posteriori*. Evolution is shown to be untrue with regard to the past. Lord Kelvin (Sir William Thompson) proves, from the cooling of the earth, that ten or one hundred millions of years ago the earth's surface was at least fifty degrees Fahrenheit hotter than now, and therefore unfit for animal or plant life. On the other side of the account stand the claims of the geologists and biologists; they have revelled in the prodigality of the ciphers which they put at the end of the earth's hypothetical life, long cribbed and cabined within the narrow bounds of our popular chronology; they have exulted wantonly in their new freedom. They have lavished their millions of years with the open hand of a prodigal heir indemnifying himself by present extravagance for the enforced self-denial of his youth. And, indeed, their theories require all, if not more, of this elbow-room, as Lord Salisbury has said.

If the mathematicians are right, the biologists cannot have what they demand. If, for the purposes of their theory, organic life must have existed on the globe more than a hundred million years ago, it must under the temperature *then* prevailing have existed in the state of vapor; the jelly-fish would have been dissipated in steam, long before he had had a chance of displaying the advantageous variation which was to make him the ancestor of the human race. The mathematicians sturdily adhere to their figures, and the biologists are quite sure the mathematicians must have made a mistake.* Weismann says candidly that he accepts natural selection, not because he can *demonstrate* the process nor even *imagine* it, but because he *must*, because the only other alternative is *assuming* the help of a principle of design—in plain words, the existence of a Creator.

And so the true reason why they wish to show that evolution is a universal law is that they want to prove that a Creator is unnecessary!

A posteriori, science is against it. Worlds as well as individuals have their birth, their growth, and their decay. In the course of centuries, the earth shall be completely oxidized, and shall become, like the moon, a dead world. Hence the theory, at least as expressing a natural and universal law, is false, both with regard to the past and with regard to the future.

---

* Inaugural Address of the Marquis of Salisbury as President of the British Association, Oxford, 1894.

19. Even if Man were descended from an Ape, the reasoning would be faulty.

But even granted that the body of man is derived from simian ancestors, does the evolution of conduct follow as a consequence? Not at all, until it is shown that the spirit also is evolved. In telling us that because the body is evolved, the intellect and will must be also a result of evolution, Mr. Spencer is guilty of the sophism called in the school, *transitus de genere ad genus*. Mr. Spencer maintains that he is not a materialist; if so, he must admit that matter and spirit are different in kind; he cannot therefore conclude from the evolution of the one the evolution of the other. Moreover, from a pretended synchronism of evolution, he concludes that the same laws govern both the development of matter and that of consciousness; another piece of common sophistry; and so, when we scan closely the bulky enumeration with which Mr. Spencer begins the rearing of his unsubstantial fabric, we find it no better than a heap of sand; it is utterly unfit to bear the foundations of human morality.

20. How did Moral Evolution begin?

Moreover, since both life and conduct are supposed to be a result of evolution, we want to know how the process began. "With a monad!" say evolutionists; and Herr Haeckel tells us that: "Monism is the only scientific theory which affords a rational interpretation of the whole universe, and satisfies the craving of our human reason for causality." (Haeckel, *Freedom in Science,* Humboldt edition, p. 11.) What, then, is that monad which makes creation unnecessary? Mr. Huxley will tell us (Huxley, Anat. Invert. An., p. 44): "The name of monad has been commonly applied to minute free or fixed rounded or oval bodies, provided with one or more long cilia, and usually provided with a nucleus, and a contracted vacuole." Very well, but to satisfy the craving for causality it is indispensable to tell us how these minute round and oval bodies have sprung into existence, how they have come by their long cilia, how they have acquired those wonderful potentialities, owing to which they have evolved into a perfect man, or even an anthropoid simian. As long as these questions remain unanswered, not only are the cravings of reason for causality unsatisfied, but the mystery of creation, far from being solved, is complicated by the mystery of evolution.

In the moral order the same problem stares us in the face: "I believe," says Mr. Spencer, "that the experiences of utility, organized and consolidated through all past generations of the human race, have been producing corresponding nervous modifications, which by continued transmission and accumulation have become in us certain facilities of moral intuition." (*Data of Ethics*, Sec. 45.) Let us, then, go back to the first man who conceived the thought conveyed by the monosyllable "ought;" did that intuition come from inherited nervous changes? "The word 'ought,'" says Kant, "expresses a species of necessity which nature does not and cannot present to the mind of man. The understanding knows nothing in nature but that which is, or has been, or will be. It would be absurd to say that anything in nature ought to be other than it is in the relations in which it stands. Indeed, the word 'ought,' when we consider merely the course of nature, has neither application nor meaning. . . . Whatever number of motives nature may present to my will, whatever sensuous impulses, it is beyond their power to pronounce the word 'ought.'" (*Critique of Pure Reason.*)

21. A *Creator* and an Eternal Law must be admitted as the foundations of the Moral Order.
Much less is it possible for those motives or those sensuous impulses to evolve into a complete moral system, sufficiently strong and consistent to control human passions and secure the foundations of society. Nothing short of an eternal law, sanctioned by an almighty ruler, can save the dignity of justice, enforce moral obligations, reward heroism, and save us from bloodshed and anarchy. We are therefore fully justified in concluding with James D. Dana: "For the development of Man, gifted with high reason and will, and thus made a power above nature, there was required, as Wallace has urged, the special act of a Being above nature, whose supreme will is not only the source of natural law, but the working force of nature herself." *

---

* New Text-book of Geology, Dana, 4th edition, p. 393, n. 4.

SIXTH LECTURE.

JUSTICE.

SEC. I. JUSTICE AS A GENERAL VIRTUE.

1. Meaning of the Latin word *jus* according to Ulpian.
The Pandects opened with the following declaration of Ulpian: "As we are going to devote our attention to the *jus* (i. e., to the foundation of law), we must know the origin of the word *jus*. It comes from justice, for, according to the correct definition of Celsus, *jus* is the practical knowledge of that which is good and equitable. For this reason men may well call us *priests*, for we worship justice, and we profess to know what is good and equitable: we mark the difference between what is just and what is unjust; we discriminate between what is lawful and what is unlawful; we try to make men good, not only by the fear of penalties, but also by the hope of rewards. Thus we uphold, not a fictitious kind of philosophy, but (as I understand it) the genuine sort of philosophy." *

We must admit that this conception of the magistrate as a wise man intrusted with a sort of priesthood which gives

---

* The *jus* is called dikaion (δίκαιον) because it is a division into two equal parts: dicha (δίχα). We might call the judge dichastes (δίχαστής), him who divides equally.

him the right to read out to men the decrees of eternal justice, is far superior to the ideal of many modern writers, who fain would make of magistrates mere defenders of society, a class of privileged policemen, better paid because they have to perform more delicate duties, but merely defending, like the humbler arms of the law, the exterior organization of society. Ulpian's concept agrees well with that of Aristotle, who thinks that the magistrate must be for other men the impersonation of justice—that is to say, a sort of living justice, which stands forth to maintain every right, be that right derived directly from nature or flowing from it indirectly through positive law. "To appeal to the judge is to appeal to justice; for the judge is but living justice." * Allow me to insist on this view of the august duties of the magistrate. Every man whom public confidence has called to the bench should bear in mind that he is delegated to exercise one of the functions of the supreme power; and that he bears an authority, which (through whatever channels derived) takes its source in eternal justice, that is, in God Himself.

2. Justice as a Virtue. But it is not of justice considered as the test of right and wrong, or as the knowledge of good and evil, that we must treat in this lecture; in ethics, justice is considered chiefly as the virtue which preserves the golden mean between excess and defect. In this sense, it offers to the mind a less universal concept, but it bears more directly on our daily actions. It is defined as follows, in the first title of the "Institutes"

---

* Ethica Nicomachea, Book V., Chap. IV., n. 50.

of Justinian: "Justice is the constant and permanent determination to give each one his due."

This definition is far-reaching, for we owe many things to God, to our fellow-men, and to the dignity of our own nature. A man who would constantly and permanently render to God, to his neighbor, and to himself everything that is due—whether the claim be imperative or based on fitness only—such a man, I say, would have all the moral perfection of which human nature is capable. He would be the just man whom antiquity praised, but could never produce. He would be one of those men whom Holy Writ praised enough when it called them *just* men.

You need not then wonder at the breadth of the definition of jurisprudence which follows in the same passage of the "Institutes," for it must evidently be coextensive with the virtue of which it contains the practical knowledge. Jurisprudence is, according to Justinian: "The knowledge of things both divine and human, the science of the *just* and of the *unjust*" (of good and evil as affecting right and wrong). "Behold, Adam is become one of us, knowing good and evil." * The first part of this definition must be qualified by the second; that is to say, the knowledge of things both divine and human must be limited to those things which concern right and wrong, moral good and moral evil. It is gratifying to find out that the English language of the present time has not discarded this broad meaning of jurisprudence; for thus the word stands defined in the Century Dictionary: "More specifically, the body

---
* Gen. iii., 22.

of unwritten or judicial law considered in the light of its underlying principles and characteristic tendencies, and as distinguished from statute or legislative law." Legislative law is a pleonasm—positive law might be better—but let us condone this verbal blunder; the definition agrees fairly with that of Justinian.

3. The standard of Justice is not arbitrary. The doctrine involved in the definitions of the Roman law does not please Austin. Referring to the text of Ulpian which we have quoted, he says: " The probable meaning of this celebrated jargon it is not very easy to detect." It did not seem difficult to such men as Blackstone or Kent, but it may seem so to a soldier turned, as Austin was, into a legist, whose mind is full of the theory that justice is but a relative term, and merely expresses equality between an act and its measure, whatever that measure may be. Austin tells us seriously: " Although it disagree with a given or assumed test, a law set by the State or a law imposed by opinion is a law which the State has set, or a law which opinion has imposed." Very likely, a law set by the State is a law which the State has set, and a law imposed by opinion is a law which opinion has imposed; we are not prepared to deny such truisms as these, but we must object to his calling jargon the noble words of Ulpian. He explains his own truisms as follows: " Just as a yard or bushel used in a town or province, but differing from the yard or bushel prescribed by the sovereign legislature, is a yard or bushel to the inhabitants of the town or province, although it is a false measure in relation to the legal standard." Yes, but if it is a false measure in relation to the legal standard, the customers who may be served according to this false measure shall have either more or less than is contemplated by law. A thing exactly equal to a wrong standard is wrong itself, and if a merchant keeps and uses false weights, the customer will not be satisfied with the declaration of the merchant, that the measure is wrong indeed if compared with the public standard, but it is all right notwithstanding, because it was measured by the merchant's own standard. If the standard is wrong, then the amount which agrees with that wrong standard must be wrong. All this strange reasoning is brought in to prove the extraordinary proposition that "Just or unjust, justice or injustice, is a term of relative and varying import;" that is, lying and robbing, arson and adultery are right or wrong, just as men are pleased to make them. Yet, with a happy turn for self-contradiction, Austin says a few lines later: "Though it signifies conformity or non-conformity to any determinate law, the term justice or injustice sometimes denotes emphatically conformity or non-conformity to the ultimate measure or test—namely, the law of God. That is the meaning annexed to justice, when law and justice are opposed." This brings us back fairly to the "celebrated jargon" of the "Institutes" and the Pandects. Let us then cling to it and say that jurisprudence is the knowledge of right and wrong, good and evil, as marked out by the divine or by the human law, and that justice as a virtue is the *constant and permanent determination to give each one his due.*

4. Perfect and imperfect Duties. That it is our duty to give each one his due none will deny; but duties, with regard to their binding force, must be divided into two kinds. Some duties carry along with them a strict obligation; they are based on claims which are clearly defined, and they can be enforced either by the holder of the corresponding right, or by the social organization to which this holder belongs. Such duties are called *perfect* or *judicial*. Others are based on *fitness, decency,* or on the claims of some virtue distinct from strict justice. Such duties are called *imperfect,* because their extent and stringency is not measured by a fixed and inflexible rule; a great amount of discretion and liberty is left to the persons on whom such duties devolve, a great deal depends on their generous impulses. Let us give an example. The duty to pay an honest debt is a perfect duty: it is measured exactly by the definite amount of the debt; it can be enforced in the civil order by the State, and in the spiritual order by the Church. The duty to assist a poor man, who needs indeed our assistance, but who can do without it, is not of that absolute character: it is an imperfect duty.

The claims of benevolence, gratitude, or fidelity are not always sharply defined and cannot be enforced in the same way. However, some sort of sanction is certain to reach in the end a disregard of the laws of benevolence, gratitude, or fidelity; but, as a rule, that sanction will come from the law of nature, or from Him who is the author of nature.

When the term justice is made to comprehend *all duties,*

even those that are *imperfect,* or that are imposed by other virtues, then justice is a *general* virtue—that is, it pervades all the other virtues, such as prudence, temperance, truthfulness, fortitude, etc., etc. The function of justice, in combination with the other virtues, is to secure the acts which such virtues require from exceeding the right measure or falling short of it.* A man who observes justice in this sense is simply a perfect man. But justice, as usually understood, does not comprise imperfect duties, but it secures the equation of what is strictly due with the satisfaction of the debt. Thus it may happen that a man is just in the limited sense of meeting the claims of strict justice, and on that account he may be unimpeachable before human tribunals, and yet is unjust in a higher sense— that is, wanting in the performance of a duty which cannot be defined by human law, but which He who is infinite justice will certainly enforce. Let us make this clear by giving an example. Let us suppose that A has signed a promissory note, payable on a certain day, without grace. The time has nearly expired, and B requires payment. A replies: " The money which I expected has not come in time, but it is perfectly safe; here is the proof that it is on its way; grant me a short delay, and you shall have the full amount with interest. If you insist on immediate payment you will ruin me and my family, and you make it impossible for me to pay you in full." Should B answer:

---

* Aristotle has described with great accuracy the various kinds of justice. Among other passages may be recommended the second chapter of the fifth book of the Ethica Nicomachea.

"I care not whether I lose or not by it, and whether yourself and your family are driven to the wall. The money is due to-day, and to-day I shall have it, or you shall be punished as a man who has failed to meet his note"—should B so answer, even though the securities given by A are sufficient, and B is not seriously inconvenienced by waiting a few days, he is unfeeling and cruel—he should evidently not drive A to the wall—but is he unjust? No if we take justice in a strict sense, and as a special virtue; yes, if we call justice that general virtue which embraces all duties perfect or imperfect, and pervades all other moral virtues. We shall have to return to the subject when we treat of the difference between justice, charity, and fidelity.

SEC II. DIVISION OF JUSTICE.

5. Commutative Justice; equality of Value, economic or contractual.

Justice, taken in its strict sense, that is to say, as a special virtue, may be divided in commutative, distributive, and legal. These three kinds must be accurately distinguished. All three suppose a certain equality, but the terms of the equality are different.

Commutative justice consists in an equality of value * between the things which are given and things that are received in exchange. Hence, if a man sell a horse and

---

* Value must be understood here as meaning *exchange value*, not *use value*.

receive for it a reasonable price, commutative justice is satisfied. The things exchanged may be equal in value, either because they are so economically, i. e., according to the rate of exchange generally accepted, and counted in labor, hours, money, or in any other quantity susceptible of economic valuation; or because they have been made equal by agreement, a common arithmetical unit being wanting. If a man buy a bushel of wheat and pay the market price for it, we have a natural equality which is arithmetically demonstrable.

If, on the contrary, a man engages to do a certain amount of work for a given price, the equality is conventional, for there is no common unit between human labor and money. Economists try to find a means of comparison in the number of hours which have been spent in acquiring and fashioning the gold or silver which is given in exchange for the work, but the intricate calculation necessary to solve such an equation as this is most unsatisfactory, and is entirely ignored in human transactions. Besides, there may be an exchange of intellectual and moral goods which defy both arithmetic and algebra. It is simpler to say that the goods exchanged must be equal either in economic value or in the appreciation of the contracting parties. We suppose, of course, that there is no fraud or deceit, for fraud and deceit will vitiate any agreement, at least when they affect the substantial value of the exchange. Commutative justice is brought into play at every moment between man and man.

6. Distributive Justice; its varied functions. Distributive justice preserves the proportion between merit, demerit, and their respective awards. Commutative justice takes no account of the good-will or of the worth of the contracting parties; but simply preserves the equality between the objects exchanged. Distributive justice, on the contrary, considers the merits of the persons and determines the award on the subjective as well as objective value of the act. In men, distributive justice is necessarily very imperfect, for often where the merit is greatest, no adequate reward can be given. How, for instance, can we reward a soldier who has died on the battle-field? By firing a few shots over his grave? What is the worth of this to the departed hero? Hence it is said truly that distributive justice is divine, for God alone can measure the award exactly on the real merit of the claimant. Yet the ruling human powers must try, as far as it is possible, to imitate the divine justice, and, in meting out the rewards and punishments, observe as far as possible the proportion which equity requires. The delicate discernment which is required when penalties have to be imposed, taxes to the utmost both the wisdom and the impartiality of magistrates. It has been said that the equality is *arithmetical* in commutative justice, and *geometrical* in distributive justice; we give this metaphor for what it is worth.

The distribution of public preferments and the repartition of public burdens come also within the province of distributive justice. The distribution of honorable and lucrative positions is a most delicate function of the supreme power, while a fair apportionment of the burdens which must be borne by citizens is a problem of great complexity. In the matter of taxation, the difficulties are such that economists have not yet succeeded in framing rules or canons which legislators may follow with perfect security; yet, if we cannot attain perfection, we must try to approach it.

7. Legal Justice; it requires a double equation. We must also draw your attention to legal and vindicative justice. Legal justice is a term which has been much abused, and taken in different acceptations. It was often used by the older schoolmen as synonymous with justice considered as a general virtue; among modern writers, it means the agreement of human acts with positive law or legality; and in this sense it is contrasted with equity, which is the application of natural law, where positive law is insufficient to maintain rights or prevent wrongs. Hence the old axiom borrowed from Aristotle: *Equum est correctio justi,* i. e., Equity corrects justice; that is to say, natural justice supplements and sometimes modifies written law and statutes. This principle was fully recognized by the older English jurists,* but there is now a tendency to eliminate equity as far as possible, and to replace it by positive legality. This tendency has the inconvenience of multiplying written laws, but it has the advantage of leaving less room for arbitrary rulings on the part of the judge. However, the advance of positive legisla-

---

* See a very important note in Pomeroy's Equity Jurisprudence, Vol. I., p. 46, § 46, n. 1.

tion can never reach a point at which equity may be dispensed with; for, the combinations of circumstances being potentially infinite, it is impossible for human ingenuity so to frame statutes as to meet all possible contingencies. Moreover, when there is a doubt with regard to the intent of the legislator, the equities of the case must guide the interpreter. The legislator must be supposed to have meant what is in accordance with natural justice; hence it becomes necessary to interpret his meaning according to the dictates of natural law. All jurists are therefore bound to study equity as well as legality.

Legal justice requires a twofold equation: the act must be in accordance with the written law, and, therefore, equal the typical act determined by law; and the citizens must be equal before that law. In other words, legislation which is partial or partisan in its character is radically unrighteous. This does not mean that all men must have the same power in the State, or that no privileges may be granted to some for the benefit of the whole community; such an equality would be impossible, and, if possible, would become disastrous, and destructive of civil order; it can be nothing more than a dream of socialists and anarchists. Every man in America cannot be President of the United States or Judge of the Supreme Court; but the equality required by legal justice is an equal protection of all the rights natural or constitutional, inborn or acquired. The poorest citizen must feel certain that the law will maintain his rights as well as those of the chief magistrate of the republic; and that, if necessary, the whole power of the State shall be employed to protect him from aggression, from whatever quarter the aggression may come. The phrase, *Civis Americanus ego sum*, must be as potent as the celebrated formula, *Civis Romanus ego sum*.

8. Vindicative Justice; its mission is to restore Order. Threefold purpose of Vindicative Justice.

Vindictive, or, rather, vindicative justice is but a derivation of distributive justice, and it consists in a proportion between the guilt of the criminal and the penalty inflicted by the tribunal. When the penalty is clearly defined by the criminal laws of the country, the judge has but to apply them faithfully. But when the statutes leave him a certain margin he has to resort to his own sense of equity —that is, to a standard which is partly subjective; and he may exercise the admirable attribute of clemency, which is as divine in its origin as the judicial power itself. In order to understand better the proportion required by vindicative justice, we must bear in mind the ends of every justly inflicted penalty.

1st. The first and principal end is to maintain, or, if need be, to re-establish the order of justice. This principle is expressed as follows by Ahrens: " The end of penalties and legal sanctions is to re-establish the order of justice assailed by crime or felony. To the law, its full sway must be restored, that it may again stand forth in its might and majesty and remain victorious if crime challenge it or revolt against it." * This is the chief and essential object of criminal legislation. Hence a penalty is insufficient if the

---

* Ahrens, Droit Naturel, p. 283.

order of justice is assailed, and justice comes out of the struggle weakened and defied. It is excessive if more pain is inflicted than the triumph of justice requires.

2d. The second end is to protect society against criminals, and, therefore, make unnecessary a personal recourse to violence. This end shall be attained whenever the supreme dominion of justice shall be fully vindicated. For law is not fully vindicated when evil-minded men are not sufficiently deterred from committing crime, so that crime is on the increase instead of retiring before the advance of morality. Here allow me to warn you against a silly tendency to make heroes of criminals, and to make their lot an object of envy for the honest man who eats his bread in the sweat of his brow. This absurd tendency turns human judicature into a demoralizing agency and a mockery of true justice.

3d. The third purpose of criminal legislation is the reformation of the criminal. It is not as essential as the maintenance of justice or the defence of society, but yet from the ethical and social point of view it is of the highest importance. In this direction there is room for improvement everywhere, and workhouses, penitentiaries, and reformatories are often as many hotbeds of corruption.

What, then, about the death penalty? For surely it cannot amend the guilty man. This is partly true, but the amendment of the criminal is not the first or most essential purpose of criminal legislation. The triumph of justice and the protection of society are more important than any individual interest. Yet an important change is often accomplished by the awful sentence of death. It often brings the criminal to a frame of mind essential for his happiness beyond the grave, a frame of mind he would probably have never reached had he continued much longer his wicked life. Nothing like the dread shadow of approaching dissolution to make a man realize the truths which are the foundation of the moral order. Moreover, the infliction of the supreme penalty has a powerful effect to deter from crime those who are tempted to take the life of a fellow-man. If, therefore, it does not amend the criminal himself, it is a sharp cure for the ills of the social body. It is objected that man is not a means for society, but a person, and consequently an end-in-self. This is doubtless true, but it is through his own free will that the guilty man has made his very being a principle of corruption for the social body. By thus attacking the existence of society, he has made himself a corrupt and corrupting member of society, and, like a necrosed limb, he may be severed from the body for which he is a permanent source of decay. Several States, after abolishing the death penalty, have been compelled to inscribe it again in their penal codes; and Ahrens himself, although strongly opposed to that awful sanction, says openly: " We must be allowed to hold with many students of criminal jurisprudence, that in the present state of society this penalty cannot be abolished." Count de Maistre puts it in a stronger and more pithy manner: " We are very willing to suppress the killing of men," says he, " but, ye murderers, please set us the example!"

SEC. III. JUSTICE, CHARITY, AND FIDELITY.

9. Justice and Charity contrasted. We have said that there are two virtues which belong to justice as a general virtue, but which differ essentially from commutative justice. Those virtues are chiefly charity and fidelity. Charity inclines us to love our neighbors like ourselves, and, as a consequence, to act by them as we would wish them to act by us. Strict justice says: "What do I owe this man, that I may pay my debt in full?" Charity says: "What does my brother-man stand in need of, that I may supply his wants as far as I am able?" The former can almost always be enforced by human law; the latter very seldom. The former exhibits a sharply defined obligation; the latter leaves a great deal to generosity. A violation of the former involves a breach of equality between man and man; an infringement of the latter a disregard of brotherhood. Injustice requires restitution, because something has been taken away from the injured man, or because he has suffered a damage and is entitled to a compensation equal to the damage itself; a breach of charity requires indeed some sort of amends, but no restitution properly so called, for nothing of economic value has been taken from the person who has been uncharitably treated. Yet there is a point where the claims of both virtues meet: it is the case of extreme necessity—that is, imminent danger of life or limb. At that point, a man has a strict right to the help of other men; and the right of property itself must yield under the pressure of extreme necessity. Yet even in this case, it is not always evident that a simple omission of the duty imposed by natural law involves the duty of restitution, for the duty neglected may have been ill-defined and imperfectly known, or the omission of which Dives is guilty may not have withheld from Lazarus any object of definite value that he could claim in strict justice. None the less, that omission cries out to heaven for vengeance; and it shall be punished, perhaps in this world, by Him who is the never-failing Friend of the poor and of the needy.

10. Justice and Fidelity. Fidelity is a virtue which makes us fulfil our promises. As it does not transfer property, no absolute right is acquired by the recipient of the promise. But two cases must be carefully distinguished: either the person who has accepted the promise incurred at the same time some corresponding burden, which remains without compensation in case of the non-fulfilment of the promise, or the contract is absolutely unilateral, and the non-fulfilment entails no other loss than that of the anticipated benefaction. In the former case, the maker of the promise has caused his disappointed friend a real damage, for which he owes *in justice* a compensation; in the latter he owes nothing *in strict justice*, but he is guilty of prevarication, and his want of truthfulness is a moral wrong, which shall be visited either in this world or in the next. We suppose, of course, that circumstances have not been materially altered since the time when the promise was made, for a substantial modification in the circumstances alters the case and annuls a mere promise.

11. The Contract of Shylock. The difference between fidelity and justice is so strongly marked that we see no need of contrasting these two virtues; but natural justice, legality, and charity are not always so clearly distinguishable. We shall, therefore, borrow from a poet a fictitious case which will allow us to make their respective boundaries more clearly visible. We take the famous contract in the *Merchant of Venice.*

> *Shy.* This kindness will I show.
> Go with me to a notary, seal me there
> Your single bond: and in a merry sport,
> If you repay me not on such a day,
> In such a place, such sum or sums, as are
> Express'd in the condition, let the forfeit
> Be nominated for an equal pound
> Of your fair flesh, to be cut off and taken
> In what part of your body pleaseth me.
> *Ant.* Content, in faith; I'll seal to such a bond.

In the first place, it is evident that such a contract is contrary to natural law: 1st. Because nobody has the right to cut off a pound of his fair flesh, hence nobody can give that right to another. 2d. There is not the necessary condition of commutative justice—that is, the equation of value between what is given and what is received. 3d. Shylock expressly states that the whole thing is a joke, a grim one indeed, but yet a *merry sport,* as he pleases to call it; but a joke is not a contract. On these grounds, the so-called contract should have been annulled at once; and a male judge would probably have gone no further. But fair

Portia, being a woman, will catch at a mere quibble instead, and reach the result by a more cunning, but less logical, process.

12. Judgment of Portia. However, let us assume that the contract was valid and could be enforced by law; otherwise the merry sport could not go on. When Antonio failed to perform his part of the contract, Shylock had a strict right to exact his pound of flesh; but *summum jus summa injuria,* an overdrawn right becomes a grievous wrong. In exacting the pound of flesh, Shylock would not have violated commutative justice, but he would have committed a very criminal act against charity; moreover, his taking the pound of flesh would have entailed the maiming or the death of his victim, either of which would have been both against natural justice and against legal justice. Hence the State could not have tolerated that merry sport of the old usurer. But we say that Portia prefers to take hold of a quibble, for had the contract been valid, it is evident that the Jew should have had the right to have the blood which was contained in the flesh; for, given the right to cut out a pound of living flesh, the right to get the blood which is in it must necessarily follow. Moreover, the Jew was not bound to take all he was entitled to. He might then have done a little carving without going against the contract. As for shedding a drop of Christian blood, that was a mere technicality, as long as he did not shed more than was contained in the pound of flesh. On the other hand, in refusing the money of Bassanio, Shylock resorted to a quibble in order to glut his revenge. Bassanio shows himself a model of fidelity. Portia acts according to strict legality in imposing the well-deserved fine which brings the usurer to his knees. In all these transactions, Portia does not show herself as wise as Solomon, but she makes a most interesting female judge, full of the cunning and keen sense of a woman; yet she ends in being herself guilty of a strange piece of misguided zeal by compelling the poor Israelite to turn a Christian in order to save his shekels. This last feature of the trial is contrary both to justice and to charity; for it is against both to coerce or bribe consciences. But had Portia been a more correct judge, or Shakespeare a less inventive poet, we should not have had so good an opportunity to test the differences between commutative justice and charity, or between natural and positive law.

SEVENTH LECTURE.

The Individual, the Family, the State.

SEC. I.   THE INDIVIDUAL.

1. Man considered as an individual Being in ancient and in modern Civilizations.

When the civilization of Rome or of Sparta is compared with that of Christian nations, a well-marked difference is at once perceptible. In antiquity, the *citizen* may have acquired a certain importance, and felt a certain tribal or national pride, but the individual, the *man* was nothing; he was either absorbed or crushed relentlessly by the State. Among modern nations, a man is conscious of his dignity as man, and his fellow-men acknowledge and respect his manhood, as well as his citizenship. In Christian countries, the infant that is born deformed, or deprived of a limb or the use of an organ, excites compassion, and is the object of the tenderest solicitude; to obtain this sympathy, it is enough that the child be a human being, born with more than its share of human woes. Among the ancients, such a human being was considered as useless and contemptible; in certain cities, as, for example, at Lacedæmon, the law did not allow the mother to nourish it, and, by the command of the magistrates charged with the regulation of birth, it was thrown down a precipice.* In our American cities, when a man bending under the weight of years, or crushed by sickness or poverty, is unable to support himself, either private charity comes to his assistance, or the State supplies him with the necessaries, if not with the comforts, of life; in Rome, an old and useless slave was taken by force, carried away to some island and left there to die. When we bear in mind that more than two-thirds of the inhabitants of the great city were *slaves*, and that insolvent debtors could be sold as *slaves*, we see at once how far this monstrous practice could be carried on *legally* in pagan Rome. What if the slave was a human being? That human being had become a burden for society, and society had cast him off as so much social refuse.† What is the reason of so striking a contrast? Simply this: Christianity has made man aware of the dignity of his nature, and of the independence inherent in personality; truth made man free, and freedom saved human society. When the individual is completely crushed or absorbed the citizen cannot long survive. Hence the despotism of Rome proved suicidal; liberty died first, and national life next. The lesson taught by the fall of Rome is of the highest importance for us. Let us bear in mind that we cannot abridge

---

* Wachsmuth, Hellenische Alterthumskunde, Vol. II., 1st Division, p. 353.

† Döllinger, The Gentile and the Jew, Darnell's translation, Vol. II., p. 264. See also Becker's Gallus, Metcalf's translation, p. 217.

individual liberty without draining the life-blood of the nation.

2. Dignity of the human Personality a consequence of the nature of Man. Kant and Aquinas. The special dignity of a human being comes from its nature. Man is not only a material, but also a spiritual being, and in the latter capacity resembles his Maker. Man has an intellect and a will, can reason, deliberate, and act freely. He is the author of his own act. As a consequence, he is, according to Kant, an end-in-self—that is to say, his end does not necessarily depend on that of his fellow-men, but he achieves it by his own exertions, whether or not others are successful. The word end-in-self used by Kant expresses a true idea, yet it may be misunderstood. It cannot mean that the felicity which is the object of his aspirations is so contained in his individual happiness that he wants no good but his own; but that the *summum bonum* which alone can satisfy his cravings is to be communicated to him individually. The happiness of his neighbor will indeed contribute to his own, but his own is not dependent on that contribution, except in so far as it cannot be obtained, unless he fulfil his duties to others.

St. Thomas Aquinas expresses the same truth accurately when he says that inferior beings are led to their ends by natural impulses, which are common to the whole kind; while man moves toward his own destiny, individually, by his own counsel and his own determination. In other words, his activity is not only *specific*, but also *individual*.*

---

* Contra. Gentes, Cap. CXIII.

3. Man is not the thing of the State.
Such is man, an image of his Maker, transcending space and time by his intellect, seeking infinite good with all the energy of his will, controlling inferior beings in virtue of his superior powers, and of his innate rights, and himself moving freely that he may frame his own destiny. Thus man is invested with a sort of kingship over the lower creation and over his own passions. Wrest from that king his circlet, take away his freedom, load him with chains, and he will pine and die. So there is a real and a philosophical meaning in those words of Patrick Henry: " Give me liberty, or give me death."

And observe that the death mentioned by Patrick Henry is not complete; the spirit itself does not die, it merely leaves for a time its earthly tenement; and so every man may say with the ancient poet: *Non omnis moriar*—I shall not wholly die. In this sense the individual outlives civil society; he cannot be wholly the thing of the State, since he must outlast the State. Individuals existed before the establishment of the commonwealths; they will exist when commonwealths have passed away; they are not created for the State, but the State is instituted for them.

4. Absolute rights, according to Chancellor Kent.
Man having his own end, controlling his own actions, and being both in concept and in fact anterior to the State, must have moral powers called rights, which cling to his personality, and which no human authority may infringe. Among these powers the principal is undoubtedly the right to work out his destiny, and, as a

necessary means, to perfect his own being morally and intellectually. Even when man lives outside of civil society, this right abides with him, it is not liable to abuse, and in the social state never conflicts with the rights of others. But there are other rights which may be assailed, and which the State is bound to maintain.

"The absolute rights of individuals," says Chancellor Kent, "may be resolved into the right of personal security, the right of personal liberty, and the right to acquire and enjoy property. These rights have been justly considered, and frequently declared by the people of this country to be natural, inherent, and unalienable. The effectual security and enjoyment of them depend upon the existence of civil liberty; and that consists in being protected and governed by laws made, or assented to, by representatives of the people, and conducive to the public welfare. Right itself, in civil society, is that which any man is entitled to have, or to do, or to require from others, within the limits prescribed by law." *

5. Individual and citizen; the citizen not the whole Man; exaggerated individualism. It is in order that these rights may be secured, that man becomes a member of a social organization; alone, he would be liable to be attacked and oppressed; united with others, he can bid defiance to his foes. Hence he is not only a human being, but also a citizen. We call *citizen* a man who belongs to a nation, and is entitled to the protection of

---

* Consult Law of Personal Rights, A. J. Willard, Appleton, 1882.

that nation; can hold property, can sue and be sued, is eligible to office, and has some share, however humble, in the conduct of public affairs. Many of the rights which we have mentioned as constituting citizenship are extended to strangers, residing in a country to which they do not belong; but this extension is not a matter of strict, natural right, it is due to the comity of nations, and consecrated by international law. In exchange for the protection, and the other privileges granted to him, the citizen is bound to obey the laws, to contribute to the common welfare, and to bear his share of the national burdens. In the performance of these duties he surrenders part of his individual freedom. National government is best when it leaves to its citizens the greatest possible amount of freedom, without impairing the strength of the nation, or permitting anarchy. To conciliate individual freedom with national unity is perhaps the most important and most difficult problem that statesmen have to deal with.

In every member of society we may find by analysis the individual first and the citizen next. Both, indeed, are combined in one person, but that person is considered in itself when we call it *individual;* and in its relations with other members of the same commonwealth when we call it *citizen.* It is important to remember that the citizen is not the whole man. Personality or individuality is inseparable from him, but citizenship may be set aside, and it is bound to cease when temporal life is at an end. Individuality clings to the spirit when the body sinks into the grave; it is born for eternity.

Yet we must beware of exaggerated individualism. It consists in acknowledging no law outside of our own person, no standard of morality outside of our own reason, no power that can require and compel obedience. Should such an individualism prevail, anarchy would be the consequence; should personal rights be infringed by the State, then tyranny would usurp the sway.

According to the pithy formula of Aristotle, man is not only a reasonable being; he is also a domestic being, and a political being. We have studied him in his personality; let us consider the two sorts of society to which he belongs by nature.

SEC. II. THE FAMILY.

6. Definition of society; three complete societies; their respective ends. A society is a group of reasonable beings aiming at and working for a common end, under a common leadership. When the end aimed at is last in its own order; when the group of human beings has or can justly claim the means to accomplish that end, then the society is said to be complete. There are in this world three kinds of complete society, the Family, the State, and the Church. The end of the family is the perpetuation and perfection of the human race. The end of civil society is the fulness of an independent and social life—in other words, the fulness of temporal well-being. The end of the Church is moral perfection as a preparation for the life to come.

When we say that each of these societies is complete, we do not mean that they co-exist in the world without any mutual relations, or without respective rights and duties—complete isolation is evidently impossible—but we assert that each one must be perfectly free with regard to its own special object. Thus *the procreation and rearing of children belongs to the family; the direction of temporal and social interests is the province of the State; spiritual and supernatural matters are in the hands of the Church.* To describe accurately the relations and interdependence of these three societies, and mark the border lines of their respective jurisdictions, is a matter of great difficulty; suffice it to say, for the present, that each one is supreme in its own sphere. We must leave to theologians and to canonists the questions of Church constitution and Church polity, and confine our present study to the two complete societies which belong to the temporal order, the family first and the State next.

7. Family, and family servants. The family, or household, is *a society consisting of husband, wife, children, and servants, having a corporate existence and a community of interests.* Why do we put in *servants?* Because perfect servants, according to natural law, form a part of the family, have at heart the interest of the family, and are within its precincts the object of affectionate consideration. When I say *servants,* I do not mean *slaves,* although where slavery is tolerated there would be no redeeming feature, if the slaves were not treated as true, though humble, members of the family. The personal rights of the slave *must* *be respected,* and no State ordinance whatever can make *chattel slavery* legitimate; *it is intrinsically bad.* Did it ever prevail in this country? We think not, surely not in theory; but during slavery times, natural law was often violated, and the laws did not sufficiently protect the personal rights of the slaves. The institution, as it existed, had to go. We wish it had gradually passed away without costing so much treasure and so much blood, but perhaps this fearful expenditure was unavoidable: every true American is glad that the struggle is over, and that freedom reigns supreme on this broad continent.

But we are not equally pleased with the disappearance of the cherished type of the family servant, whose interest was centred in the household and who received from all its members the most affectionate consideration; the hireling who cares little for those among whom his lot is cast for a short time, and who may be dismissed at any moment, is but a poor substitute for the family servant, and cannot be counted as a member of the household. Practically the relation of master to servant is a thing of the past, at least among us. It is not indispensable, yet its absence takes away one of the charms of family life.

8. Union of husband and wife; it originates in a sacred Contract. But an association which is absolutely necessary, and which constitutes the very essence of the family, is that of husband and wife, founded on mutual love, and hallowed by a sacred contract. "The primary and most important of the domestic relations," says Chancellor Kent,

" is that of husband and wife. It has its foundation in nature, and is the only lawful relation by which Providence has permitted the continuance of the human race. In every age it has had a propitious influence on the moral improvement and happiness of mankind. It is one of the chief foundations of the social order."

" The relation of marriage," says Parsons, " is founded upon the will of God and the nature of man; and it is the foundation of all moral improvements and all true happiness. No legal topic surpasses this in importance." This relation, being contractual in its nature, and requiring mutual love from the contracting parties, must be based originally on mutual consent. " Mutual consent even without solemnity constitutes betrothal," says Ulpian. (Digest LXXIII., Tit. 1, Section 4.) " The daughter is supposed to be of one mind with her father when she does not clearly express her dissent." (Ibid., Paulus, Section 7.) " Betrothals, as well as marriages, are made by the mutual consent of the contracting parties." (Ibid., Julianus, Section 11.) Canon law considers the contract itself as raised to the dignity of a sacrament; that is to say, of a rite instituted by Christ to convey supernatural grace. The necessity of a mutual consent is admitted both by English and by American authorities. "Chancellor Kent," says Parsons, "quotes another passage from the Digest: *Nuptias non concubitus sed consensus facit.* This is the language of the common and canon law, and of common sense."*

---

* Parsons on Contracts, Vol. II., Book III., Chap. X., § IV., p. 557.

9. Marriage did not originate either in violence or in promiscuous intercourse. How McLennan could have imagined that primitive marriage originated in successful rape, and how some modern writers could say that, at first, it was nothing but a promiscuous intercourse between a group of men and a group of women, we do not attempt to explain; the freaks of imagination cannot be accounted for. In vain the sacred books of India describe the rites of matrimony; in vain the history of Egypt, the Assyrian inscriptions, and the narrative of the most ancient and most sacred of all books proclaim that from the beginning matrimony was a sacred contract; all those historical monuments are useless for a man who, like McLennan, seriously tells us: " Apart from the test of truth afforded by the minute knowledge of primitive modes of life, and their classification as more or less archaic, *nothing can be more delusive than written history.*" Yes, there is a thing far more delusive than written history; it is the unbridled fancy of a man who draws on his imagination for his facts.

Some writers pretend to find in the rape of the Sabines the type of primitive marriage; they forget Livy's narrative. "Romulus in person," says the Roman historian, " went about and declared . . . that they (the Sabine maidens) should be joined in lawful wedlock to the Roman youths; they would participate in all the possessions and civil privileges of their husbands. He begged them to moderate the fierceness of their anger, and cheerfully surrender their affections. . . . They should find them (the Romans) kinder husbands, because each of them, besides performing his conjugal duty, would endeavor to his utmost to make up for the absence of their parents and the loss of their country." (Liv. I. 9.) "The minds of the ravished virgins were soon appeased," says Livy, and he proves that they were devoted to their husbands no less than to their fathers. A war had begun between the Romans and the parents of their willing captives. What is the behavior of the Sabine women? Do they run away? No. "With hair dishevelled and garments rent, the timidity of their sex being overcome by their anxiety to stop the bloodshed, they had the courage to throw themselves between the flashing swords . . . they parted the incensed warriors; imploring their fathers, on the one side, their husbands on the other, that as fathers-in-law and sons-in-law they should not contaminate their hands with the blood of relatives, or leave the stain of parricide, the ones on their grandchildren, the others on their children." (Chap. XIII.)

This is quite enough; who does not see that the real marriage was not MADE by the rape, but by the succeeding wedlock? McLennan seems to have a special talent to refute himself. He tells us that "the symbol of capture occurs whenever after a CONTRACT OF MARRIAGE it is necessary for the constitution of the relationship of husband and wife that the bridegroom or his friends should go through the form of feigning to steal the bride." Then in such cases there is a preceding contract; is it the sham fight or the contract which constitutes marriage? One would naturally suppose that a real contract was a more effective cause than a sham fight. The same writer tells us that " the difference between the Welsh and Muscovite practice lay in this, that in Wales, in the celebration of marriage, betrothal came first, and the sham fight afterward; while among the Muscovites an actual invasion came first, and if the bridegroom party succeeded in carrying off the lady, there followed the consent of the parents and the SPONSALIA." Very well; but according to his own statement there was a marriage contract in both cases. He quotes the Latin text of Olaus,* who says explicitly that the girl BEING LET FREE to oppose the marriage, " began sham lamentations to bring about a conflict." Then the same author adds the following significant sentence: " It is considered by all nations a disgraceful crime, if before the performance of the sacred rites the girl's modesty is not preserved in its integrity. Nay more, the maidens used the utmost care to avoid a premature intercourse, for otherwise they, and with them their offspring, would incur perpetual infamy." How does this authority show that marriage did not originate in a contract?

10. Chief end of Matrimony; duties resulting from the Marriage relation.

The conjugal union of man and woman has for its natural consequence the continuance of the family and the permanency of human society. Hence the main purpose of matrimony is the raising and education of children till they have reached the

---

* Olaus, Archbishop of Upsala, Historia de Gentibus Septentrionalibus, Rome, 1555.

fulness of manhood or womanhood. But this is not the only purpose of married life. Each sex is imperfect, insomuch as neither contains all the potentialities of human nature; as a consequence, the complete type of humanity unites both sexes in the bonds of conjugal love. When God created man, *Male and female He created them.* (Gen., Chap. I., verse 27.)

Hence the secondary purpose of matrimony is the complement, physical and moral, of both sexes.

If we condense in a short formula what we have said of the nature of marriage, the result will be the following definition: *Marriage is the union of one man and of one woman in a community of life, hallowed by conjugal love, formed by the united consent of both parties to last until death part them, ordained by nature for the continuance and increase of the human race and the complement of both sexes.*

It will be observed that we have not said, *raised by Christ to the dignity of a sacrament.* We have left out this important clause because it is theological in its character, and would prevent our definition from being universal. But we are not blind to the fact that to take away from marriage its character as a sacred rite is to tear down the strongest barrier that can be opposed to mere animal passions. Replying to those who said that pure and happy marriages were not dreams, but facts, Count Tolstoï says somewhere: "All that was possible when marriage was a sacrament." There is more in this remark than a fling at modern society. When marriage is not a sacrament, it is apt to become a mere temporary association, from which all sacredness has departed, and which is not secure enough to be the foundation of civil society.

Passing over in silence the reciprocal duties of married persons, duties which are commonly well known, if not always faithfully observed, we shall come to the duties of parents to their children. By Blackstone they are reduced to three: maintenance, protection, education. Four evident reasons show that this threefold duty follows directly from natural law: 1st, Every moral agent is accountable for the consequences of his own acts, so far as he can foresee them; on him it is incumbent to provide that those consequences be not hurtful, but beneficial. But the birth of children is the result of an act of the free will of their parents. Therefore it is the bounden duty of the parents to see that the life which they have given be not a curse, but a blessing. It could not be a blessing were the duties mentioned, especially that of education, neglected; therefore it is the duty of the parents to provide for the maintenance, protection, and *education* of their children; and that duty would exist of necessity even if positive law should fail to sanction it; for even in that case the natural relation of parents to children would remain essentially unchanged.

2d. As we have seen, the end of nature in the marriage relation is to secure the continuance and perfection of the human race; but this purpose would evidently be defeated if the three obligations above-mentioned were neglected by the parents; therefore those obligations are laid upon them by nature itself. Blackstone says: "The last duty of parents to their children is that of giving them an education suitable to their station in life; a duty pointed out by reason, and of far the greatest importance of any. For, as Puffendorf very well observes, it is not easy to imagine or allow that a parent has conferred any considerable benefit upon his child by bringing him into the world, if he afterward entirely neglects his culture and education, and suffers him to grow up like a mere beast, to lead a life useless to others and shameful to himself."*

We must add that by this neglect the parent not only sins against the child and against society, but also thwarts the beneficent purpose of the Creator in instituting matrimony.

11. Natural impulse and natural fitness of Parents to educate their Children.

3d. A universal impulse which is not only rational and human, but which is reproduced in the instinct of animals, is, according to Roman jurisconsults and to reason itself, the unmistakable token of natural law. But such is the impulse of parents to accomplish the three duties mentioned, and it finds its counterpart even in the instinct of animals. Therefore those duties are imposed by natural law. We quote in full the celebrated text of Ulpian: "Natural law is that which nature has taught all living beings, for it is not the exclusive property of man, but it reaches all the animals which live in the air, on the earth, or in the depths of the sea. Hence flow the union of man and woman, which we

---

* Blackstone's Commentaries, Vol. I., n. 451.

call matrimony; hence the procreation of children; *hence their education."*

4th. Where there is a special and natural fitness, there also is laid a special and natural duty; but parents have a special and natural fitness to educate their own children; hence it is their special and natural duty. The minor premise is evidenced by observation both of private and of social life. Nothing can supply the love of a mother or the mild firmness of a father. Young orphans are at a disadvantage from the start, as keen observers of human nature well know. After insisting on the duty of the parents to educate their children in a manner suitable to their station and calling, Chancellor Kent makes the following important observation: "Several of the States of antiquity were too solicitous to form their youth for the various duties of civil life, even to intrust their education solely to the parent; but this, as in Crete and Sparta, was upon the principle, totally inadmissible in the modern civilized world, of the absorption of the individual in the body politic, and of his entire subjection to the despotism of the State."

History has proved that it is unwise to depart from natural law either by encroaching on parental rights, or by conferring on parents rights which natural law does not sanction. One of the Grecian States, Sparta, shifted the responsibility from the parents to the State. It interfered with nature's law, and the consequence was that Sparta did not produce a single poet, a single orator, a single statesman of superior ability, unless it be Lycurgus, who invented the system, but was not reared according to it. For a time it had warriors, but even these at last were wanting, and Sparta was conquered by the other commonwealths, on which in the beginning she was wont to impose her will. Rome committed another fault, that of giving by law to the father an authority which had no warrant in nature; but although she paid the forfeit in the end, yet she can boast of a succession of great men down to the last period of decline.

"The father," says Blackstone, "may delegate part of his parental authority, during his life, to the tutor or schoolmaster of his child, who is then *in loco parentis,* and has such a portion of the power of the parent committed to his charge, namely, that of restraint and correction, as may be necessary to answer the purpose for which he is employed. . . . The power of the parents over their children is derived from . . . their duty."

12. Duties of Children; their personal Rights must be respected. The duties of the children offer no serious ethical difficulty; they are often explained, but seldom enforced sufficiently. They owe to their parents reverence, obedience, and love; they must help their parents to support the family, and give them maintenance when strength and resources fail them. To the performance of those duties they are bound in strict justice, but they have also their rights. They are not the *things* of their parents; they are human persons, holding the moral powers inherent to personality, and entitled to the necessary means to work out their destiny.

The family is a complete society, having its own organization, its own rights, and its own directing power; by nature itself this power is vested in the father, the head of the household, and in the mother, who has her own sphere of action, and must have her share of parental authority. Within its own sphere—that is, with regard to marriage, *to the raising and education of children*—the family does not depend on the State. The family, both in concept and in fact, existed before the commonwealth, and therefore cannot have derived its special rights and duties from the commonwealth. The *personal* rights of the individual must be respected by the family, and the special rights of the household must be protected by the State. In order to protect the family against all aggressions within and without the commonwealth, the State is armed with extensive powers, which, according as they are used justly or unjustly, may secure liberty or crush it.

SEC. III. THE COMMONWEALTH.

13. The Individual enters civil society through the Family. Why the Individual is not a perfect social Unit. It is through the family that the individual enters the commonwealth. Alone, he is indeed an element of civil society, but he is not a perfect unit, for several reasons. 1st. There is lacking the condition of permanency required in a perfect social unit. 2d. The individual cannot represent the highest interests of the race which cluster around the cradles. 3d. During a part of his existence, he is unable to perform the duties of citizenship.

What, then, is a civil society or commonwealth? *A civil society is a community of freemen, comprising smaller groups and families, bound together to obtain by combined action the fulness of a perfect and autonomous existence.* Such is substantially the definition of Aristotle.* We say a community of *freemen,* because slaves do not constitute a civil society; yet they may live in it, and if they do, must retain their personal rights. We say *comprising smaller groups and families,* because a civil society must contain several municipal communities and families, each possessing its own municipal or domestic organization, but subordinated to the central government. We assert that the end of that combination is to obtain the fulness of life, because many of the acts and of the enjoyments of life would remain inaccessible to isolated persons, or to families cut off from the rest of mankind; lastly, the social life is called autonomous, because where there is no self-government there is no complete society.

14. Civil society a body politic. A civil society is a body politic; that is to say, it is in the political order what a living body is in the material world. It must consist of organisms, incomplete in themselves, but supplying by their several functions all the essential elements of social life. Like a living body, it must have *its own life principle,* its own *central force,* which makes its combined action *corporate,* preserves its identity, and makes it accountable as a moral being or person, for whatever is accomplished by the nation as a body politic.

---
* Politic, Book III., Chap. IX.

"In calling the State an organism," says Bluntschli, " we are not thinking of the activities by which plants and animals seek, consume, and assimilate nourishment, and reproduce their species. We are thinking rather of the following characteristics of natural organism: (*a*) Every organism is a union of soul and body, i. e., of material elements and vital forces. (*b*) Although an organism is and remains a whole, yet in its parts it has members, which are animated by special motives and capacities in order to satisfy in various ways the varying needs of the whole itself. (*c*) The organism develops itself from within outwards, and has an external growth. In all three respects the organic nature of the State is evident."*

This concept is indispensable; without it we have a multitude, or at best an aggregate, of moral beings, but no social life. Moreover, an important conclusion flows from this truth. As the perfection of a living body results both from the perfect play of the several organisms which enter into its composition, and from the harmony with which those various organisms concur to sustain and develop *one* life; so the civil organization will be most perfect when all the elements of the body politic have full liberty to accomplish the special functions to which they are adapted, and when those various activities are so harmonized as to be available for combined action. In other words, *Unity*

---

* The Theory of the State, Oxford, Clarendon Press, 1892, p. 19.
The author carries his theory too far when he makes the State *masculine* and the Church *feminine,* but the statement which we have quoted is perfectly true and very clearly put.　[R. I. H.

and *Liberty* are both essential for the well-being of the body politic.

We have said that the family alone was a perfect social unit, but the citizens constitute the first elements of the body politic. They may be considered as perfect units when they represent family interests; imperfect when they stand as mere individuals with only personal responsibilities.

After describing the social units, we must determine the principle which binds them together. Doubtless the oneness of a common purpose is in itself a bond of union; yet as the minds of men, however agreed with regard to the end, are apt to disagree in reference to the means, as the social units are many and various in their nature, as oppositions will arise and must be overcome, as contending interests must be harmonized, nothing short of the supreme power, the *Majestas* of the Romans, can secure a powerful corporate action. By *Majestas* we mean *the right to control exterior individual actions, and to direct national activity, insomuch as it is necessary in order to attain the end of civil organization.*

15. Did society originate in a compact? Hobbes and Rousseau.
Did society originate in a compact or is it the work of nature itself? In the first supposition it is an artificial and accidental creation; according to the second it is a necessary growth, whose laws are both natural and imperative. Opposite schools of sociology must spring from contrary answers to this fundamental question. Hobbes and Rousseau tell us that the whole social organ-

ism originated in a contract. Both go back to the primitive state, which, in the opinion of both, was barbarism. But according to Hobbes that barbarism was the state of war of everybody with everybody else; Rousseau is not quite so unkind to his forefathers; he makes them innocent, benevolent, and upright, but uncivilized. Neither of our *compactists* accounts for the fact that our earliest historical records bear testimony to some sort of primitive civilization, and that, in order to go beyond these records, a man has to draw on his imagination for his facts; they also ignore popular and poetic traditions which refer to a golden age; all these lovely legends are meaningless for such grave philosophers. Some time or other, the men of Hobbes found out that they had to fight or be kept from fighting by an absolute ruler; and those of Rousseau loathed the simple food supplied by the untilled soil. In both cases dissatisfaction led to a contract, the record of which has unfortunately been lost long ago; but its tenor has been recovered both by Hobbes and by Rousseau. The two texts do not agree very well, but the substance of both amounts to this: everybody gave himself up, soul and body, to everybody else, in order to be handed over in due time to the governing power; then these primitive beings chose the man or men who were to be intrusted with that supreme power, and immediately the absolute ruler called by Hobbes, *Leviathan,* arose from the deep; or the universal democracy of Rousseau ruled the world. Hobbes gave his monster-king unlimited power, made him not only the arbiter, but the creator of right and wrong, and forbade insurrection. One hundred years before Hobbes, Bodin had asserted the absolute power of the State, but he had left the following restriction:* *"When we say that in the commonwealth the supreme power is above all the laws, we did not mean either the law of God or natural law."* Hobbes frees Leviathan from such shackles: *"Whatever is the object of any man's appetite or desire, that is which he calleth good; and the object of his hate and aversion, evil. . . . Nothing is simply or absolutely so; nor any common rule of good and evil is to be taken from the nature of the objects themselves, but from the person of the man, where there is no commonwealth; or in a commonwealth from the person that representeth it; or from an arbitrator or judge whom men disagreeing shall by consent set, and make his sentence the rule thereof."*†

The contract may be expressed in the following terms: " I authorize and I give up my right of governing myself to this man or this assembly of men, on this condition, that thou give up thy right to him, and authorize all his actions in like manner. This done, the multitude so united in one person is called a commonwealth, in Latin, *civitas*. This is the generation of that great Leviathan, or rather, to speak more reverently, of that *mortal god* ‡ to whom we owe under the immortal God our peace and defence." §

---

* Frederick Pollock, History of the Science of Politics, Chap. IV.
† Lev., Chap. VI.
‡ Italics ours.
§ Lev., Chap. CVIII.

We have seen the generation of the god Leviathan described by Hobbes.

Let us see how the Marianne of J. J. Rousseau was ushered into this world: "Each one of us turns over to the general will his own person and all his powers, and receives in exchange every member of the community as an inseparable part of the whole body. Directly, instead of the individual parties to the contract, the act of association brings to life a collective moral body, with as many members as the community has suffrages. This collective being derives from the same act its unity, its *ego*, its life and its will. The moral person, which is the aggregate of all the individual units, was of yore called *City;* it is now named commonwealth or body politic. By its members it is called the *State;* when actually ruling it becomes the *Sovereign;* when compared with other States it is called a *Power.* The members, taken collectively, constitute the *People;* taken distributively, they are termed *Citizens,* when sharing in the supreme authority; *Subjects,* when yielding obedience to the laws of the State."* Such are the two systems of Hobbes and Rousseau; they are both liable to very obvious objections.

16. Both Contracts inadmissible. 1st. If such a contract was ever made no trace of it remains in history. 2d. Such a contract would be invalid, because individuals could not confer on the State powers which they had not themselves—e. g., the power to inflict the death penalty. 3d. Acting in their individual capacity,

* Contrat Social, Chap. VI.

they could not bind their successors. 4th. The contract would involve a curious vicious circle, for the State would receive its rights from the individuals, and the individuals would receive their rights from the State. Besides, the authority being an aggregate of individual rights would sink or swell with the number of social units. Thus a little State would have less authority than a large one. 5th. Both systems involve the surrender of what men hold most dear, their liberty and their personality; as a compensation, they would have an infinitesimal fraction of everybody else. Where is the man who would accept such an exchange?

17. Civil society originated in Human Nature. This plexus of absurdities shows us evidently that civil society did not originate in a contract, but in nature itself. Men, in entering commonwealth, merely obey natural law. The following reasons show it directly and conclusively:

1st. By a natural impulse, man seeks the company of his fellow-men. This want is so imperative that protracted isolation stunts his powers, and often dethrones his reason. Such could not be the case if the social condition were not a natural, but an artificial one. Hence man is naturally a social being.

2d. Man has received from nature the power of speech; lower animals utter sounds, but those sounds are not articulate; they express feelings, not concepts. Now, the end or purpose of speech is chiefly an interchange of ideas, which involves society. Domestic society may be for a time sufficient, but it is totally inadequate to bring out all the possibilities of human intercourse. Therefore man is destined not only to *domestic,* but also to *civil* society.

3d. So far is it from truth that the natural state of man is that of universal war, that nature has implanted in his heart strong sympathies for his fellow-men. Love and pity spontaneously arise within the human breast, and when directed by reason may attain the dignity of the highest virtues. What Hobbes has mistaken for a natural state is the predominance of animal instincts. Man is an animal, but a reasonable one, a being not only gregarious as some of the lower animals, but destined to civil society.

4th. Man naturally seeks the measure of happiness which is attainable in this world. But this happiness requires a division of labor and a variety of functions which cannot be realized out of society. Hence man is impelled by nature itself to a social life.

5th. Man is bound in duty to himself to develop, as far as practicable, his physical, mental and moral powers. But this evolution requires social intercourse; it is promoted by the advance of civilization, which is impossible outside of civil society. Therefore man is naturally destined to civil society.

18. Authority comes originally from God, but the consent of the People determines the Ruler.
If civil society springs from nature itself, whence comes that authority which transforms a multitude into a nation; or, as Mr. Spencer has it, *discharges in the social economy functions that are comparable with those of the brain in a vertebrate animal?* It does not come originally from

the multitude, for the multitude has it not; at least so long as that multitude is not organized into a commonwealth. It is not the sum or total of the individual powers of each man over himself, for the cession of these powers would have to be proved by clear historical documents, and *a priori,* it is absurd; no one *would* yield the control of his own liberty, nobody *could* give power over his own life. We have therefore to seek the first origin of State authority in a power superior to man, and extending over the whole human race. Such a power is evidently divine in its source. Let not this doctrine be mistaken for the *divine power of kings,* such as it was advocated by James II. and some Oxford divines, nor for the "divine power of majorities," as Mr. Spencer calls the "great modern superstition." We do not say that God appoints rulers and gives them unlimited power, but that if we trace State authority to its first source, we find it to be nature itself —i. e., the Author of nature. Moreover, we aver that this authority is limited to the objects for which it is given. Lastly we assert that the first fact by which it is conveyed to the rulers is the consent of the people, either explicit or implied. On this point the reasoning of Zigliara seems to us apodictic. Here is the argument of that eminent writer: "The moral duties which bind one man to another must either flow spontaneously from nature, or be the consequences of an act of free will; but the obligation to obey this or that man as a ruler does not flow spontaneously from nature (for nobody is born either king or subject), therefore it must be the consequence of an act of free will; that is to say, it must be the result of a choice."

19. Legislative, Executive, and Judiciary power. State authority necessarily comprises the legislative power, because free men must be governed by laws, not by the arbitrary will of the ruler; the executive power, because laws must be carried out and enforced, otherwise they would prove worse than useless; the judiciary power, both in civil and criminal cases; in civil cases, because the State must protect the rights of all, and prevent conflicts and appeals to violence; in criminal cases, because otherwise justice and the majesty of law could be defied with impunity.

Besides the legislative, executive, and judiciary powers, the State must have also the right of eminent domain. We mean by eminent domain, " The right inherent in the supreme power of civil society to use the property of its members, when it is indispensable for the *being* or well-being of the commonwealth; with the understanding that a suitable compensation shall be given whenever public burdens would, without that compensation, fall unequally on the various units of the body politic."

Observe that this is not *a right of property,* but merely an application of *State jurisdiction.* Were the State to absorb the property of the citizens, it would destroy what it is bound by its very institution to defend and to maintain.

Many authors consider the right of taxation as a consequence of the eminent domain. The importance and the extreme complexity of the subject oblige us to devote to it a special lecture. It cannot be properly treated as an incident of eminent domain.

The combination of powers which makes up the supreme State authority is truly formidable, and when wielded by strong and unscrupulous men may imperil the liberty of the citizens. To divide these powers without impairing the strength and unity of the nation has been the most difficult problem with which the framers of constitutions have had to grapple. The solution given by our Constitution has proved so far successful. Perfection is not attainable in human institutions, and it would be extremely unwise to make new experiments; it is better to let *well enough* alone.

20. Unity and Liberty; State Atomism; Nihilism; State Fetichism. Another problem which is no less important and no less difficult to solve is to conciliate the corporate strength of the nation with the greatest possible amount of individual freedom. W. Von Humboldt,[*] J. S. Mill,[†] and Herbert Spencer [‡] have warned the world against the coming slavery, and there is doubtless throughout the world an impulse toward centralization and the absolutism of majorities; but these authors seem at times to incline to *State Atomism,* which ignores the rights of minor societies within the State, or to what Mr. Huxley calls *Administrative Nihilism,* which

---

[*] W. Von Humboldt. Die Grenzen der Wirksamkeit des Staats.
[†] J. S. Mill on Liberty.
[‡] H. Spencer, The Coming Slavery, the Sins of Legislators, etc.

would make State influence *negative* rather than *positive*. On the other hand, professorial socialists clamor for a more active intervention of the State powers. The system which they advocate is often called *Paternal Government;* perhaps it might as well be called *State Fetichism.* It is impossible to mark with hard and inflexible lines the boundaries of State action, but statesmen must always keep before their eyes the end of civil government, bearing in mind this principle of Mr. Spencer, in which we fully concur: "*State authority . . . is a means to an end, and has no validity save as subserving* that end." This end he describes as comprising the enforcement of justice, the maintenance of equitable relations, and protection against external enemies. We wish he had mentioned also the unification of individual forces whenever corporate action is imperative. We are justified in making this addition, since Mr. Spencer himself has said that the Houses of Parliament discharge in the social economy functions comparable to those discharged by the cerebral masses in a vertebrate animal.

21. Practical rules of State polity. In the light of the principles laid down in this lecture, the following rules will, it is hoped, commend themselves to your acceptance:

1st. The State must not remain inactive when an object essential to the public welfare can be attained only by corporate action.

2d. Whenever an object can be attained as well by private enterprise, leave it to private enterprise.

3d. The State must not attempt to displace private industry in order to become itself a trader.

4th. Since the State must enforce contracts, it must beware of lending its sanction to fraudulent or iniquitous contracts.

5th. Never frame a new law without being certain that it is a notable improvement on previous legislation.

6th. Never put a new restriction on the liberty of the citizen, unless order and peace require this limitation *imperatively.*

7th. The State must protect children as well as other defenceless persons; but it would commit a breach of natural law were it to substitute its authority for that of the parents.

8th. No plurality of suffrage can justify the invasion of the rights of the minority by the majority, however large the majority may be. The majority may be overwhelming, it may be able to crush the minority, but *Might is not Right.* The former is a material, the latter a moral power.

EIGHTH LECTURE.

PROPERTY.

SEC. I. WHAT IS PROPERTY?

1. What is the Right of Property? It may be limited in its exercise.

PROPERTY, according to Webster, *is the exclusive right of possessing, enjoying, and disposing of a thing.* This is equivalent to the definition of the Roman jurists: "The right of fully disposing of a material object, when not forbidden by law." The last clause is inserted to convey the idea that, however perfect ownership may be, it must not be considered as absolute or unlimited; no human right can be, if we except that of growing in moral perfection. Every other right may be limited and regulated in its exercise, both by natural and by positive law. A right is limited by natural law when it happens, in a particular case, to conflict with another natural right. Thus the extreme necessity of a man who is on the point of perishing of hunger is a stronger claim than private ownership, however lawfully the possession may have been acquired, and the owner of a loaf of bread cannot prevent a starving man from consuming the loaf or so much of it as is necessary to save the indigent from death—unless, however, the owner of the bread be himself reduced to the same extremity, in which case the owner has a twofold claim, necessity and possession combined. The right of property is limited by positive law, when the legislative power enacts rules to prevent conflicts, or to secure the recognition of the right of property; but in order to do so effectually, imposes conditions which restrict the exercise of the right. For, as it is the province of the civil government to maintain the rights of its subjects, it is necessary either to prevent conflicts by the exercise of the legislative power, or to decide judicially, when conflicts have arisen, which right must prevail. But the power of the State cannot go beyond the limits which are marked out by the end or purpose for which this power is given.

To remove all obscurities and equivocations, we shall expand a little the Roman concise formula and define property: "The right, not limited in duration, fully and exclusively to dispose of a material object, within the limits assigned by natural law, or by civil law, when the latter does but interpret and apply the former."

2. Explanation of the definition. We say a *right,* i.e., a moral power that other men are bound to respect; **to** *dispose* of, i.e., to use, to modify, to consume, if the thing be perishable; also to transfer or to sell; we say, *an exclusive power,* for if other men could take the object from the possessor or use it against his will, the possessor could not be said to *own* the object; we add, *not limited in duration,* for otherwise the object would be loaned to the possessor, but not *owned* by him; we say, *a material object,* for we speak of things which can be held visibly by men, and in whose possession the owners may be maintained by law. Lastly, we say that the control of the owner is limited by natural law itself, for in using your right you are bound to respect the rights of others, and to yield to other men, if they urge a claim superior to your own. With regard to civil law, it cannot abrogate a right which comes from God more directly than human positive laws, but as long as the State uses its power to prevent the clashing of rights, or to apply the principles of natural law, it is entitled to the obedience of the subjects. Thus the elements of the definition consist in the following concepts: *Right, Permanency, Disposal, full and exclusive, regulated by Law.* To give an accurate idea of the nature of ownership we had to bring into the definition all these various elements, but for practical purposes we may define property with Webster: "The exclusive right of possessing, enjoying, and disposing of a thing." To own the thing itself is to be the *proprietor;* a right to the use, but not to the full and exclusive disposal of the thing itself, is called *usufruct.* A man who is proprietor, but cannot make use of his property as he pleases, because the right of using or the use-value has been transferred to another, and the man who enjoys only the use-value without being the owner of the object itself, have, both, an *imperfect* dominion. Neither enjoys property in its full sense. Some modern writers, leaning toward socialism or communism, have held that man could never have the full property of anything, but only the usufruct; or, to use the less bar-

barous Latin expression, the useful domain, *dominium utile*.* The reverse is the case. Man may very well own the thing itself, say a house, or a field which produces a certain amount of food supplies, and yet be bound in certain cases to let others have some share in the benefit which is derived from these possessions. It is only a duty of charity to help the needy when their wants are only pressing, but it becomes a duty of strict justice when those wants are extreme. Man does not live for himself alone, but also for his brother-men.

3. All Human Rights beget Duties. All the rights bring duties in their train, and ownership is no exception to the rule. Those duties vary with the nature of the objects which are possessed by man. The owner of a tenement house is bound to see that the building is properly ventilated, that hygienic precautions are taken, that everything is substantial, so that there be no reason to fear that the whole fabric may tumble about the ears of the inmates. The owner of a ship is bound to assure himself of the fact that the ship is seaworthy, he must take care that the vessel be free from infectious diseases, properly equipped and supplied, manned by a reliable crew, and commanded by competent officers. The owner of a factory must take care of the security, health, and general well-being of the workmen; he must pay them fair wages at the proper time, and avoid everything like the sweating system, or undue pressure to compel them to do

---
* See the definition of *Usufruct* in Bouvier's Dictionary, Vol. II., p. 617.

more than is expressed or implied in the contract, etc., etc. It is enough to say that every kind of wealth has its obligations, which cling to it and cannot be disregarded without crime. The wealthy man is a responsible man: he is responsible both to God and to the law of the land. Such is the right of property which is sanctioned by the law of God and by the law of man. Ownership without responsibility is opposed to both of these laws.

SEC. II. SOURCE OF THE RIGHT OF PROPERTY.

4. Socialists and Communists. The Right of Property is founded on Natural Law. Two classes of political dreamers attack the right of property, and seek in its restriction or complete suppression a remedy to all the ills of human society.

Socialists would take from their owners both land and capital, which, united with labor, constitute wealth-producing agencies. They would leave to the workman his wages and to the rich man his gold; but as soon as wealth becomes productive, in other words, as soon as it is turned into capital, they would put it in the hands of the Government.

Communists are more radical: they would abolish private property altogether. Everything in the State would belong to everybody; and out of the common fund the State would dole out the daily pittance necessary to each one.

These two great social heresies have not yet made much progress in this country, yet we do not know what may come to pass before this mighty republic has reached the end of another century. Let us remember eternal vigilance is the price of liberty, and let us beware of playing with dangerous weapons, such as the doctrine that private property is a creation of the State, and has no better warrant than positive law. Were it so, then it could be abolished to-morrow, if a majority judged fit to pass a law to that effect. Now, socialists and communists, that is, those of a mild type, do not ask for anything else. They insist that they do not contemplate violence, but they will work incessantly for the repeal of the property laws which now govern the land. This repeal they hope to secure by keeping up a legal agitation until they succeed in securing the desired majority.

Nothing of the kind could be apprehended in the days of Blackstone; hence we need not be astonished to find in his Commentaries, Book II., Chap. I., the following statement:

" There is indeed some difference among the writers on natural law, concerning the reason why occupancy should convey this right (the original right to the permanent property in the substance of the earth itself), and invest one with absolute property: Grotius and Puffendorf insisting that this right of occupancy is founded on a tacit and implied assent of all mankind, that the occupant should become the owner; and Barbeyrac, Titius, Mr. Locke and others, holding that there is no such implied assent, neither is it necessary that there should be; for that the very act of occupancy alone, being a degree of bodily labor, is from a principle of natural justice, without any consent or compact, sufficient of itself to gain a title. A dispute that savors too much of nice and scholastic refinement."

Whereupon the commentators observe:

"But it is of great importance that moral obligations and the rudiment of laws should be referred to true and intelligible principles."

Chancellor Kent had a stronger hold on the truth, and without hesitation he traced the right of property back to natural law: "The sense of property," says the illustrious American jurist, "is inherent in the human breast, and the general enlargement and cultivation of that sense, from its feeble force in the savage state to its full vigor and maturity among polished nations, forms a very instructive portion of the history of civil society. Man was fitted and intended by the Author of his being for society and government, and for the acquisition and enjoyment of property. It is, to speak correctly, the law of his nature; and by obedience to this law, he brings all his faculties into exercise, and is enabled to display the various and exalted powers of the human mind." *

Truly said and nobly. In proving the right of individual property, I shall do almost nothing more than develop the doctrine contained in this passage. And in proving that the great Chancellor is right, I shall defend the American Constitution, which places the right of property among those inalienable rights which come from the Au-

---

* Lecture XXXIV., Part V., a little before n. 319.

thor of nature, and which human governments have no power to abolish.*

"The absolute right of individuals," says Kent, "may be resolved into the right of personal security, the right of personal liberty, and the right to acquire and enjoy property. These rights have been justly considered, and frequently declared by the people of this country to be natural, inherent, and inalienable." †

We shall now proceed directly to demonstrate the right of property, basing our demonstration on acknowledged principles of natural law.

SEC. III. DEMONSTRATION OF THE RIGHT OF PROPERTY.

5. Man is a reasonable Being, compelled to supply his daily wants, and bound to provide for the future.

We shall not discuss the right of using or consuming material objects (*dominium transiens*), for nobody in his senses ever questioned it. We have to deal only with permanent dominion (*dominium stabile.*)

1st. Man has the duty, and, therefore, the right to accomplish those acts which are necessary to attain the end of his being, and work out his destiny; but in order to do so, man is bound to appropriate many exterior objects; hence the right of appropriating such objects unquestionably

---

* It is one thing to originate or create a right; another to regulate its exercise. Hobbes seems to have been unable to understand this distinction. [R. I. II.

† Lecture XXIV.

springs from an essential duty. This appropriation must be permanent; for man cannot incessantly continue the struggle for existence; he has other duties to perform which prevent him from being constantly engaged in the work of appropriation. Should the effect of appropriation be transient, these duties would become impracticable. Besides, nature has compelled him to cease his labor at times. Now, if during those intervals the effect of appropriation should cease, he might lose the means of renewing his labors, and this would defeat the purpose of appropriation.

2d. Nature directs man to give his faculties the fullest development that is practically attainable; but without permanent dominion, this development would be unattainable. For, should a man devote his attention to the cultivation of science, he would have either to starve or to rely on the charity of other people. The former is evidently against his duty to himself; the latter would compel him to rely on the kindness of others, and the supply would be both insecure and enslaving. Besides, the contributor must have hoarded up something over and above his actual wants, for the use either of himself or of his friends. Over that something he must have a perfect ownership, since he can give it away. But this very hypothesis proves permanency, for those savings have remained his, even after he has ceased to need them; it proves *exclusiveness,* because he could not hoard up first, and give up afterward, what any one might have appropriated while the holder of the property did not actually use it. We have then the three characteristics of ownership, permanency, exclusiveness, free disposal.

3d. Nature constantly teaches man the necessity of providing for the future. Man is subject to sickness, and must reach old age, unless overtaken by death; when old or sick, he cannot procure what is necessary to satisfy his wants. He must therefore lay by enough for a rainy day. Nature teaches the lesson most strikingly in the little ant and bee, which, in obedience to instinct, amass and lay by their tiny stores against the oncoming winter.

6. Man must provide for others, and support the State.
4th. Man, in the sententious phrase of Aristotle, is *animal domesticum*, or destined to live in domestic society; to raise children who shall owe him their existence and in whom he will perpetuate himself. The permanency and progress of the species depend on his faithful discharge of those duties. But in order to fulfil them, he must have permanent domain, for otherwise he might die, leaving his children unprovided for. If parents left nothing to their offspring, then every generation would have to begin the work over again, and each man would be a Danaid, forever pouring water into a bottomless barrel.

5th. Although man is *animal domesticum magis quam politicum,* that is to say, more of a domestic than of a political being, yet he is by his very nature destined to national life. Now, in a nation or political society, men must have various functions; they must be able to exchange and barter, to give, to produce and to consume. This needs no proof. Now, the performance of all these functions supposes the free disposal of the things appropriated; this free disposal itself implies exclusiveness, and exclusiveness, in turn, supposes permanency; and so we come back to the three characteristics of ownership—disposal, exclusiveness, permanency.

7. Joint ownership presupposes Individual rights. A disciple of Cabet would say: "We grant you that each man is in duty bound to provide for himself and family, and that in order to do so he must own something permanently, but could he not fulfil his duty just as well if he held that property jointly with others?" Not as well, if we take warning from the fate of the phalansterians, yet, under exceptional circumstances, it might be tried. But suppose the experiment successful, what would have been accomplished? Each one would have shifted a part of his burden on others, and taken a part of their burden in exchange. The duties and rights of the community would be the aggregate duties and rights of the members. Let us make this plainer by a simple illustration:

Let us suppose that two pioneers have settled side by side in a new country. After some time each one finds that his neighbor has some implement without which his own labor remains almost unprofitable. Their respective wants prompt them to resort to joint ownership. They put up a house on the very line which before divided the two estates, establish their families in that house, and make all their goods and chattels the common property of both households. On both settlers now devolves the duty of supporting the two families; to both jointly belong the rights without which their joint duties could not be performed. From what source spring the duties and consequently the rights of the association? From the duties and rights of both partners. Take away that foundation, and nothing can remain standing. Thus the rights of a community presuppose the rights of its members. Whether our friends have acted wisely, is quite another question. Often do we find a house which is too large for one family; seldom do we find one large enough for two.

8. Why Collective ownership cannot replace Private ownership. Modern dreamers believe that collective ownership is the great nostrum which will cure all social distempers. Repeated failures do not dispel their illusions, but merely excite their wonder. St. Thomas gives three very good reasons why collective ownership should fail, and experience has made good his assertions.

"With regard to exterior objects, man has two powers —to acquire and dispose" (i.e., according to the dictates of reason). "With regard to both acquisition and dispensation, the holding of property is not only lawful, but also necessary for human life; and this for three reasons: First, because man displays more thrift in acquiring that which must remain his own than that which is destined to many or to all; for (as it happens where servants are in considerable number) each one, shirking toil, leaves to his neighbor the care of supplying the wants of the community. Secondly, because human interest will be better promoted if each man has the care of supplying a particular kind of commodity; should every one busy himself about everything a great confusion would be the result. Thirdly, because by this division the peace of society is better secured, because each one must be content with his own portion." *

With regard to the division of property, Puffendorf very justly observes, that the distinction of *meum* and *tuum* has been doubtless the occasion of many quarrels and many wars, but that, if we wipe it out, we come at once to the condition imagined by Hobbes, the war of all against all—in fact, a general grabbing match in which every one tries to hustle every one else out of the way.

" But," says Mr. George, " every one is not selfish." Happily not, but there are and there will ever be a great many selfish men. Human nature left to itself is essentially selfish, and it is only supernatural virtue which raises men, habitually, at least, above self-interest; or, as Puffendorf says: " It is easy to imagine men as they might be, but impossible to find them in actual life such as they are in our fancy."

9. Communistic societies. Dreamers may object that some societies, based on collective ownership, have existed—nay, that some are yet in existence. We reply that *political* societies of this kind either have never existed, or have been invariably swept away by the advances of civilization. The nearest approach to a common wealth of the kind was made by the reductions of Paraguay; but unfortunately the greed of merchants and the

* Summa Theol. 1ª, 2ᵃᵉ, 9-66, A. 2º.

anti-religious frenzy of such men as Carvalho put an end to the experiment before it was completed. Should some friend of the human race desire to make another attempt, we wish him Godspeed; but let him make the experiment where it will not interfere with vested rights and existing social institutions. We object to have things pulled down while we hold nothing but a mortgage on Dreamland or Utopia.

With regard to small communities which have not the political character, such experiments are indeed possible, but they require exceptional conditions which cannot prevail in a sovereign State. We quote on this subject a few words of R. J. Wright, which appear to us to sum up the whole question: " Communism is not merely, nor chiefly, a tenure of property, but rather a form of government for a corporation or even a precinct, in which the highest attainable perfection of human nature is supposed to be the chief object of the individual, and is established as the chief object of the society. . . . It must be a highly obeyed system of government, both in one's individual soul and in the association. . . . The successful communities in every age of the world have included nearly all the following principles: (1) that community life is to be sought as a means of perfection; (2) that the government of them is to be in the hands of good men; (3) that the governors are supposed to be *saints,* or to be leading lives of some sort of inspiration or peculiar consecration." *

---

* R. J. Wright, Principia of Social Science, p. 463.

10. Mr. Thiers' argument, drawn from personality. We have proved the right of appropriation from the end and duties of man; let us derive another proof from his personality and from the nature and range of his faculties. We shall give it in the words of Thiers, who was President of the French Republic.

"There is a kind of ownership which will not be called usurpation, the ownership of my own person first, and of my mental and physical powers next. My feet, my hands, my eyes, my brain; in one word, my soul and my body.

"Here is a first property which cannot be questioned or divided; with regard to it no agrarian law has ever been devised; it has never been a ground of complaint against me, against society, or against social legislation."*

"I sum up: man has a first ownership in his self and his inborn powers; a second less closely united with his very being, but no less inviolable, in the product of those powers. This product includes all that is called earthly possessions, which society is bound to warrant to him. For without that warranted deed, there is no labor; without labor, no civilization, not even the necessaries of life, nothing but wretchedness, high-handed robbery, and barbarism." . . . †

"Those accumulations of wealth, which so readily catch the popular eye, are neither as numerous nor as vast as fancy pictures them. Should men get it into their heads to divide them, but a trifling amount could be allotted to each of the sharers. We would have taken away the incentive which conjures up labor, and the means of paying

---

* Le droit de propriété, Chap. IV., p. 37.
† Ibid., Chap. V., p. 47.

for the noblest efforts of skill. In a word, the plan of God would have been marred, and nobody would have grown wealthier." *

They have objected against this argument that man with all his powers does not belong to himself, but to his Maker. This objection is not serious. God gave all these things to man when He made him a person, a responsible being, standing in his own rights, and accountable for his acts. The right of man is derived from that of God, and it is this origin that makes this right inviolable.

11. Blind impulses and instincts show that the Law is universal. We have applied the deductive or *a priori* process to the doctrine of individual ownership; let us now try induction. If the right of acquiring and holding property is based on nature itself, then, according to the Roman jurisconsults, we shall find some traces of it in the instinct of lower animals. This index is not wanting, if we believe Taparelli, and our own daily observations.

" The rational proof which we have adduced to show that nature has established the right of property, is confirmed by a *fact* of instinct, which is observable in man and even in the brute; thus, in both, a feeling of natural indignation springs up when one attempts to snatch from the owner what he holds in possession. Take two little children who run a race for an apple. The winner of the race could well have borne the loss of the apple had he been beaten in speed by his rival; but with what indignation is he not carried away, if the latter, availing himself of

---

* Ibid., p. 33.

superior strength, strives to wrest the prize from his hands. And how will not the mastiff growl, if one dare deprive him of his favorite bone. Far be it from me to attribute to a dog the *idea of right;* the animal moves itself, or rather is moved by natural instinct. But this instinct shows us that creative Providence saw that peaceful possession of the good occupied was necessary for the wellbeing of the animal, and hence it impressed upon the very brute a certain natural respect, which not unfrequently restrains the strongest in presence of the weakest." *

12. Evolution of the Right of Property. We may add that the ant will fight for its hill, the bee for its hive, the bird for its nest, the dog for its kennel; to every animal its chosen abode is a castle which stronger animals will fear to invade. In man this instinctive clinging to ownership becomes an inclination, sanctioned by reason, and growing with human personality.

" Man, thriftless at first, cares but little for the ground which yields nothing but wild berries. . . . But he soon divides land, improves it, and strongly clings to his share. When people gather their strength to wrest it from him, he blends his energy with the corporate strength of his nation. If the onslaught is committed within the city, he appeals to a judge for redress. Thus, as he develops himself, he grows fonder and fonder of his own estate; in a word, he becomes more and more a proprietor." †

In scanning nature, we have not only struck a group of phenomena, we have met a general law. But is that law

---

* Taparelli d'Azeglio, Natural Right, Book II., Chap. IV., n. 403.
† A. Thiers, De la Propriete, Vol. I., p. 27.

a social as well as an individual one? Let us propose the question to a standard authority, Mr. Cliffe Leslie:

"The term *Natural* has been indeed a source of so much confusion and error in both the philosophy of Law and Political Economy that it might be well to expel it altogether from the terminology of both (we have cleared away the confusion, with the help of Emperor Justinian); but it could not be more legitimately applied than in the proposition that there is a natural movement, as society advances, from common to separate property in lands and chattels. This movement is perceptible even among the Slav nations themselves, and is closely connected with the movement from the *status* to *contract,* which Sir H. Maine has shown to be one of the principal phases of civilization." *

Let us hear W. Roscher, the founder of the historical school of political economy:

"The progress of civilization demands an ever increasing fixity, and a more pronounced shaping of landed property, in the interest of all who share in this progress, and even of those who own no landed property. Were there no property in land, every one would find it more difficult and laborious to gratify his want of agricultural products, and the products themselves would be of an inferior kind." †

We turn to Mr. de Laveleye, who had decidedly socialist tendencies, and lo, he tells us the same tale:

---

* Introduction to Laveleye, p. 13.
† Political Economy, Book I., § 87. Translated by J. Lalor, Henry Holt & Co., N. Y.

"The flourishing appearance of Bulgaria shows decisively that the system (patriarchial ownership) is not antagonistic to good cultivation. And yet this organization, in spite of many advantages, is falling to ruin, and disappearing wherever it comes into contact with modern ideas. The reason is that these institutions are suited to the stationary condition of a primitive age, but cannot easily withstand the condition of a state of society in which men are striving to improve their own lot as well as the political and social organization under which they live."

To the end of time, men will try to improve their own lot as well as the political organization under which they live; to the end of time, the laws which govern the advance of civilization will remain substantially the same; therefore the attempt to substitute collectivism for private property will prove abortive, if not mischievous.

SEC. IV. WHAT CAN WE OWN, AND HOW CAN WE BECOME OWNERS?

13. How an abstract right becomes a concrete right. So far we have proved that the right of acquiring and holding property comes from nature, but two questions remain to be answered: what can we own? and in what manner does the mere abstract right of acquiring property become the concrete right of holding property; in other words, how is it exercised, how does it pass from speculation into practice? We know that an abstract right becomes concrete when the subject-matter to which it is applied is clearly defined, and when the conditions under which the right may be exercised are determined. This determination always involves a certain expenditure of human activity. A little later we shall prove that occupancy is the first fact which transforms the right of acquiring property into the right of holding property; but we must show first what material objects may be appropriated. In this connection, we need not mention the good which must perish in order to be useful—the difficulty does not lie there—but we must consider objects which are not consumed at once, but remain the subject-matter of proprietary rights—that is, which are permanently valuable, or which bear fruit for their owners. To be appropriated, objects must be useful or at least agreeable, for otherwise they could not serve man's purpose, or be the means to attain his end. They must not be unlimited, for, if they were unlimited, every one could help himself without diminishing the owner's wealth. They must be in some way confined or capable of being confined, for otherwise no man could impress on them the stamp of his ownership and personality. Hence, the air of the atmosphere; the water, when unconfined, when not brought artificially to a place nor obtained by the skill of the chemist; the light of the sun; the depth of the sea, and its broad expanse; the stars in the heavens; heat when not artificially produced; all the forces of nature, so long as they have not been brought under human control; the wild beasts, so long as they roam in the wilderness; all these things are common property; none can be claimed exclusively by any man.

14. Property in land. But what about land? Mr. H. George tells us that "in every essential, land differs from those things which, being the product of human labor, are rightfully property. It is the creation of God: they are produced by man. It is fixed in quantity: they may be increased illimitably."

Let us examine the logical value of these antitheses. Land is the creation of God certainly, and so is everything else. Man creates absolutely nothing. He modifies with his labor what God has created; he sets free forces which before were held in equilibrium; he causes to spring into existence new forms, which matter had not yet evolved; but the power to evolve them lay dormant in nature. To awaken that power and start it into full activity is indeed a noble achievement, but it is not creation. What Mr. Henry George means is that the share of labor is greater in industrial products than in the raising and reaping of harvests. Suppose that it were so, we would have a difference in degree, not in kind. In both cases matter and force are supplied by our great Maker, and labor avails itself of both.

"Earth is fixed in quantity and the products of labor are illimited." They are limited by the material, which cannot be greater than the earth from which it is drawn, unless we suppose that the contents can be greater than the container. They are limited by human energy, which is not infinite. By *fixed in quantity* we must understand actually measured or measurable. In this sense, only, is it true that the earth itself is a fixed quantity; for if to the energies which it holds in its bosom we add human labor, the product defies human calculation. In other words, the bulk of the earth is a fixed quantity, but the productiveness of the earth is a variable one. It may be that it is easier to approximate the probable yield of the earth than the output of the industrial production; but here again we meet a difference in *degree,* not in *kind.*

"Earth exists though generations come and go." Yes, but gold and diamonds also are more lasting than man, and yet Mr. George does not oppose ownership either in diamonds or in gold. In fact, most of our earthly possessions can outlast us. Nothing sublunary will last forever. The differences mentioned by Mr. George are real, but not specific. Everything which may be owned by man differs from other things equally destined to his use; and from those differences spring various duties. The owner of a ship, or of a tenement house, has duties which are not common to the ironmaster or the cotton-grower, and conversely; yet all those have a perfect right to their property, even according to Mr. George.

When we wish to find out whether a particular object may be held as property, we must examine whether it has the test qualifications recognized by moralists; whether it is useful or at least agreeable, capable of receiving the impress of man, or at least of being confined by its owner; whether it is limited, so that the use made of it by another man would abridge the owner's right.

Now, land possesses these characteristics in an eminent degree. It is not only useful, but indispensable, it can receive the impress of man so as to acquire, and permanently retain, a utility and value which it may take a long time and much labor to impart to it. In point of fact, land, as brute material, has ceased to exist in civilized countries, and the soil has acquired an economic value, like any other bounty of nature that man has appropriated.

Logically, denial of land ownership leads to a denial of ownership in capital. This, in turn, leads inevitably to communism. It is the special and eminent qualifications of land to be appropriated, which explains why authors who set about treating of property in general so often refer to land property as an illustration.

15. First title, occupancy. But if land can be appropriated, by what process can the appropriation be made? By labor or by occupancy? We answer that every kind of occupancy involves a certain amount of labor, but that the labor involved in mere legal occupancy need not be considerable; while labor which gives it a new value, or what they call *effective occupancy*, supposes a considerable expense of human energy. The former gives a *prima facie* title, it is indispensable in order that labor and capital be invested in land; but the title is perfected by the labor which gives land its economic value.

"Occupancy," says Chancellor Kent, "doubtless gave the first title to property in lands and movables. It is the natural and original method of acquiring it; and upon the principle of universal law, that title continues so long as occupancy continues. There is no person even in his rudest state who does not feel and acknowledge, in a greater or less degree, the justice of this title. The right of property, founded on occupancy, is suggested to the human mind by feeling and reason prior to the influence of positive institutions. There have been modern theorists who have considered separate and exclusive property and inequalities of property as the cause of injustice, and the unhappy result of government and artificial institutions. But human society would be in a most unnatural and miserable condition if-it were possible to be instituted or reorganized upon the basis of such speculations. The sense of property is graciously bestowed on mankind for the purpose of rousing them from sloth, and stimulating them to action; and so long as the right of acquisition is exercised in conformity to the social relations, and the moral obligations which spring from them, it ought to be sacredly protected," etc.*

16. Accession or increment. Accession is the second of the titles which legists have called primary. It may be natural, artificial, or mixed. I need not dwell on this subject, for it is carefully treated in other branches of jurisprudence. But is the increase of value which is due to the concourse of population, and which J. S. Mill called the unearned increment, a legitimate accession to the owner's property? Everybody thought so until John Stuart Mill told us that mankind was all wrong. Let us see whether society is right. 1st. It is an admitted axiom that the accident follows the substance; but the so-called unearned increment is an accident of property; therefore

* Lecture XXIV., p. 1.

it ought to follow property. 2d. That increment is rarely accruing to the property, without some exercise of the owner's foresight and penetration; often it is brought about by exerting considerable ingenuity. It is not altogether unearned; it would be extremely unwise for any society to snatch the prize of those human qualities which have so much influence on social progress, even though in some cases the improvement in fortune should not be altogether deserved.

3d. Who could claim a better title than the owner? Not those who have raised the value of the property by repairing to that place; for they did it, not to benefit the owner or the public, but to improve their own condition by selecting a more favorable place for their own comfort or for the benefit of their trade. Not the rest of the population, for they have done nothing at all toward improving the rent. Not the State, for the State did not cause the rise by any governmental activity. It remains, therefore, to say that the owner has the best title.

4th. Should the State confiscate the increment, it should make good the losses. The State has no intention whatever to make good the losses, therefore it should leave the increment to him who has risked his capital in the venture.

5th. As the value of land increases, the value of everything which is upon it increases. Must, then, the State confiscate all that surplus value? It would be a deathblow to industry and the ruin of real estate.

Therefore, the so-called unearned increment must, according to justice, revert to the owner of the property.

SEC. V. OBJECTIONS.

17. Appropriations of the whole world. While proving the existence of the right of property, we have already met several objections; others need not delay us much, for they are not to the point. Such is the following: If some portions of the earth are appropriated, others may be, and so the whole world may become the exclusive property of a certain number; whither will the rest of mankind betake themselves? We answer, whether the land is occupied or rented, the problem is just the same. Those who occupy the land need the labor of the others, and are compelled by self-interest to give up in their favor a part of the produce. But should they be foolish enough to let the produce perish rather than share it with others, or leave the land uncultivated, or exclude other men from so much of it as is necessary to carry on trades and the business of life, then the right of eminent domain would come into play and recall them to the observance of their duties as landowners and citizens. If the objector insist and say that, after all, the land might become insufficient for the wants of mankind, I answer that this calamity is very far off. If anything could bring it nearer our times, it would be the folly of confiscating the rent, for by discouraging permanent improvements, and the investing of capital in land property, it would soon diminish and eventually stop production. Universal starvation would be the consequence.

18. Mr. Herbert Spencer's Cosmopolite. But there is a more serious objection: everybody has the right to the land; but the man who appropriates deprives other men from this common right; hence the landowner is a thief. Mr. Spencer puts this objection on the lips of a *cosmopolite;* we call these people *tramps* in this country.

"Hallo, you sir," cries the cosmopolite to some backwoodsman, smoking at the door of his shanty, "by what authority do you take possession of these acres that you have cleared?" (Reluctantly we must shorten the dialogue.)

Settler—"I squatted there. I have cut down the wood and ploughed and cropped the ground."

Cos.—"Ay, so you all say." (Tramps could not say that much.) "Now I want to understand how, by exterminating one set of plants, and making the soil bear another in their place, you have constituted yourself lord of the soil for all succeeding time."

Settler—"I have caused the earth to bring forth things good for food—things that help to give life and happiness."

Cosmopolites do not acknowledge a right founded either on labor or on a new utility or value imparted by labor. They object to labor in any form.

Cos.—"Still you have not shown why such a process makes the portion of the earth you have so modified yours. By what magic have these acts made you sole owner of that vast mass of matter, having for its base the surface of your estate, and for its apex the centre of the globe?"

No landowner claims a spheroidal sector: common-sense people claim only as much of that mass of matter as they need for cultivation. As men in quest of minerals might undermine the field which is already appropriated, in many countries positive law gives to the first settler the first claim to the ore under his field, or obliges those who wish to dig it out to obtain his consent; but neither the squatter nor the miner has the slightest inclination to claim the point at the centre of the earth.

Settler—"If it isn't mine, whose is it? I have dispossessed nobody. When I crossed the Mississippi yonder, I found nothing but the silent woods. If some one else had settled here, and made this clearing, he would have had as good a right to the location as I have."

Had our squatter studied Kant, he could have answered that he had projected his own individuality on that field, and that he fell back on the postulatum, that a law by which "a thing subject to his free action should be made *res nullius*" would be a very unjust law. But our friend has not read Kant: he goes on boldly, and says rashly: "While they were unreclaimed, these lands belonged to all men." Our friend might have avoided this slip by committing to memory the following words of Prof. Woolsey: "If the world was common, it was in the sense of being unappropriated, and not in the sense of being held in joint property." *

The cosmopolitan is not the man to let the slip pass unnoticed. "You say truly when you say that ' while they were unreclaimed these lands belonged to all men.' And it is my duty to tell you that your improvements cannot

---

* Woolsey, Social Science, p. 49.

vitiate the claim of all men" (tramps included). "Let me put you a case. . . . Suppose now that in the course of your wanderings, you come upon an empty house. You paint and paper and whitewash. On some fatal day a stranger is announced who turns out to be the heir to whom this house has been bequeathed. Do they (your improvements) quash the title of the original claimant?"

Settler—"No."

In the case of untilled lands the first settler is the first claimant, hence the argument of the cosmopolitan is fatal to his contention. But Mr. Spencer makes the settler remain so confused that he is glad to accept a promise that the improvements should be paid for, and to surrender his claim to the land. Our settler might have said that the whole human kind being the owner, the settler could keep his property until the whole human kind showed cause why it should dispossess an honest man and deprive him of the fruits of his labor. He might have denied point-blank that the earth was the joint property of all men. He would have been supported by the consent, morally unanimous, of philosophers, in averring that the community of ownership, which had been assumed as the primitive condition of mankind, was negative, not *positive;* that is to say, that land was common to all in so far as it belonged to nobody in particular. Or more simply he might have said that what belongs to everybody belongs to nobody.

All these answers would have been valid, but Mr. Spencer makes the honest pioneer speechless. Even worse, he advises the State to compound a felony. For, according to him, the State should take the rent, but warrant the ownership to the holders of the land. Practically, the State would tell the landowners: "You are a pack of thieves; but just pay the rent to me, and I will connive at your unlawful proceedings."

Let us add that Mr. Spencer has reconsidered the problem, and admitted with commendable literary candor, in his book on justice, and elsewhere, that, after all, the present system of ownership is more than any other in accordance with natural equity. It is, therefore, our duty to defend it against all the sophists, and all the inventors of political nostrums.

NINTH LECTURE.

ON TAXATION.

SEC. I. RIGHT OF TAXATION.

1. Nature and necessity of the taxing Power. "The taxing power is an incident of sovereignty, and is possessed by the Government without being *expressly* conferred by the people. . . . It is a *legislative* power, . . . it is not arbitrary, but rests on fixed principles of justice. . . . Taxes are the enforced proportional contributions from persons and property, levied by the State by virtue of its sovereignty, for the support of Government, and for all public needs. . . . Tax legislation means the making of laws that are to furnish the measure of each man's duty in support of public burdens, and the means of enforcing it."

These words which we have borrowed from the opening chapter of the *Law of Taxation*, by Judge Thos. M. Cooley, contain a sufficiently accurate description of the important State function which is the subject of this lecture; but some of the statements being severed from the context require a short explanation.

The learned judge states that the taxing power need not

be *expressly* conferred by the people. This does not mean that it does not come from the people, but that the conferring of this power follows, as a necessary consequence, the framing of a constitution and the establishment of a supreme civil authority. It is conferred by the very fact that a supreme power is lawfully constituted. The people may divide this power, determine who shall wield it, and in what manner it shall be exercised by those to whom it may be intrusted; but it is essential to sovereignty, and is substantially the same in every State which possesses the plenitude of the sovereign power—without it no perfect civil society is possible. The proof of this position is evident. Whenever a physical or moral person is intrusted with a duty strictly binding, this moral or physical person receives explicitly or implicitly the rights which are necessary for the performance of that duty; but it is indispensable for the performance of State duties that the supreme power should apportion the burdens of the Government among those who live under its protection; in other words, that it should tax its subjects, therefore every supreme power has the right to tax its subjects; that is to say, the taxing power is an incident of sovereignty.

2. It is neither an Evil, nor the result of a Contract or of a Partnership. Some writers have considered taxation in the light of a *necessary* evil. It is no more an evil than the expenditure of energy which is essential to the material life of man. Let us not call the paying of taxes a *necessary evil*, but a bounden duty. Some have wished to derive this duty from an implied contract; the

State would say *implicitly:* "I will protect you and you shall support me." As a rule, a compact of this kind has no historical foundation, but the binding force which is attributed to it is the result of the relations existing between the citizens and the social power. These relations do not originate in oral or written compacts, but in the nature of things. It has also been said that the obligation to pay taxes is the outcome of a *partnership* between the Government and the subject. The State would say equivalently: "Take me as a joint owner, and I will guarantee our joint estate."

This is another figure of speech which must not be taken literally; this sort of warrant would resemble too much the sort of insurance granted by a captain of a banditti to the peasants who pay him a tribute. Let us not deal too much in metaphors, they are often misleading; the plain truth is that the assessment and enforcement of taxes is a governmental duty, that the paying of taxes is a duty of the citizen, and that both arise from the obligation of promoting the end of civil society, which is binding both on the rulers and on the people. And yet these metaphors, although not to be construed in a literal sense, may serve to illustrate two principles, which legislators must always bear in mind when they impose a taxation on the people.

3. Taxation and Protection. Taxation and Representation. 1st. Protection and taxation are correlative terms; that is to say, a government *de jure,* when unwilling or powerless to *protect,* has no right to *tax;* and conversely, even an illegal or unconstitutional government, provided it exists *de facto,* and affords adequate protection to its subjects, may impose taxes for national ends; but the obligation to pay the taxes does not in the two cases rest exactly on the same ethical foundation. When the Government is *de jure* as well *de facto,* the duty of obedience to the lawfully established authority is the first principle from which the obligation of the citizen is derived; the duty of making a return for the benefits conferred by the State comes next in order. Both duties are deduced from the relations existing between the citizen and the State. When the Government exists only *de facto,* no *direct allegiance* is due to it, but compliance to its decrees is made obligatory solely by the necessity of preserving social order and national unity. A government *de facto* is better than no government at all; and so long as no government *de jure* is attainable, it remains incumbent on the citizens to make use of the only means at their disposal to preserve the existence of society. The second principle which the contractual hypothesis may serve to illustrate is the interdependence of taxation and representation. We have seen that taxation and protection are correlative; can the same thing be said of taxation and representation? From the standpoint of the English and American constitutional legislation, the answer must be distinctly affirmative; but it cannot at once be applied to all nations and all states of society. *Natural Law* itself makes *Taxation* and *Protection* correlative; Constitutional Law, in accordance with natural equity, and breathing its spirit, binds together *the power of taxing,* which exists in the

State, with the right of being represented in the councils of the nation, which abides in the subject. A society which would sever these two rights would, under ordinary circumstances, act unwisely, yet it could not be said in all cases that an inalienable right has been violated. The right to be represented *directly,* viz., by men of our own choice, cannot be grounded on natural law alone; but the right to be represented, at least indirectly, that is to say, by some one whose duty it is to protect our interests, this right of indirect representation is essential to every member of any civil society, whatever the constitution of that society may be.

SEC. II. EXTENT OF THE RIGHT OF TAXATION.

4. The Right of Taxation extends to all subjects and all kinds of property. Since the power of taxing is an incident of sovereignty, it is evident that it extends to all the subjects and all kinds of property within the limits of its jurisdiction.

Judge Marshall says:* "All subjects over which the sovereign power of the State extends are objects of taxation, but those over which it does not extend are on the soundest principles exempt from taxation. The sovereign power of the State extends to everything which exists by its own authority or is introduced by its permission."

We will add that natural equity demands that all the citizens should be made to bear equally the burdens of the

---

* 4th Wheaton, 431.

State as far as an equal distribution of public burdens is possible. This does not mean that the State cannot exempt *any one,* but that, if it grant exemptions, it must be on the ground that the people will be more benefited by such exemptions than it would have been by the collection of the taxes from which an exemption has been granted. It is on this ground that schools and churches are exempted. A similar plea might be used to justify certain exemptions granted temporarily to industries which could not otherwise be introduced, and which are calculated to bring more wealth to the community, or to make it independent from foreign exactions. Universally, both taxation and the exemption from taxes must have for their *sole purpose* the interest of the people. Any other ground is insufficient. Is then the granting of rebates or bounties a legitimate exercise of the supreme power? It may be sometimes legitimate, but under one condition, that it benefits the community rather than the individual. As a temporary measure it may sometimes benefit the community by increasing notably the wealth produced, by developing resources which otherwise would have remained latent, or by enabling the nation to protect itself against commercial or military aggression, but in every instance it must be justified by the *evident interest* of the nation, *not* by the interest of individual citizens, or of a privileged class.

Since taxation and protection are correlative terms, it seems evident that the State cannot tax what it cannot protect.

"A system which would recognize in each State the

power of regulating persons or things beyond its territory, would exclude the equality of rights among different States, and the exclusive sovereignty which belongs to each of them." *

In 15 Wallace, 306, 328, we find a decision of the Supreme Court of the United States containing the following words: " The power of taxation, however vast in its character, and searching in its extent, is necessarily limited to subjects within the jurisdiction of the State. Property lying beyond the jurisdiction of the State is not a subject upon which her taxing power can be legitimately exercised. Indeed, it would seem that no adjudication should be necessary to establish so obvious a proposition."

5. Is the taxing Power unlimited in its application? It must be admitted with Judge Cooley that "nothing but express constitutional limitation upon legislative authority can exclude anything to which the authority extends from the grasp of the taxing power, if the legislature, in its discretion, shall at any time select it for revenue purposes." That is to say, every subject and every kind of property within the State may be taxed by the State. But we cannot agree with him when he adds that this power is *unlimited in its very nature,* nor with Judge Marshall when he says: † " The power to tax involves the power to destroy. If the right to tax exists, it is a right which in its nature acknowledges no limit." As a qualification to this strong statement, we beg leave to add the fol-

---

* Wheaton's International Law, Chap. II., § 2.

† McCulloch vs. Maryland, 4 Wheatstone, 316.

lowing words of Mr. Herbert Spencer: "State authority is a means to an end: if the end is not subserved, the authority, by the hypothesis, does not exist."* This is ethically and rationally correct: no human power is in its very nature unlimited. It is true that extreme contingencies may be imagined, in which taxation might absorb a man's wealth, or even a source of public revenue; but this must be accidental, and it must be a matter of life and death for the nation to justify the State in destroying what, under ordinary circumstances, it is bound to protect. Outside of these extreme cases, in which the State is compelled to destroy some kind of wealth, in order to save what is more necessary to national life, the power of taxing is not *destructive,* but *constructive.* The State does not exist to absorb or destroy the rights of the citizens, but to protect these rights. In the exercise of its power, if it takes from the citizens so much as one penny for any purpose but a well-proven public need, it commits an act of legalized robbery.

SEC. III. EQUITY OF TAXATION.

6. Absolute Equity is impossible. Relative Equity is obligatory. In the passage quoted at the beginning of this paper, Judge Cooley states that the taxing power "is not arbitrary, but rests upon fixed principles of justice." Very few men will question this statement, but it is not an easy task to define these fixed principles.

---

* The Great Modern Superstition, by H. Spencer.

In fact, McCulloch, in his masterly article on taxation in the 8th edition of the British Encyclopedia, gives up the attempt. " Practically," says this very able writer, " it is impossible to attain anything like perfect equality in taxation; and provided no tax be imposed in the view of trenching on this principle (the principle of equality), or of making a class or order of people pay more in proportion to their means than others, equality of pressure is of inferior importance. In this, as in most departments of politics, we have only a choice of difficulties; and what is absolutely right must often give way to what is expedient and practicable."

In order to be correct ethically, this last sentence should be amended as follows: " And what would be *absolutely* right *in theory,* when impossible of attainment, must give way to what is *relatively* right, and at the same time both expedient and practicable."

But this impossibility of reaching an absolute standard of right is not peculiar to the theory of taxation. All human laws show the limitations of human wisdom and human power; nothing short of infinite wisdom and infinite might can administer either legal or distributive justice without some accidental inequalities. Hence the general principle, that a *general* law does not lose its binding force *on account of individual hardships.* This truth is clearly set forth by Judge Cooley in the following lines: " The *apparent equity* of any particular exaction cannot support it as a tax unless it is made in accordance with law; nor, on the other hand, can the *seeming injustice* of a levy actually authorized by law defeat it, provided it is made under such general rules as the wisdom of the legislature has determined are needful and proper for the general good. The impossibility that government should be administered even by the most conscientious ruler without unjust consequences is universally recognized." *

It is evident that if the ruler is conscientious, the inequalities will be few and accidental, yet they will remain and betray some imperfections, either in the law itself or in its application. What then? Do men cease to draw circles because a perfect circle is an impossibility? Not at all. Mathematicians approach the limit as nearly as they can, and are content to make *absolutely* imperfect but *relatively* perfect geometrical figures. Ideally, a perfect tax should be like the atmosphere, whose pressure, being sensibly equal in every direction, is not felt by those whom it surrounds. But this ideal perfection is not attainable; all that man can do is to approach it as closely as possible.

7. The diffusion of Taxation tends to equalize pressure. Happily there is a property of taxation which tends to equalize the pressure. This quality is *diffusiveness,* and its operation is described in the following maxim: *Proportional taxes on all things of any given class will be diffused and equalized on all other kinds of property.*

This axiom may be understood easily if one considers that every exaction, however legitimate, diminishes the purchasing power of the person who pays it; and, there-

---

* The Law of Taxation, Chap. I.

fore, the amount which might otherwise be distributed among persons manufacturing or selling other goods is proportionally reduced. This reduction affects the market value of the untaxed articles by diminishing the demand for them. Hence the pressure may extend with diminishing intensity, until it has reached the whole expanse of social wealth.

Lord Mansfield said, in his famous speech on taxing the colonies: " I hold it to be true that a **tax** laid in any place is like a pebble falling into and making a circle in a lake, till one circle produces and gives motion to another, and the whole circumference is agitated from the centre."

This, no doubt, is a beautiful simile, but in the case which was then considered it was ill applied: the pebble had not fallen in the centre of the British empire, but in the harbor of Boston, where it raised a mighty storm. We must not carry these theories too far. No doubt taxation has a tendency to diffuse itself, and riches constantly seek their level; but when an unwise measure has been adopted, it often takes a long time before the equilibrium is restored, and the ripples on the ocean of wealth often become mighty waves and swallow up many a frail craft.

8. Incidence and repercussion. The diffusion of taxation presupposes the *incidence*—that is, the pressure brought to bear on those who pay the taxes; and, as this pressure has a tendency to expand, the important problem both in equity and in economy is to find out the *final incidence*—that is to say, the person who pays in the last resort. Moreover, the pressure when apparently reaching its limit is reflected back to the point where it originated; hence arises what they call the *repercussion of taxation,* which may be defined *the recoil of the pressure of taxation on those by whom it has been caused or propagated.* Let us suppose that a heavy tax is laid on beer; apparently the pressure bears on brewers, for they have to pay it first. This is the first incidence; but as they do not wish, and perhaps cannot pay it without compensation, they raise the price of the keg of beer, and this increase is paid by the retailers. This is a second incidence of the tax; but retailers in their turn raise the price of a glass, or, what is worse, lower the quality, and the difference in either case is paid by the consumer. Here is, as far as we know, the last incidence. But here also the recoil begins. The workman who has paid more for his beer has less money left for other commodities, and those who sell these commodities suffer proportionately; if the trade is seriously injured the State receives less taxes and feels also the repercussion. As it is essential that this economic phenomenon be thoroughly understood, let us give other illustrations. We will suppose that on some imports, wool for instance, the State lays a heavy tax. The trade may be seriously checked, and the importers may be less able than before to pay taxes. Let the duty be so high that it becomes prohibitive, and the money previously received by the Government ceases to flow into its coffers. This is repercussion reaching destructiveness. Once more illustration. Let an ironmaster be placed by governmental action in such a condition that he cannot sell his iron at the same price as before, and that the margin of profit is considerably narrowed. He will resort either to a lockout or to a lowering of wages; if the workmen accept a reduction, they will have less money to spend; and, ten to one, the stores of the company will have to reduce the volume of their business. Here is a repercussion caused by a reduction of wages, which will strike the manufacturer; but the recoil may not stop there. If business become dull and the plant become almost worthless, the amount of taxes will be affected, and the Government will suffer. If a strike or a lockout of considerable importance and duration be the consequence, then the production of wealth will cease, and both the private citizens and the State itself must suffer. These illustrations might be multiplied *ad infinitum*, but enough has been said to show that in the assessment of taxes *incidence, diffusion*, and *repercussion* must be taken into account. Unfortunately the economic problems attending the exercise of the taxing power are of so complex a nature that it is next to impossible to calculate with accuracy the fluctuations of wealth which may be caused by legislation; hence the formidable difficulties with which legislators have to contend. However, the two following rules may be considered as practically correct, and may serve to eliminate negligible quantities:

1st. The choice of the commodities selected as the objects of taxation is *relatively* of minor importance, if all the goods of the same class are equally taxed, and if no producer gets an advantage over the other producers of the same kind of commodity.

2d. When a tax is extremely light and hardly felt, it may act as a stimulant, cause greater exertions, spur on invention, and result in an increase of production and of taxable wealth. But admitting that these rules are sound, and may be followed in practice, who does not see how difficult it is to draw the line where taxation begins to be productive instead of *destructive,* with regard to the industry which is directly affected by it?

This difficulty is chiefly felt in *Internal Revenue* taxes, which fall more or less directly on production; hence the United States have generally drawn their revenues from other sources, or have retained on the list of taxable commodities only those objects whose production they were willing to check, such as whiskey and tobacco.*

9. Infinitesimal system. Social dividends. Equality of ability; Equality of sacrifice; Equality of benefit.

These considerations are economic rather than ethical, but equity no less than economy claims the attention of legislators. In order to approximate equity, several systems have been devised. We shall just mention them, and add a few words showing their inadequacy. The fact is that this difficult question is partly ethical and partly economic, and to arrive at practical rules, data drawn from sociology, ethics, and economics must be brought together and carefully combined. This the framers of rules or canons of taxation have endeavored to do; we shall see a little later the result of their labors.

---

* However, the chief reason why the United States resort only to indirect taxes, is that direct taxation is left to the several States.

For the present it will be sufficient to mention the various systems adopted by the various schools of political economy and sociology.

The first system may be called *infinitesimal*. It might be formulated as follows: " Let the rate be low, but follow property everywhere; and let not the smallest item escape the grasp of taxation." This system would be extremely vexatious, extremely costly, and often altogether impracticable; besides, the diffusiveness of taxation makes it almost unnecessary.

The second is the *social dividend theory:* " So divide the assessments that, after the paying of the tax, each citizen may remain in the same *relative* condition as before, with regard to wealth." The rule is fair enough in theory, but practically inapplicable.

The third system is the *equality of ability.* " Tax each citizen according to his ability to meet the demands of the Government." This sounds all right, but how shall we measure that ability?

The fourth is the *equality of sacrifice.* " So tax each citizen that he may feel the pressure of taxation neither more nor less than any other citizen." How shall we measure the amount of sacrifice? Moreover, individual sacrifice is a subjective standard, and consequently unfit to become a standard of legislation.

The fifth is: " Tax each one in proportion to the benefits which he receives from society." In that case the indigents ought to be taxed most, for society often feeds and clothes them.

Evidently these five standards are inadequate, yet each one brings forward a consideration which must not be neglected by the ruling power; taken singly, none is unfit to become the basis of taxation.

10. Proportional, progressive, and progressional rates. But before we propose the practical rules of Adam Smith and others, we must mention the divisions of taxation according to the rate adopted. With regard to the rate, taxation may be divided into proportional, progressive, and progressional.

A proportional tax is that which grows at the same rate as the wealth which is taxed. If A, possessing $10,000, pays $500, B, who owns $20,000, will pay $1,000, C, who owns $30,000, will be taxed $1,500, and so on, the rate of increase of the wealth taxed being always the same as the rate of increase of the tax. This system is perfectly equitable in itself, but we must acknowledge the fact that the great mass of the people wishes the richest members of the community to be more heavily taxed, even *proportionately*, than their poorer fellow citizens; and it might be good policy on the part of the wealthy to yield something to the demands of the masses, even though the grounds on which this sacrifice is required may not be sufficient to prove that it is due in strict justice.

In progressive taxation, the tax rate increases faster than the wealth. If the rate be 2 per cent. for $1,000, the amount collected being $20.00, it may become $2\frac{1}{2}$ per cent. for $2,000, 3 per cent. for $3,000, or $90.00, and so on. Now, it is evident that this mode of taxation is radically unjust, and amounts to a confiscation of very large estates; for we have two progressions, the one arithmetical and the other geometrical; as wealth increases arithmetically, the rate of taxation increases geometrically; hence, whatever be the starting-point and the rate, there will be a moment when the tax will equal the property taxed, and confiscation will be the result. This system of taxation is the dream of socialists; they wish to prevent the accumulations of wealth, and they know that progressive taxation will do it. Do not tell them that a rich man has just as much right to his millions as a poor man has to his thousand; that by preventing accumulation of capital they strike at the dynamics of production; that the recoil means starvation for the masses of laboring men. They are deaf to all these considerations; envy is their ruling passion, and the rich they must destroy, be the consequences what they may. This gives you the key to the saying of French socialists in 1848: " Before the Revolution taxation was proportional; then it was unjust. To be truly equitable, taxation must be progressive."

Progressional taxation is a compromise between proportional and progressive taxation. Up to a certain point the tax rate increases progressively, but when a certain maximum is reached it becomes proportional. This system is illogical, but it does not involve confiscation. It may take various forms, and under some forms it is comparatively harmless, because it checks its own increase. Such is the form mentioned by the lamented Prof. Francis A. Walker in his *Political Economy*, resulting from the exemption of small revenues and from the income tax. We will let the eminent economist speak for himself: "Suppose the constant amount exempted to be $1,000 and the rate of taxation on the excess to be 10 per cent., incomes of different amounts will be taxed as follows:

Income.	Income Subject to Taxation.	Amount of Tax.	Rate on Total Income.
$1,500	$500	$50	3.33 per cent.
2,000	1,000	100	5.00 per cent.
2,500	1,500	150	6.00 per cent.
3,000	2,000	200	6.66 per cent.
3,500	2,500	250	7.14 per cent.

etc."

By carefully examining these figures, and continuing the same kind of calculation, it will be found:

1st. That the tax rate on the whole revenue is constantly approaching the tax rate on the surplus, but by a constantly retarded motion; hence it will never reach it.

2d. As a consequence, the taxation on the whole income cannot go beyond a certain limit; it is checked automatically by the very law of its progress. Hence there is no need of an arbitrary maximum. This system is perfectly justifiable on ethical grounds, for the duty incumbent on the citizen to support himself and his family precedes in ethical order the duty of supporting the State, unless the State be in just as great necessity as the family, in which case the right of the State should prevail. But as this case never happens, it is perfectly equitable to exempt from taxation that part of the income or of the property which is necessary for his support and that of his family.

11. The three Systems contrasted. In order to illustrate the differences between the three systems of taxation, proportional, progressive, and progressional, we shall apply all three to the same sums, beginning with $4,000 and ending with $10,000. Whether these sums represent various properties or various incomes is not material to the present inquiry.

PROPORTIONAL.			PROGRESSIVE.		
Basis or Amt. Taxed.	Rate of Taxation.	Amount of Tax.	Basis.	Rate.	Amount of Tax.
$4,000	5 per cent.	$200	$4,000	5 per cent.	$200
5,000	5 per cent.	250	5,000	6 per cent.	300
6,000	5 per cent.	300	6,000	7 per cent.	420
7,000	5 per cent.	350	7,000	8 per cent.	500
8,000	5 per cent.	400	8,000	9 per cent.	720
9,000	5 per cent.	450	9,000	10 per cent.	900
10,000	5 per cent.	500	10,000	11 per cent.	1,100

In progressive taxation, it is evident that, when the rate will have reached $\frac{100}{100}$, the whole property or income will be absorbed by the State. This absurd result is precisely what extreme socialists aim at; it makes large fortunes impossible and practically destroys the right of property, whenever the amount is large enough to allow wealth to be readily turned into capital.

But all socialists are not extreme in their views; hence many have advocated a rate which would be progressive, until it reaches a certain limit, say 10 per cent., and then for all would become stationary—i. e., remain 10 per cent. for all larger amounts. It is evident that this system is inconsistent, for it ceases to operate precisely when accumulations of wealth become very large.

There is another system which has never been proposed, and which would prevent the rate ever reaching $\frac{100}{100}$. It is a rate constantly increasing, but at a constantly diminishing rate of increase. The various rates might be, for instance:

5%	5%
$5 + 1$	6
$5 + 1 + \frac{1}{2}$	$6\frac{1}{2}$
$5 + 1 + \frac{1}{2} + \frac{1}{4}$	$6\frac{3}{4}$
$5 + 1 + \frac{1}{2} + \frac{1}{4} + \frac{1}{8}$	$6\frac{7}{8}$
$5 + 1 + \frac{1}{2} + \frac{1}{4} + \frac{1}{8} + \frac{1}{16}$	$6\frac{15}{16}$
$5 + 1 + \frac{1}{2} + \frac{1}{4} + \frac{1}{8} + \frac{1}{16} + \frac{1}{32}$, etc.,	$6\frac{31}{32}$

It is evident that this system would be as arbitrary and as unjust as the preceding one; yet it would have the advantage of following the same rule throughout. Moreover, however high the original rate of taxation might be, it would never, in its progress, reach confiscation.

Let us now come to a progressional system which is not necessarily against equity. We will suppose that $4,000 are exempt from taxation.

Total Amt. of Property or Income.	Amount Taxed.	Amount to be Paid.	Rate to the Amt. Taxed.	Rate to Total Property or Income.
$4,000	$0	$0	0 per cent.	0 per cent.
5,000	1,000	50	5 per cent.	1 per cent.
6,000	2,000	100	5 per cent.	1.66 per cent.
7,000	3,000	150	5 per cent.	2.14 per cent.
8,000	4,000	200	5 per cent.	2.5 per cent.
9,000	5,000	250	5 per cent.	2.77 per cent.
10,000	6,000	300	5 per cent.	3 per cent.

On examining these figures a peculiar property of this kind of progressional taxation will become prominent. While the legal rate of taxation on the amount of property which is not exempted remains constant, the rate on the whole property or income, both taxed and untaxed, gravitates toward the legal rate without ever reaching it, until the difference between the two rates is less than any assignable quantity.

As the State should, as far as possible, exempt from taxation the amount necessary for the support of its citizens, there is nothing unjust in the progressional rate, which is an incident of the exemption. But as the ethical ground of this exemption is the duty of the citizen to support himself and family, the State should never exempt surplus wealth, unless it be used for the benefit of the community.

SEC. IV. CANONS OF TAXATION.

12. Canons of Taxation, according to Adam Smith. The canons of Adam Smith are not free from objections, yet they have never been superseded. They will be found in full in his *Inquiry into the Nature and Causes of the Wealth of Nations* (Book V., Chap. II., Part II.). They are four in number, and might be styled respectively, rule of ability, of certainty, of convenience, of economy.

The first amounts to this: " The subjects of every State ought to contribute toward the support of the Government as nearly as possible in proportion with their respective abilities; that is, in proportion to the revenue which they respectively enjoy under the protection of the Government."

Many objections are urged against this rule. It supposes that a man ought to be taxed because he *can* pay, while the true legal and ethical ground is that he ought to pay. It assumes the value of the benefits received and paid for as another standard. Then he who buys the protection wholesale, as the large capitalist, ought to pay least. Moreover, the poor cost relatively more to the State than the rich. Lastly, it sets up two standards which do not always agree.

Against the first rule or canon of Adam Smith, Prof. F. A. Walker raises the objection that it sets up two different standards of taxation: " Does it put forward ability to contribute, or protection, as affording the true basis of taxation? Which? If both, on what principles and by what means are the two to be combined in practice?" Perhaps the question may be answered in the following manner: Protection is not here understood in its broadest sense by Dr. Smith, and does not mean every kind of assistance extended by the Government; for it is perfectly true that the State, in this sense, does more for the indigent than for the rich; but let us understand *protection* as *securing property*, then the two standards agree, for he is most protected in this limited sense who holds *securely* the greatest amount of property, owing to the protection of the Government. The rule is somewhat vaguely worded, and is extremely difficult to apply, but the apparent verbal inconsistency can be reconciled.

The second rule, which might be called the rule of certainty, is briefly this: " The tax which each individual is bound to pay ought to be certain and not arbitrary. The time of the payment, the manner of payment, the quantity to be paid ought all to be clear to the contributor and to every other person."

Adam Smith adds that uncertainty encourages extortion and corruption, and he concludes with the following words: " The certainty of what each individual ought to pay is, in taxation, a matter of so great importance that a very considerable degree of inequality, it appears, I believe, from the experience of all nations, is not near so great an evil as a very small degree of uncertainty."

This is plain common sense, and it leads to this important conclusion, that legislators ought to be very cautious in changing the laws of taxation. Even tariffs should not be changed too often. Capital is the most sensitive of barometers, and a small degree of uncertainty will often compel capital to hide itself and remain inert.

The third rule may be summed up in one word, *convenience*. " Every tax ought to be levied at the time, or in the manner in which it is most likely to be convenient for the contributors to pay it."

The author illustrates this rule in a very clear and happy manner. It comes in the end to the famous saying attributed by some to Turgot, and by others to Colbert: " In taxation, the art consists in so plucking the goose that we obtain the greatest amount of feathers with the least amount of squealing."

Economy is the fourth rule: " Every tax ought to be so contrived as both to take out and to keep out of the pockets of the people as little as possible over and above what it brings into the public treasury."

This is an excellent advice; the cost of collection of a tax is a subject to be seriously taken into account. Taxes have been imposed with so little attention to this plain common-sense rule, that the expenses of collection equalled one-half, sixty per cent., or even the whole amount collected.

13. Canons of Sismondi, and supplementary rule of Mr. Atkinson. Mr. Sismondi, quoted by de Paricu, suggests four maxims which will be found useful in practice. We shall slightly modify the order and the wording, and name them respectively: saving of productive wealth, preservation of the income, security of fugitive values, exemption of a minimum.

1st. Let the taxes be taken out of the revenue, but leave intact the productive capital. As long as the State consumes only a part of the revenue, it acts as a prudent manager; when it consumes a part of the productive capital, it destroys its own support and that of the citizens.

2d. Taxation must never fall on that part of the income which is necessary for the continuance of that income. Hence gross product and net income must be carefully distinguished. That part of the revenue which is necessary to preserve or replenish the fixed capital must be left untouched.

3d. Taxes must not fall heavily on wealth which might be carried elsewhere, or for which the owners would be likely to seek an investment in foreign countries.

4th. Whereas taxes are a price paid by the rich to enjoy their wealth, those who have nothing to enjoy, but are reduced to the bare necessaries, should not be taxed at all. The reason given for this rule is not valid, but the rule itself is sound; for, as we have seen before, the person and the family of the citizen have a prior claim to the necessaries which the State would wring from the needy, should a tax be levied on the minimum which is indispensable for the being or well-being of the poor.

The observation of Sismondi with regard to a confusion of gross product with the net income is supplemented by the following apt remark of Mr. Edward Atkinson: "The burden or injurious effect of a tax on production and exchange is not to be measured by the ratio which the tax may bear to the gross value of the subjects of taxation, but rather by the proportion which the tax bears to the profit which might normally or naturally result from undertaking a certain line of industry or product."

That is, as we understand it, that a tax will be injurious when it will place competitors under different conditions, so as to compel some to give up producing; or, worse yet, when it will altogether destroy a productive industry. This destructive effect does not depend so much on the *rate* of the tax as on its influence on profit and production.

SEC. V. SUBJECTS OF TAXATION.

14. Direct and indirect Taxation. Poll tax. As every tax takes something from the wealth of the individual citizen, and as most taxes are necessarily consumed by the Government to meet actual wants rather than to help production, there can be no tax that is not subject to some inconveniences. These inconveniences must be carefully weighed and compared by statesmen and legislators, so that Government consumption may be reduced to the lowest figure compatible with the public welfare.

To make this comparison easier, it is best to divide taxes according to the subjects upon which they fall.

Taxes are often divided into direct and indirect. A direct tax is laid on persons, their property, their business, or their income. It is supposed to be paid in the first instance by the person who must bear the weight of it; a supposition which, upon analysis, will be found gratuitous.

An indirect tax is laid on commodities before they reach the consumer. Usually it is less felt, because it is confounded with the price of the commodity. The income tax is considered by some as direct, and by others as indirect.*

A tax on persons is called a Capitation, head or poll tax. Legal equality requires it to be the same for every citizen,

---

* This distinction of direct and indirect taxation seems at first sight more subtle than useful; yet it becomes a very important matter when the income tax is discussed. According to the Constitution, the general government must be supported by indirect taxes, while direct taxation is left to the several States in their individual capacity.

for all citizens are equal before the law: it is not *unjust*, but it is singularly *distasteful*, and this is a sufficient reason for not resorting to it. A poll tax, imposed on those only who cast their votes at elections, has the inconvenience of fining the man for the performance of a duty, because this duty happens to be also a civil privilege.

15. Taxes paid in labor. Taxes on property, real or personal, on profits and on rent. Taxes paid in labor, such, for instance, as the days of labor imposed for keeping country roads in repairs, are very wasteful, and therefore expensive. Turgot has demonstrated, by actual calculation on a large scale, that the waste amounted fully to 30 per cent. Yet, as in country districts cash is not readily forthcoming, it may be less obnoxious to the people than contributions in money.

A tax on property may be laid on real or personal property. In both cases it is difficult to collect; but the difficulty is far greater when the property is personal. Real estate can be seen and assessed with a certain amount of certainty. Yet even this tax has its inconveniences. Property may be productive or unproductive. If unproductive, it seems unfair to assess it, and yet if it be not assessed, an unproductive use of wealth is encouraged. On the other hand, if productive property is assessed, the taxation seems to bear on labor. It is probably best to tax both: taxing unproductive property acts either as an incentive to make it productive, or as a compensation which the owner pays to the State for his failure to increase the volume or value of social wealth. Productive property cannot be exempted, for the production and the benefit derived from it must be protected by the State; it is therefore just that the State should be compensated for the cost of this protection.

For the same reason, profits may be taxed; but the tax must be extremely moderate, otherwise production and accumulation of wealth, which are absolutely indispensable for the maintenance and progress of social welfare, will languish and eventually cease.

Rent, or the compensation for the use of land belonging to another man, and interest, or the compensation for the use of capital, are subject to the same ethical and economic laws. He who gives to another man the use of his land, or the use of his money, places at his disposal an instrument of labor and a source of profit, and is a partial cause of the profit which is gained, and therefore has a right to share in this profit. But because the State enforces the contracts under which he receives his share, he is also bound to pay tax for State protection, unless this tax is already paid by the farmer or borrower, and already deducted from the amount paid to the landowner or capitalist. It is evident that the same value must not be taxed twice, which would happen if the whole product of the farm would be taxed as it comes from the hands of the farmer, and then the landowner's share were taxed besides.

A tax on personal property is extremely difficult to collect, or even to assess. Frauds are so common and so easy, that personal property often escapes the grasp of the law. It may seem a libel on human nature, but it is a fact that when men can easily evade an obligation, conscience becomes blunted, and men, in other circumstances honorable and law-abiding, easily become guilty of falsehood, sometimes of perjury, when their interest is at stake, and when fraud is almost sure to pass undetected. For this reason it is best that such a tax should be so light that the incentive to evade the law be reduced to a minimum.

16. Income Tax. The income tax is at first sight the most equitable and the most easily assessed. It seems to be exactly in accordance with the first rule of Adam Smith. Practically, however, it is exposed to very serious difficulties.

1st. In order that it be at all equitable, the assessors have either to pry into the private concerns of every family, or to rely entirely on the sworn statement of the contributors. In the first supposition, the privacy of family interests is rudely interfered with, and the inquisitorial process becomes most offensive to high-minded citizens. In the second, every kind of evasion will be resorted to, and the outcome of the impost will be comparatively trifling. In fact, honest men will have to pay the full tax, while dishonest men will escape through the meshes of the law. Moreover, a great part of the income may be consumed in replenishing the capital. How can this part be distinguished from the rest? Lastly, the permanence of the income becomes a very serious question. It depends on the health, sometimes on the popularity of the person, especially when we consider the income of professional men. To have any approximation to justice it would be necessary to " deduct from the income of the professional man such a portion as would effect an insurance on his life, equivalent to the present value of his income. Here we are met at the very outset by the difficulty of deciding as to the standard by which to estimate his expectation of life."

Probably the only way of escaping all these difficulties, a way which is somewhat arbitrary and inconsistent, but which would avoid the complications and hardships, would be to adopt some sort of *progressional,* not *progressive,* taxation at an extreme low rate, and with the exemption of a minimum. It would be a concession to the public demand. England adopted an income tax as a war measure, under Pitt, in 1797, repealed in 1802, revived in 1803, under the name of property tax, repealed again in 1816. The present tax was proposed by Sir Robert Peel, to enable him to carry out important reforms, such as the famous Corn Laws. With some modifications it is yet in existence, and seems to be borne without very serious complaints.*

17. Internal revenue, Excise, duties on Imports and Exports. The income tax is considered by some as *indirect,*† but the internal tax must more justly be called so, because, although apparently charged to the producer, it is almost immediately paid by the consumer. As it cramps production and invites both corruption and fraud, it should never be resorted to, except as a temporary

---

* Vide McCulloch, Art. Taxation, British Cyclopedia, 8th Edition, Vol. XXI., p. 50, § IV.

† The Supreme Court has rejected the income tax on constitutional grounds.

measure, or it should be laid only on such commodities as carry along with them very serious abuses.

Excise is a sort of Government monopoly, which is objectionable, as well as all other monopolies of the kind.

Duties on exports are paid by foreign nations, but they have a tendency to cripple trade, and consequently should never be resorted to, except when it becomes necessary to keep at home a sufficient supply of certain commodities, the unchecked exportation of which might leave the country destitute of necessaries or of war resources. It is in its nature a temporary measure.

Duties on imports are an excellent source of revenue, provided that the schedules be not so high as to be prohibitive, for if they become prohibitive they defeat their purpose. They may be used also to support an industry, without which an important source of wealth would remain unproductive, or the destruction of which would render the State defenceless against commercial or warlike aggression.

18. Sole Tax. One word more about what they call *Sole Tax*. Under the pretence of *simplicity* and *economy*, some political charlatans would advocate the reduction of all the taxes to a single one from which all the revenues of the State should be derived. Some put this single tax on income, others on land values. Income tax as a *sole tax* is highly objectionable. All the defects inherent to a taxation of revenue would become a hundred times aggravated if the income would bear the whole weight of taxation. Simplicity is an excellent thing, but it must not be carried too far. "The mere circumstance of the taxes being very numerous, in order to raise a certain sum," says Sir Arthur Young, "is a considerable step toward equality in the burden falling on the people. If I were to define a good system of taxation it should be that of bearing lightly upon an infinite number of points, heavily on none."

But objectionable as a sole tax on income must be, a single tax on land is worse yet. It puts the whole burden of State support on a capital which must be preserved in its integrity. Were it adopted, it would, in its first incidence, oppress the husbandman; in its second incidence, it would raise the price of necessaries of life, and by its repercussion it would destroy the most permanent source of State revenues. An attempt to apply it in part to the ground values of a town not far from Washington* brought out, as its result, loud complaints and a contraction of the municipal resources. But before the experiment had been fully carried out, it was brought to an end by a decision of the Court of Appeals of Maryland.

---

* Hyattsville, Md.

TENTH LECTURE.

Conflict of Rights.*

SEC. I. DIFFICULTY OF THE QUESTION: THE CONFLICT OF RIGHTS IS OVER A WIDER FIELD THAN THE CONFLICT OF LAWS.

1. Law is the common source of Duties and of Rights; but Rights extend over a wider field than laws.

Every jurisconsult agrees that in the whole range of jurisprudence, if there is a matter full of difficult problems it is the conflict of laws. Hertius,† a very high authority on this subject, says openly: " With regard to the conflict of laws, the controversy is wide in its diffusion and doubtful in its results; and I do not know a single author who has attempted to treat the whole subject." But if to harmonize opposite legislations is a dif-

---

* As between two points lying in the same plane, one straight line only can be drawn, thus, under well-defined conditions, one line of conduct only perfectly coincides with strict duty. Hence, there can be no real objective conflict either of rights or of laws, and the word conflict is a real misnomer. Yet as it expresses pointedly the subjective aspect of opposite moral claims we shall retain the term and use it as it is commonly used by legal and ethical authorities.

† Joannes Nicolaus Hertius, born in Giessen, A.D. 1651; wrote a treatise De Conflictu Legum. Died in 1710.

ficult task, it is harder yet to reconcile opposite rights and opposite duties. The reason is obvious. Rights as well as duties originate in natural or in positive law, but extend beyond the range of legislation; at least, beyond that part of legislation which is strictly imperative or prohibitive. Man may do many things which are neither commanded nor forbidden, for, being the artisan of his own destiny, he may use, in order to attain it, all the means that are neither evil in themselves nor injurious to others. And yet we have said that both rights and duties originate in law. To show that these two statements do not conflict, let us consider this wonderful moral chain, by which the whole world of reasonable and free beings is connected with the throne of eternal justice. The first link is in the hand of God; in Him we find no duties properly so called, nothing but the eternal law of His divine essence, His supreme dominion, and the prototype of the natural law which He has imposed on His creatures. When we reach man, we meet first the impress of his Maker's intellect and will, which we call natural law. To this he is bound to submit, beginning his existence with the paramount duty of accomplishing the destiny which is marked out for him by the law of his nature, and which will bring him back to his first principle. In order to perform this task he must use the necessary means, perfect his mind, his will, all his powers and faculties. These means he has *the right* to use. If they be absolutely indispensable, his right is absolute; if they be only useful, it is conditioned on the rights of others and on the laws which may be justly imposed upon him by those who have received from God their authority. His fellow-men must respect his rights, and he must respect the rights of others; hence arise mutual duties which weld together the whole human race in mutual interdependence. Thus both rights and duties originate in the immutable law which is common to all; but, as the application of that law is to a certain extent left to individual free will, it spreads beyond the limits of strict precept and strict prohibition.

2. In cases of conflict, both authority of the Law and its connection with the Right claimed must be considered. This theory supplies us with one of the means to find out the relative merits of contending claims. With what law is each chain connected? And is the connection of the one with the law from which it has sprung more necessary than the connection of the other with its own juridical principle? Which law is higher, more universal, more imperative? And if both laws are equal, or if the same law is the common source of both rights, on which side is the greater moral or physical necessity to accomplish the act or refrain from it? The answer to these questions will often supply the solution of the problem.

Before proceeding further, it is necessary to define what is meant by *right* and by duties.

SEC. II. NATURE OF RIGHTS AND DUTIES.

3. Definition of Right. *A right is a moral power vested in a person, owing to which the holder of the power may claim something as due to him, or as already* *belonging to him,* or *demand of others that they shall perform some acts or abstain from them.* We say *moral power* to distinguish *right from might,* which is the physical power to enforce obedience.* For Determinists this distinction is useless; all acts being alike necessary, there can be no reason to distinguish a moral bond from a physical necessity. But for those who believe that men are free, *sui juris* and responsible, the distinction is essential. Might must be subservient to right, not conversely.

We add *rested in a person,* for if it be a moral power it must reside in a moral agent; but only a *person* is a moral agent; hence a right properly so called must be held by a person.

We say *to claim something as due to him, or already belonging to him,* because the thing claimed may or may not be in the power of him who claims it. As long as the object is not yet possessed, the right is called by jurists *jus ad rem (right to claim,* or simply, *claim).* When the object is already held by the claimant, the right becomes *jus in re* (lawful possession or ownership). Instead of demanding a material object or thing, the holder of a right may claim that others are bound to perform certain acts in his behalf, or at his request; for instance, the executive power, so long as it does not exceed its constitutional limits, has a right to have its mandates carried out and its prohibitions respected by all the citizens.

Such is the definition of right in general. Chancellor

---

* When contrasted with wrong, right is conformity to the rule of justice.

Kent [*] has a much simpler one, which is quite sufficient for legal purposes: " Right, in civil society, is that which any man is entitled to have, or to do, or to require from others, within the limits prescribed by law."

This brief and lucid definition of Kent will serve all ordinary purposes in the practice of law; but we must bear in mind, first, that some rights, and consequently some duties, are antecedent to civil society. Thus Adam had a perfect right to exert his powers, and to avail himself of the bounty of nature; he was in duty bound to worship his Creator. Robinson Crusoe had a right to capture goats and consume the stores which he had rescued from the wreck. He was bound to observe the natural law, so far as it refers to the individual man, even before he had seen in the sand the footprints of other men.

Secondly, we must not forget that a moral power supposes a moral being, and consequently a person. Here we must dispose of a side issue which is not without its legal importance. Have insane persons or children, before they have reached the age of reason, any rights properly so called? We answer at once affirmatively. Essential rights cling to personality, not to the condition of the person. If a person be deprived of the use of reason, and therefore incapable of performing acts perfectly human, that human being is debarred from the exercise of rights and exempt from the fulfilment of duties which require the use of reason, but the rights remain rooted in personality; they are merely in abeyance with regard to their

[*] Part IV., Lecture XXIV.

exercise, so far as the person thus incapacitated is concerned.

This principle is fully recognized by the codes of all civilized nations. Take, for instance, the following passage of Blackstone: " Life begins, in the contemplation of the law, as soon as the infant is able to stir in the mother's womb." And he quotes Bracton, who himself re-echoes both civil and canon law: " If any man strike a woman with child, or give her poison whereby abortion is caused, chiefly if the child be animated, that man is guilty of homicide."

Before civil law, as before natural law, a man deprived of the use of reason becomes irresponsible; but he is a man yet.

4. Definition of Duty. Rights and Duties are interdependent. *Duty is a moral bond, owing to which a man must perform, or refrain from performing, certain acts, in obedience to the lawful claims of another.* Right produces duty, for if a person is invested with rights, other rational beings are bound to respect those rights, and a moral tie is thereby created. In turn, duties beget rights; for if a man be bound to accomplish a certain purpose, he must be able to use the necessary means; or, if he cannot use them, either because they are beyond his reach or because, under the circumstances, they happen to be unlawful, then the duty is in abeyance. We speak advisedly when we speak of means which are accidentally unlawful, because means intrinsically wrong can never be made subservient to duty: man can never have the right to do anything wrong himself, much less to require wrong from others. But there are many acts indifferent in themselves, such as reading, speaking, walking, etc. These acts become positively good when performed in obedience to duty, and distinctly bad when opposed to it. Again, there are some acts which under ordinary circumstances may be bad physically, and under exceptional circumstances become morally good. Thus, under ordinary circumstances, it is a crime to inflict suffering by the use of a knife, but if it be done to relieve the sufferer from intense pain, without abridging his life, it becomes a work of mercy. The use of the knife is often both a right and a duty for the surgeon; it is a crime for an unskilled hand, or for a man who tries to maim or to kill. But lying, perjury, treason, are wrong in their essence, and can never be justified by any necessity whatever. With regard to those acts which are not wrong, either in themselves or on account of circumstances, a duty confers the right to resort to them; sometimes it obliges a man to do so, for although such acts are indifferent in themselves, they may become necessary for the accomplishment of a purpose which divine or human law has made obligatory.

Although originating in law, and therefore presupposing duty as far as man is concerned, right is more extensive than duty; for the latter applies only to the acts which are either commanded or forbidden, while the former extends to all the acts which are permitted explicitly or implicitly. Yet the connection between the two is not disrupted, because the foundation of the right is the obligation of accomplishing the purpose marked out by law. As the utility or necessity of the means becomes more and more stringent, the right becomes more and more entitled to respect.

SEC. III. CLASSIFICATION OF RIGHTS AND DUTIES.

5. We owe Duties to God, to ourselves, and to our fellow-men. After defining rights and duties, it becomes necessary to classify them. As the two terms connote each other, we may spare ourselves a double classification and omit, for the present, a discussion on the relative imperativeness of duties, by stating briefly that all our duties as men may be divided into duties to God, duties to ourselves, and duties to our fellow-men. At first sight it may seem that man can have no duty to himself, for duty involves a sort of moral subjection; and to say that man owes duties to himself seems to imply that man is both superior and inferior to himself, a contradiction, or at least a dualism, which is at variance with the oneness of the Ego.

Kant, in the *Critique of Practical Reason,* strives not very successfully to account for this dualism. This difficulty comes from ignoring the objective reality of God. So long as man has no higher ideal of goodness to realize than the subjective excellence of his own reason, he cannot be superior to himself; but when we consider him as bearing in his nature the outlines of a divine concept which he is destined to express in his conduct, under the guidance of the law which in its source is eternal, then, owing to the power derived from this superior law, he is invested with a sort of kingship over himself, and over the lower orders of creation. To the godlike man the animal man is bound to yield obedience. Thus the highest term of our duties is God, the next is our own person, insomuch as it bears the stamp of its Creator. We place our duties to ourselves before our duties to others, not because they are of a higher kind, but because our love of ourselves must be the pattern of the love we bear to our brother-men. Altruists may require a sort of self-denial which would ignore *self* altogether, but this altruism is suicidal; for when we take away the *Ego*, then no *Alter* is even thinkable. The gospel rule is the acme of human perfection: we must love our neighbors like ourselves, and love both ourselves and our neighbor for God's sake. This is the true juridical order. Without insisting on the classification of duties, let us come to the division of rights.

6. Rights natural and legal; absolute and relative. These moral powers may be *natural* or *legal,* according as they emanate directly from Nature, or are conferred by law. The rights to life, liberty, and the pursuit of happiness are natural rights; the rights of suffrage and eligibility are legal. *All other things equal,* a natural right is superior to a right founded on positive law alone.

"Rights of persons in private life," says Chancellor Kent, " are either *absolute*, being such as belong to an individual in a single unconnected state, or *relative*, being those which arise from civil and domestic relations."

About this distinction three remarks must be made.

1st. *Relative rights* may be derived from nature as directly as *absolute rights;* hence absolute rights *as such* may have no superiority. 2d. *Absolute,* as used by Kent, Blackstone, and other legists, often means *natural;* and in this particular sense it is not fitly contrasted with *relative,* since a relative right may be natural. 3d. When philosophers use the term *absolute* in connection with a right, they mean to say that it is unconditioned, and not limitable by any other right. The only human right which is absolute in this sense is the right to acquire virtue and grow in moral excellence. This right can never conflict with any other.

7. Rights inborn or acquired, abstract or concrete, personal or real.

Inborn rights are those which are co-extensive with human existence. Inborn rights are natural, unless we apply the term to *hereditary* rights, which may be partly natural and partly legal.

Acquired rights are those which owe their existence to an act of the free will of man, and which are not co-extensive with human existence. This distinction may be referred to that of *natural* and *legal.*

An *abstract* right is that which has never been applied to any definite matter, and for this reason remains, as it were, potential. The right of acquiring and enjoying property is abstract, as long as appropriation has not taken place. But when occupancy or any other legitimate title has determined what can be possessed, then it is transformed into ownership, which is a concrete right. An abstract right, being incomplete, is far inferior to a concrete one. Its only effect is to inhibit others from unjustly preventing us from giving it a concrete existence.

The terms *real* and *personal* next claim our attention. *Personal rights* adhere to the person; that is to say, they belong to a man precisely because he is an individual and rational being. Of this kind is the right of self-defence. *Real rights* belong to a man on account of a property which he has either acquired or inherited. To this class belongs the right to defend property against thieves and robbers. Observe that the words *real* and *personal* have a different technical meaning when applied to the property itself. A *real property* is not movable, a *personal property* follows its master, either really, or in the contemplation of the law. Personal rights are of a higher grade than real rights, because the former cling to personality, while the latter depend on the place, or on the nature of the object which is claimed or possessed.

8. Direct and indirect Rights. Another distinction is of great importance, the distinction of *direct* and *indirect*. A right is *direct* when the thing claimed is comprised in or coincides with the specific aim of the moral power which is granted. It is therefore limited only by the scope or purpose of that power. It is *indirect* when the thing claimed is not necessarily and, in the nature of things, within the range of the power granted, but becomes connected with it accidentally, or as a means to an end.

Thus, the Chairman of the House has a direct right to maintain its dignity, *to carry out its regulations,* and to forward its business; for such are the specific purposes for which he has been placed at the head of that august body; but his right to send his marshal to visit the houses and hotels of Washington is *indirect,* because consequent upon the necessity of securing a quorum for the transaction of business. He has not been appointed for the specific purpose of ordering the arrest of Representatives, but he might be driven to do so should they attempt to evade their legislative duties. And indirect right is limited not only by the purpose of the power given, but by its subordination to that power. As the connection of an indirect right with a direct one is often difficult to ascertain, it should, when possible, be defined by positive regulations.

Many other distinctions should be introduced, were this a treatise on rights; but, for our present limited purpose, it will be sufficient to bear in mind the meaning of such terms as Natural and Legal, Absolute and Relative, Inborn and Acquired, Abstract and Concrete, Direct and Indirect.

SEC. IV. NATURE AND CAUSES OF JURAL CONFLICTS.

9. Three sources of conflicts: uncertainty of Legislation, divided Allegiance, and incompatibility of Claims.

After defining rights and mentioning the principal kinds of right which may be vested in a person, the moralist is confronted with the following questions: Can rights conflict? Can duties conflict? Can rights conflict with duties? Three questions which may be reduced to one by expressing duties in terms of rights.

For if one duty conflicts with another, it is because the respective rights which impose these duties cannot easily be reconciled. If a duty conflicts with a right, it is because the right of the person from whom the duty is required is inconsistent with the claim which is made upon that person. Thus the matter is reduced to a conflict of rights, or rather, as we shall see, to a conflict of claims. To make this matter plainer, let us mention some of the causes from which conflicts may arise.

1st. There may be an opposition, real or apparent, between the laws from which the rights have sprung, or under which they have been sanctioned; thus, what is lawful marriage in one State may be considered adultery in another. Again, there may be inconsistencies in the rulings of different judges, or in the decisions rendered at different times. Thus it is not an easy task to reconcile the decisions rendered by different judges in England and in America, with regard to the opposite claims of capital and labor.

2d. The same person or persons may owe allegiance to several distinct powers, which may have opposite claims. Thus a man residing in a country which is not his own, either by birth or by adoption, may in some cases be subject to a divided allegiance, for his fatherland and the country where he resides have both jurisdiction over him.

3d. The object contended for may be inadequate to satisfy several claims, in which case it becomes necessary to consider: First, the nature and authority of the laws under which the several claims have sprung up; and, secondly, the value of the titles by which such claims are substantiated. Contentions of this sort are perpetually before the civil courts.

After all, the whole matter may be reduced to a conflict of claims; for, as justice cannot contradict itself, among conflicting rights there can be but one that is entitled to be enforced. But it is often very difficult to find which one must prevail. By far most conflicts arise from the fact that the same object is claimed by two or more persons, and that only one can have it.

10. Opposite Material forces are partly like, and partly unlike opposite Moral forces.

When moral forces are opposed, there are, in the conflict, some features which remind us of the composition of mechanical forces, and others that show the difference between the material and the spiritual world. Rights, or at least *claims,* may conflict and do conflict, but there can be but one resultant right, and that one must prevail. A hundred different forces may solicit one element of matter in opposite directions, but unless all these forces are so combined as to produce perfect equilibrium, the element of matter will follow the direction of the resultant. In presence of contrary and opposite moral forces, a perfect moral equilibrium is almost unthinkable. But if it should become a fact, the object claimed, or its value, should be divided, unless the contending parties agree to a compromise. The comparison which we have drawn from material forces, though illustrating the opposition of moral forces, is far from perfect. Yet in exposing its imperfections, we shall set off the working of moral forces more clearly than we could have done without the simile.

When a material body follows the line of the resultant, every force that enters into the composition of that resultant has its full effect. Not so in moral conflicts. It is often discovered that many claims are not valid, and must, therefore, be simply eliminated; at other times the conflicting claims are all valid, but some must remain in abeyance, while stronger ones have their full effect. For instance, a father has a perfect right in his old age to be supported by his son; on the other hand the State may be reduced to the necessity of calling to arms all the male adult population. The right of the father is sacred, so is the right of society; but the right of society is more universal and must prevail. Of course society in this case is bound to support the father if it be at all possible. A right in abeyance is not annulled, it is merely prevented from having its effect, insomuch as it is held in check by a higher act; it retains its potentiality, which is ever ready to pass into actuality, as soon and as far as the higher right will permit. Yet this sort of suspense of a moral power which we call abeyance does not exist in the composition of physical forces.

The doctrine which treats of the conflict of rights and duties is commonly called by moralists *Casuistry*. It was for a time despised, but its importance is now recognized. As it reaches its conclusions by referring to laws which are the common sources of rights and duties, something must be said of the relative authority and conflict of laws.

SEC. V.   SUBORDINATION OF LAWS.

11. Divine Law and the Law of Nature. Canon Law and State Law.

Highest of all laws and paramount in authority is the revealed divine law founded on the attributes of God and on the essential fitness of things. It is but a declaration of the immutable will of God and a more explicit and solemn promulgation of the precepts already contained in the law of nature. It is eternal, immutable, and universal; and with it no real conflict is possible.

But there are also divine commands which depend only on the free will of God, or were issued to meet special wants. These constitute the *divine positive law,* and have not the same immutability as the precepts of the essential law of God which is founded on His attributes.

The law of nature needs no definition, for it is accurately described by Blackstone, and we have made his words the subject of a previous lecture. It is evident that no conflict is possible between the essential divine law and the law of nature, the latter being but an imperfect manifestation of the former. "No human laws are of any validity if contrary to it (Natural Law), and such of them as are valid derive all their force and their authority, mediately or immediately, from this original." *

Not even the divine positive law, should it accidentally seem to conflict, can prevail against natural law. For instance, abstaining from bodily work on the Sabbath day

---

* Blackstone, § 2, n. 40.

is admitted by all Christians to be commanded by the divine positive law, yet a person would do wrong in neglecting the care of the sick or any other imperative duty required by natural law, in order to obey the positive divine command. Of course, the conflict is only apparent, since the will of God, which is the common principle of both laws, is absolute in one case and conditional in the other.

A conflict is possible between Canon Law and Civil Law. Objectively, Canon Law is superior and should prevail; practically, Canon Law yields whenever it is possible to do so without violating the law of God, and this is the only conduct which prudence can sanction.

12. Constitutional Law supreme. Public International Law partly natural and partly conventional.
Among human laws, constitutional or fundamental laws hold the precedence, because they are based on a fundamental compact, explicit or implied. The laws of the several States must yield to the Constitution of the United States, but there is but little danger of conflict.

We must come now to the International Law, which offers serious difficulties. A part of it should be called the law of nations, and is based on natural law. It is called by Wolf necessary international, *jus gentium necessarium,* and it has the stability of natural law itself. The other part is conventional and binds only the contracting parties. But it would be very bad policy to object to an agreement which most nations have adopted as conducive to the general welfare of the world. As conflicts of International

Law occur between sovereign States, the only means to bring them to a pacific issue is to resort to arbitration.

13. Private International Law. *Lex fori, situs, domicilii*. Personal, real and mixed Statutes.

But the difficulty is most perplexing in cases of private International Law, where the one and the same person is subject to several legislations equally supreme and conflicting. Theodore D. Woolsey shows this perplexity in the strongest light when he says: "A man may change his domicil from one country to another, and may hold property in both; he may in a third execute a contract to be fulfilled in a fourth; he may inherit from relatives in another, and have heirs in another still; in short, with the increase of commerce and of emigration, in modern times, private jural relations extend far beyond the bounds of any one territory where an individual has his domicil." *

Is that extension due solely to the comity of nations? Opinions differ, but it seems evident that in many cases it is due to natural equity. For instance, natural equity requires that a man who has been married lawfully and validly in the country where the union was contracted should be considered in all countries as lawfully and validly married. But which legislation must prevail? *Lex Fori, Lex Situs,* or *Lex Domicilii?* † The answers of

---

* Woolsey's International Law, §§ 68, 69, 70, 71, 72, 73, 74, 75.

† *Lex Fori*, the law in force where the court has jurisdiction; *Lex Situs* or *reisitœ*, the law of the land where the property is situated; *Lex Domicilii*, the law of the country where the party or parties have their domicils.

legists suppose a subtle distinction between personal, real, and mixed statutes.

"Personal statutes," says Judge Story, "are those which have principally for their object the *person*, and treat only of property incidentally; such are those which regard birth, legitimacy, etc.

"Real statutes are those which have principally for their object property; such are those which concern the disposition which one may make of his property, either living or by testament.

"Mixed statutes are those which concern at once both persons and property.

"Equity seems to require that, in general, when the contention has been decided anywhere by a competent tribunal, the *lex fori* should obtain; when the contention is about persons, the *lex domicilii* should prevail, and when the suit is about property, the *lex situs* should be preferred. This, of course, would be subject to many exceptions. As it is impossible to enter into details, I shall give you the three rules of Huberus,* which, although often questioned, are yet substantially admitted:

"1st. The laws of every empire have force only within the limits of its government, and bind all those who are subjects thereof, but not beyond those limits.

"2d. All persons who are found within the limits of a government, whether their residence is permanent or temporary, are to be deemed subjects thereof.

"3d. The rulers of every empire, for the sake of security, admit that laws of every people in force within its own limits ought to have the same force everywhere."

---

* Ulric Huberus, born in Dokkum, 1635, wrote on the Conflict of Laws; died in 1694.

All that can be done in this lecture is to draw attention to the weighty matters contained in this difficult branch of jurisprudence: by their able works on *the conflict of laws,* Wharton and Story have opened the path for their successors, but much remains yet to be done.

We shall conclude these remarks with a few rules which may prove serviceable in ascertaining the relative merits of contending claims.

SEC. VI.   RULES TO DECIDE CONFLICTS.

14. Rules of Judicature. In the first place we must distinguish the right itself from its exercise; that is to say, the moral power from its application to individual cases. An inalienable right cannot be validly resigned, but if its actual exercise be not imperative, it must be suspended whenever more evil than good would result from the act. This is in obedience to the higher principle of ethics that man must do good and avoid evil.

In general, a higher law imposes a more stringent obligation and confers a higher right, yet the urgency of the occasion is to be taken into account. For instance, the divine law forbids work on Sunday, yet magistrates may order a work to be done on the Lord's day if it be necessary and cannot be postponed; the higher law yields in presence of necessity. We suppose that the act commanded is not bad in itself, for an act intrinsically bad can never be performed, much less commanded.

Necessity is also to be considered in conflicting claims

of the same order. Thus a starving man may take a loaf of bread which belongs to another man who does not need it. The right of appropriating what is absolutely necessary to save life is superior to the right of property, although both are founded on natural law. We suppose, of course, that the needy cannot obtain the bread by working or asking for it. In the contrary supposition, the right of property should evidently prevail.

In claims made upon us, universality and the ties of blood, relationship, or beneficence constitute a superiority. Thus individual interest must yield to those of the community. If two persons claim your assistance, the one closer to you by relationship, or by benefits conferred upon you, has the better claim. Thus in a conflagration or a shipwreck, if you can save but one person, and you have the choice between your father and another man, you must save your father.

If you abstract both from law and from duty, and consider rights alone, the following proposition will hold good: *In the conflict of rights, that must prevail which is morally stronger; that is morally stronger which belongs to a more universal order, has a more important object, or is supported by a better title.* The universality of the order proves that the purpose of the right is beneficial to a greater number of human beings; the importance of the object shows greater utility or greater excellence in the good which is sought after; the greater perfection of the title shows a more evident connection between the good claimed and the person who claims it.

This last remark may serve to explain the common axiom that *possession is nine points of the law.* Possession itself does not constitute a right, but it is a *prima facie* evidence that the right exists. This evidence may be rebutted, but a clear case must be made against the holder of a right, or of a piece of property, before he can be dispossessed.

The very best maxims to follow in practice are doubtless the rules of judicature placed in the *Corpus Juris Civilis,* at the end of the imperial constitution, and in the *Corpus Juris Canonici,* after the constitutions of Boniface VIII.

ELEVENTH LECTURE.

Combinations of Capital, and Labor Organizations.

Sec. I. The Law to Protect Trade against Monopoly.

1. Capital and labor are interdependent—yet conflicts must arise. Why?

When natural equity and even self-interest require interdependence and harmony, human greed and human jealousies often create discord, and cause wars which prove equally destructive for all the contending parties. The ruinous nature of unnatural conflicts is nowhere better illustrated than in the strife between capital and labor, two forces naturally allied, both essential to society, and whose combination is so necessary for the public welfare, that without it production cannot meet the wants of men, nay, must cease altogether. Yet, as capitalists will probably go on trying to obtain as much labor as possible for the smallest amount of compensation, and as workingmen will probably continue to ask as much money as they can hope to get for the smallest expenditure of energy for which that compensation may be exacted, struggles are unavoidable. To prevent or to quell outbreaks which might be disastrous to society, physical force is inadequate; if might is to prevail over lawlessness, it must be panoplied by justice and legality. Sometimes in self-defence, and sometimes in order to obtain the mastery, capitalists form combinations, and workingmen organize. Both have a perfect right to do so as long as they do not aim at taking an undue advantage of their opponents; the right of association is natural to man, and the State has no power to abridge it, so long as the boundaries of justice are not overstepped. But in the excitement inseparable from the conflict, trespasses occur which call for State interference. In this lecture we shall mention some of these trespasses, and as capital is probably, at least for the present, the more formidable of the two contending parties, we shall first devote our attention to the transgressions of capital as described in the act " to protect trade and commerce against unlawful restraint and monopoly, approved July 2, 1890." The act is as follows:

" Chap. 647. An act to protect trade and commerce against unlawful restraint and monopoly.*

2. Text of the Act to protect trade. " Be it enacted, etc. Section 1. Every contract, combination, in the form of trust, or otherwise, or conspiracy, in restraint of trade or commerce among the several States, or with foreign nations, is hereby declared to be illegal. Every person who shall make any contract or engage in any such combination or conspiracy shall be deemed guilty of a misdemeanor, and, on conviction thereof, shall be punished by a fine not exceeding Five thousand dollars,

* Supplement to the Revised Statutes U. S. A. Richardson.

or by imprisonment not exceeding one year, or by both said punishments, in the discretion of the court.

"Section 2. Every person who shall monopolize, or attempt to monopolize, or combine or conspire with any other person or persons, to monopolize any part of the trade or commerce among the several States, or with foreign nations, shall be deemed guilty of a misdemeanor, and, on conviction thereof, shall be punished by a fine not exceeding Five thousand dollars, or by imprisonment not exceeding one year, or by both said punishments, in the discretion of the court.

"Section 3. Every contract, combination in form of trust, or otherwise, or conspiracy in restraint of trade or commerce in any territory of the United States or of the District of Columbia, or in restraint of trade or commerce between any such territory and another, or between any such territory or territories, and any State or States or the District of Columbia, or with foreign nations, or between the District of Columbia and any State or States or foreign nations, is hereby declared to be illegal.

"Every person who shall make any such contract or engage in any such combination or conspiracy shall be deemed guilty of a misdemeanor, and, on conviction thereof, shall be punished by a fine not exceeding Five thousand dollars, or by imprisonment not exceeding one year, or by both said punishments, in the discretion of the court.

"Section 4. The several circuit courts of the United States are hereby invested with jurisdiction to prevent and restrain violations of this act; and it shall be the duty of the several district attorneys of the United States, in their respective districts under the direction of the attorney-general, to institute proceedings in equity to prevent and restrain such violation.

"Such proceeding may be by way of petition, setting forth the case and praying that such violation shall be enjoined or otherwise prohibited.

"When the parties complained of shall have been duly notified of such petition, the court shall proceed, as soon as may be, to the hearing and determination of the case; and pending such petition, and before final decree, the court may, at any time, make such temporary restraining order or prohibition as shall be deemed just in the premises.

"Section 5. When it shall appear to the court before which any proceeding under Section four of this act may be pending, that the ends of justice require that other parties should be brought before the court, the court may cause them to be summoned, whether they reside in the district in which the court was held or not; and subpœnas to that end may be served in any district by the marshal thereof.

"Section 6. Any property owned under any contract or by any combination or pursuant to any conspiracy (and being the subject thereof), mentioned in Section one of this act, and being in the course of transportation from one State to another or to a foreign country, shall be forfeited to the United States, and may be seized and condemned by like proceedings as those provided by law for the forfeiture, seizure, and condemnation of property imported into the United States contrary to law.

"Section 7. Any person who shall be injured in his business or property by any other person or corporation by reason of anything forbidden or declared to be unlawful by this act, may sue therefor in any circuit court of the United States in the district in which the defendant resides or his family, without respect to the amount in controversy, and shall recover threefold the damages by him sustained and the costs of the suit, including a reasonable attorney's fee.

"Section 8. That the word 'person' or 'persons' wherever used in this act shall be deemed to include corporations and associations existing under or authorized by the laws of either the United States or the laws of any of the territories, the laws of any State, or the laws of any foreign country.

"Approved July 2, 1890."

This law, no doubt, is stringent and comprehensive enough, and sufficiently sanctioned, but it is not easy of application. The word *conspiracy* is so difficult to define accurately, and to apply to the facts in a given case, that the *conspirators* are almost certain to break through the meshes of the law. Bouvier defines conspiracy: "An agreement between two or more persons to do an unlawful act, or an act which may become by the combination injurious to others." He also quotes the revised statutes of the State of New York in which the various kinds of conspiracies are briefly mentioned: *

3. Definition of Conspiracy. "It is enacted that if any two or more persons shall conspire, either, 1, To commit any offence; or, 2, Falsely and maliciously to indict another for any offence; or, 3, Falsely to move or maintain any suit; or, 4, To cheat or defraud any person of any property, by any means which are in themselves

---

* The extreme difficulty of proving a criminal conspiracy will be best understood by carefully reading both the decision of Chief Justice Fuller, and the dissenting opinion of Justice Harlan, in the case of U. S. against E. C. Knight Company; U. S. Reports, Vol. 156, 1894.

criminal; or, 5, To cheat or defraud any person of any property, by means which, if executed, would amount to a cheat, or to obtaining property by false pretences; or, 6, To commit any act injurious to the public health, or public morals, or to trade or commerce, or for the perversion or obstruction of justice, or the due administration of the laws; let him be guilty of a misdemeanor. No other conspiracies are there punishable criminally. And no agreement, except to commit a felony upon the person of another or to commit arson or burglary, shall be deemed a conspiracy, unless some act besides such agreement to be done to effect the object thereof, by one or more of the parties to such agreement.

"When a felony has been committed in pursuance of a conspiracy, the latter, which is only a misdemeanor, is merged in the former; but when a misdemeanor only has been committed in pursuance of such conspiracy, the two crimes being of equal degree, there can be no legal technical merger."

4. Ethical and Legal aspects of Conspiracies. From the standpoint of ethics, the definition of conspiracy offers no special difficulty: *any combination of two or more persons to do an unlawful act or to inflict an injury on themselves or some other person or persons* is a conspiracy. The evil intent need not be exteriorly manifested; moral law seeks it in the depths of human conscience. A man who resolves in his heart to do wrong is already guilty; if he carries out his intent the guilt is intensified; if he combines with others to accomplish his wrongful purpose, he multiplies his guilt, for he shares in the guilt of every one of his associates, and, as a consequence, becomes responsible for the result of the combined action. The guilt and the responsibility are at the same time individual and corporate. This is true, even though the means to which the conspirators resort be indifferent or lawful in themselves. For if a good purpose cannot justify evil means, much less can indifferent or lawful means justify an evil purpose. *Bonum ex integra causa.*

Natural law reproves conspiracy, even when the criminal intent lies hidden within the consciences of the conspirators; but human law cannot penetrate the recesses of the human conscience—it must have exterior manifestations of the criminal intent before it can condemn the guilty; hence the necessity of describing the facts which prove a criminal conspiracy: as these facts are many, and conflict with rights of various kinds and orders, it is next to impossible to mention them all. *The Law on Criminal Conspiracies and Agreements,* by Wright and Carson, Chap. III., p. 138, will probably be found to contain the most complete, if not the most accurate, catalogue of indictable conspiracies.

I shall now proceed to consider a certain number of combinations of capital which may easily lead to such monopolies as the act first quoted evidently aims at preventing. In so doing I shall have to use my own definitions, for I am not acquainted with any author who has attempted to differentiate accurately the various contracts which lead to vast accumulations of wealth, and which may, at the same time, bring about forbidden monopolies.

SEC. II. CONTRACTS WHICH MAY LEAD TO MONOPOLIES.

5. Syndicates, Trusts, and Pools. The contracts which most easily lead to monopolies are probably the following: syndicates, trusts, pools, combinations or *combines,* corners, to which we may be allowed to add lockouts, which may be as mischievous as the preceding transactions, although not necessarily connected with express or implied contracts.

A *syndicate,* properly so called, is a corporation which absorbs two or more companies by means of purchase, or otherwise, so as to place the properties, charters, assets, and liabilities under the control of one board of directors. A syndicate is not necessarily unjust or illegal; it may sometimes be useful, because enterprises which, left to a divided direction, are unprofitable may, by a condensation of capital and unity of control, become remunerative. But in the framing and granting of charters, legislators should foresee and forestall the possibility of a combination which would secure to the corporation a real and permanent monopoly by giving it the means to crush all competition. When the letter or spirit of the several charters, or of any one of them, has been violated, then such charters should be forfeited. And when such combinations would amount to "a conspiracy in *restraint of trade,"* it would be the duty of the district attorney to proceed by petition or otherwise, according to Section 4 *of the act to protect trade.*

Trusts are much more objectionable than syndicates. They consist in deeding the property of the several companies, individual manufacturers, or retail dealers, belonging to the combination, to one or several trustees, who need not be real owners of any part of the property thus intrusted to them. The members of the association get in exchange stock or certificates which warrant to them a pro rata of the profits of the trust. It becomes for them a matter of indifference whether their particular business is contracted or expanded, provided that the corporation makes large profits. Hence the trustees can increase and diminish production, open or close stores, just as it suits the interest of the corporation, and without any regard for the public benefit. They can easily get rid of competitors by underselling them, for mere local losses are comparatively of little consequence. That such combinations naturally lead to monopolies *in restraint of trade or commerce* needs no demonstration, yet it is not always possible to prove a conspiracy, and many trusts entered into with unlawful purposes escape the clutches of the law by means of technicalities. The words *trust* and *syndicate* are often used indiscriminately, yet there is a substantial difference. In a syndicate the legal owners are the real ones; in a trust the apparent or legal owners are not the true proprietors, but mere trustees. A trust involves a sort of legal fiction, a syndicate does not.

Pools come next. We do not speak here of those aleatory contracts the issue of which depends on betting, and which differ from ordinary gambling only by the extent of merited losses and ill-gotten gains. Pools, in the sense here contemplated, are agreements owing to which several persons or several corporations put together their respective profits and losses, or their profits only, to be afterward divided, according to a proportion determined by a previous contract. They are resorted to chiefly by competing railroad lines, in order to avoid the evil of unchecked competition, and what they call *cut-throat rates*. Pools, as a temporary expedient, are sometimes excusable, but they often lead to a restraint of trade or to unjust discriminations, and thus fall under the law to protect trade and commerce, or under the interstate law which forbids discrimination. Moreover, the agreement is seldom of long duration, on account of the conflict of interests, and of suspected frauds, or alleged unfairness. In the case of common carriers, pooling is expressly forbidden by Section 5 of the *Act to Regulate Commerce* (published by the Interstate Commerce Commission, Washington, 1893). Section 5 runs as follows: " It shall be unlawful for any common carrier, subject to the provisions of this act, to enter into any contract, agreement, or combination with any other common carrier or carriers for the pooling of freights of different and competing railroads, or to divide between them the aggregate or net proceeds of the earnings of said railroads, or any portion thereof; and in any case of an agreement for the pooling of freights as aforesaid, each day of its continuance shall be deemed a separate offence."

6. Combinations, Corners, and Lockouts. *Combinations,* properly so called, or *combines,* as these compacts are sometimes called, involve no transfer of property, and no pooling of profits; they are merely agreements to carry on business according to certain methods and at given rates, in order to avoid a ruinous competition. When free from any conspiracy to restrain trade or crush competitors, they do not seem to involve any moral obliquity, but, like pools, they are commonly short-lived.

It has been advanced that these various combinations ought to be left to the regulating influence of economic laws. For either they are conducted on sound business principles, and then they have a tendency to lower prices; for, on the one hand, condensed capital produces cheaper commodities, and, on the other, it is the interest of the corporations to meet the wishes of the public, lest they should rouse antagonism and stimulate competition; or they are conducted on unsound principles, and they are sure to collapse. The great international copper syndicate is held as an example. It tried in vain to maintain the price of copper, but that powerful combination failed and went to pieces. Mr. Andrew Carnegie had predicted its fall, and other sharp business men fully expected it. It is perfectly true that condensed capital produces more cheaply. It is also true that corporations must be conducted on sound business principles, and must take into account the wants and wishes of the public, or come to grief; but in the meantime expansion and contraction may take place and profoundly disturb the market. The water of the ocean as well as any other liquid constantly seeks its level, but nevertheless it is often convulsed by storms that may sink the mightiest navies. No doubt the State must avoid over-government, and meddling unnecessarily with trade, but it must also protect the weak against the strong, and save the people from conspiracies against which it would be defenceless.

Corners consist in buying up the whole or the greater part of the supply of a given commodity when that commodity is very cheap, in order to force the prices to an unnatural level, and oblige the buyers to pay such prices when necessity compels them to obtain the commodity at any cost. It is perfectly lawful to buy at the cheapest market and sell at the dearest, or to purchase when articles are cheap and sell when they have appreciated; but it is immoral by means of a monopoly to give commodities a fictitious value. Yet this is the usual purpose of corners. It is evident that such a purpose cannot be accomplished without conspiring to restrain commerce, but the fact of the conspiracy can seldom be proven legally. Happily for the community, most of the corners bring disaster on their authors: should corners raise the price of the necessaries of life so high as to cause to the people real suffering, the State would be justified in exercising its right of eminent domain.

Lockouts consist in interruptions or stoppings of production, which leave the workmen unemployed. They may sometimes be unavoidable, for nobody can be compelled to run a factory at a loss to himself or to the company which he represents. Hence, unless a conspiracy can be proved—and this is seldom the case—there is no legal remedy. It is often caused by a misunderstanding between employer and employees. Both parties should resort to arbitration. On this important subject, which cannot be treated in this lecture, I strongly advise the reading of a very able report of Col. Carroll D. Wright, bearing the title of *Industrial Conciliation and Arbitration.* (Boston, Rand, Avery & Co., 117 Franklin Street, 1881.) Also the second *Special Report of the Commissioner of Labor, on Labor Laws.* (Washington, Government Printing Office, 1892.)

Other trespasses of capitalists, such as a resort to the sweating system, deferred payments, or payments in scrip —that is to say, in paper money issued by the company, which is redeemed only in certain stores, and for which nothing but inadequate values are obtained—are so evidently contrary to law and justice that we need not discuss them. We will merely observe that, practically, workingmen are not sufficiently protected against possible abuses of capitalistic speculation.

SEC. III. LABOR ORGANIZATIONS.

7. Interstate Law. Ann Arbor case. In order successfully to resist the apparently overwhelming power of capital, labor is compelled to organize, and to resort to strikes and boycotts. To make these desperate remedies effective, they are exposed to have recourse to violence or conspiracy, to break contracts, cause contracts to be broken, to violate, or cause to be violated, the third section of the *Interstate Law.* Let us give the text of this important Section.

"Section 3. It shall be unlawful for any common carrier subject to the provisions of this act to make or give any undue or unreasonable preference or advantage to any particular person, company, firm, corporation, or locality, or any particular description of traffic, in any respect whatsoever, or to subject any particular person, company, firm, corporation, or locality, or any particular description of traffic, to any undue or unreasonable prejudice or disadvantage in any respect whatsoever.

"Every common carrier subject to the provisions of this act shall, according to their respective powers, afford all reasonable, proper, and equal facilities for the interchange of traffic between their respective lines, and for the receiving, forwarding, and delivering of passengers and property to and from their several lines and those connecting therewith, and shall not discriminate in their rates and charges between such connecting lines; but this shall not be construed as requiring any such common carrier to give the use of its tracks, or terminal facilities, to another carrier engaged in like business."

They may also find out that they have run foul of such a proviso against boycotts, as we find in a very equitable statute of the State of Colorado:

"Section 1. It shall not be unlawful for any two or more persons to unite, or combine, or agree, in any manner, to advise or encourage, by peaceable means, any person or persons to enter into any combination in relation to entering into or remaining in the employment of any person, persons, or corporation, or in relation to the amount of wages or compensation to be paid for labor, or for the purpose of regulating the hours of labor, or for the procuring of fair and just treatment for employees, or for the purpose of aiding or protecting their welfare and interest in any other manner, not in violation of the constitution of this State or the laws made in pursuance thereof: *Provided*, That this act shall not be so construed as to permit two or more persons, by threats or either bodily or financial injury, or by any display of force, to prevent or intimidate any other person from continuing in such employment as he may see fit, or to boycott, or intimidate any employer of labor." *

Illinois, New Hampshire, New York, North Dakota, Oregon, Rhode Island, South Dakota, Texas, Vermont, and Wisconsin have similar statutes.

We can best illustrate both the ethics of the case and the workings of the law by taking as the text of our remarks a decision of Judges Taft and Ricks rendered in Toledo, Ohio, April 3, 1893.† The case was briefly this: The engineers and firemen of the Ann Arbor railroad had struck. To make their strike more effective, Grand-Master Arthur had drawn the attention of engineers and firemen in the employment of other companies to a rule of their organization which required them to boycott the cars of a company against which a strike had been declared. An injunction of both judges had been powerless to prevent the boycotting, and a suit was instituted against the companies which had failed to send the cars to their destination, and against the engineers and firemen who had refused to handle them. The decision at the time created a great sensation, for it covered the following important

---

* Labor Laws, pp. 90, 91.
† Federal Reporter, Vol. LIV., p. 730, also p. 746.

grounds: 1st. The ownership of man in his own labor; in other words, the right to work and quit working. 2d. The freedom of contracts. 3d. The right of association. 4th. The lawfulness or unlawfulness of boycotts.

We shall advert briefly to each one of these issues:

I.

8. Ownership of man in his own labor. This ownership is not unconditioned. That man owns his own labor cannot be seriously disputed. Labor is essentially *personal,* it is something of the person, it is the exertion of personal energy, called into existence by the command of personal will. No doubt, like man himself, it belongs primarily to the Maker of man and to the Preserver of human existence and activity; but by the makeup of his own being, man becomes a sharer in the ownership of his Maker, he possesses a rational nature, is free, and *sui juris;* that is to say, he stands in his own right, but dependent on the superior will of his Maker.

But if the ownership of man in his own labor is unquestionable and founded on nature itself, it does not follow that it is absolutely unconditioned and unlimited. It has already been mentioned that his right is derived from the supreme domain of God, and must remain dependent on the divine will. Moreover, man is a *social* being, and from his sociability arise relations of interdependence and claims on his labor. He must support those whom nature itself has made dependent on him for their subsistence. He must bear his share of social burdens.

He must help his brother-men when his help is indispensable. All these are *liens* on his labor; these liens are beneficial not only to others, but to the owner himself; for they prove his ownership, and compel him to use his activity to the best advantage, yet they fence in with conditions the exercise of his ownership.

Man must fulfil his duties to his fellow-men taken individually; and to society, which consists of the same men taken collectively, or in their corporate capacity. He must meet the claims which his own free will has created by entering into contracts, especially those contracts which jurists call *commutative,* because they involve an exchange of values. He must refrain from so exercising his activity as to inflict an injury on others, or to hinder them in the legitimate exercise of their own powers. But when all these conditions are met, his labor belongs to him and to him alone; he can " work and quit working " without having to answer for it before any tribunal but God's and his own reason's.

If the workingmen have the right to " quit working," they have the right to " strike," provided they do not break a valid contract, resort to violence, inflict positive injury on any one or omit the performance of a duty imposed by justice or charity. With these reservations (which affect the exercise of other natural rights as well as the right to " quit working ") it is evident that, since their work is *theirs,* they can withhold it when they have reasonable grounds to do so. Take away this right, and you reduce the workingman to the condition of a slave, and leave him absolutely defenceless against the aggressions of capital. It is as natural to him as the right of self-defence. Nor is it enough to grant to workingmen the right to quit work *individually:* they must be able to do so *collectively,* for otherwise they cannot protect themselves against their employers, let alone combinations of organized capital.

The right to strike is not questioned by the court. Judge Ricks says explicitly: " In ordinary conditions, as between employer and employee, the privilege of the latter to quit the former's service cannot be prevented by restraint or force."

Judge Taft held that the damages caused to the companies by the mere cessation of work are a lawful means of self-defence. " The probable inconvenience or loss imposed on the complainant company by withholding their labor (the labor of engineers and firemen) would, under ordinary circumstances, be a legitimate means available to them for inducing a compliance with their demands."

Thus the learned judges maintained the right to work and quit working, but their contention was that in the cases submitted to them there were, besides a conspiracy, a boycott, and in one instance a breach of implied contract. With this contention we are not concerned; it is a judicial question which must be left to the higher court.

9. When has the State the right to make men work? An order of the court to do a specific work naturally suggests the question: *Has the State the right and power to make men work, on the ground that the public needs such work?* If we take the word " public " in its usual sense—that is, as a collection of men taken in their individual capacity—we say that the State has no such special and direct right. The State has no more right to take the labor of one man and give it to another man, or to several other men, than it has to put its hand into the pocket of one citizen and hand the cash found in this pocket to another citizen, or to a corporation. The State is not the owner of the property of private citizens, and the labor of the workingman is private and personal. But the State acquires a right when it acts in pursuance of its own duties. As it is unquestionably one of the State functions to protect the rights of all, when a citizen or a corporation complains of injuries, or of the non-fulfilment of a contract, the State is obliged to interfere and secure to each one his right. This action of the State may affect private property or private labor, and yet is perfectly legitimate, not on account of an ownership that has no real existence, but on account of a duty whose immediate and direct object is the security of individual rights. Again, the State may exact money and labor to carry out *necessary* State purposes. We say *necessary,* because it is the plea or title of necessity which justifies the apparent invasion of individual rights. Thus the civil power may not compel trainmen to bring to their destination any number of citizens seeking their own pleasure, or intent on their own private business (unless there be a contract, either express or implied, between these trainmen and the passengers); but it has a perfect right to impress both engineers and firemen, if it be necessary to send troops to a threatened point, or to revictual a city.

But, it is asked, where does the public come in? Any man belonging to the public can sue those who have made a contract with him, or who have neglected their functions as public carriers. Now, it is neither the engineers nor the firemen that have made the contract or received the charter; hence the public must go elsewhere for redress. It is true, as Judge Taft says in his decision, that "A corporation acts only through its officers and employees, and it is through them only that its action can be restrained or compelled. *While doing the work of the company,* the employee is the company." But observe the important reservation of the learned judge; if the employee becomes the company, it is only while doing the work of the company—that is to say, while under a contract. The employee is directly responsible to the company, and indirectly to the public; it is through the company that he becomes responsible to the public. Hence, in order to prove that by quitting work he has done a wrong to the public, it must first be shown that, at the time, he was under a contract to the company. This brings us to the second question, or to the freedom of contract.

II.

10. Nature of a Contract. Freedom essential to Contracts. "A contract is a compact between two or more persons. An express contract is one where the terms of agreement are openly uttered and avowed at the time of making; implied contracts are such as reason and justice dictate, and which, therefore, the law presumes every man undertakes to perform; as, if a man employs another to do any business for him, or perform any work, the law implies that the former contracted or undertook to pay the latter as much as his labor is worth. Commutative contracts are those in which what is done, given, or promised by one party is considered as equivalent to, or in consideration of what is done, given, or promised by the other."

These definitions, taken from Bouvier's *Law Dictionary*, show at once that freedom is an essential condition of contracts. If they are *agreements, compacts, reciprocal promises*, the things promised must belong to the contracting parties; to prevent rational beings from making such use of their own as reason dictates to them, is to assail human personality. This is especially true when the respective considerations are, on the one side, *labor*, which is essentially *personal*, and, on the other, capital, which is the product of preceding labor. It need hardly be said that the exercise of this freedom, like that of any other natural right, is subject to the dictates of natural equity. These principles are most clearly brought out in the encyclical on the condition of workmen:

"Rights must be religiously respected wherever they are found. . . . Let it be granted that, as a rule, workman and employer should make free agreements, and in particular should freely agree as to wages. Nevertheless, there is a dictate of nature more imperious and more ancient than any bargain between man and man, that the remuneration must be enough to support the wage-earner in reasonable and frugal comfort."

11. Duties of the State with regard to Contracts. But if, within the bounds of natural equity, employers and employees may frame their contracts as they think best, must the State remain a disinterested spectator? By no means. The State, being essentially the protector of all the rights of its citizens, is called upon to enforce equitable contracts with perfect impartiality. This could not be done without knowing the conditions of the agreement, and ascertaining whether these conditions are just or unjust, and whether they have been observed or set aside by one or by both of the contracting parties. This is the department of the judiciary power. The Government has also legislative duties, for "Laws should lend their influence and authority to the removal in good time of the causes which lead to conflicts between masters and those whom they employ."* The State does not *make* the contract, but *sanctions* it, when it is just and equitable. It has been said that Judge Ricks was illogical in fining Engineer Lennon and discharging Engineers Clark, Rutger, and Conley; to make good such an objection one should prove that all left their engines before performing their part of a valid contract, either express or implied; the learned judge contends that Engineer Lennon alone was working under a contract, and that he was, moreover, disobeying an order of the court enforcing that contract.

"An engineer and a fireman who start from Toledo with a train of cars filled with passengers destined for Cleveland begin that journey under contract to drive their en-

---

* Leo XIII., De Conditione Opificum.

gine and draw the cars to the destination agreed upon. Will it be claimed that this engineer and this fireman could quit their employment when the train is part way on its route and abandon it at some point where the lives of the passengers would be imperilled and the safety of the property jeopardized?

"The simple statement of the proposition carries its own condemnation with it. The very nature of their service, involving as it does the custody of human life and the safety of millions of property, imposes upon them obligations and duties commensurate with the character of the trusts committed to them.

"The evidence shows that, according to the rules and customs of the company, the engineers were paid $3.75 for a run of 100 miles and were paid for overwork. The time for computing compensation began at the hour when they were called to leave the yard and ended when they gave up their engines in the yard, and they were entitled to pay for that time, even though their engines did not move a wheel. Their service was therefore due to the company from the hour when their compensation began. That period of service continued during the time usually occupied in making the run for which they were called. During that period they were constantly subject to the orders of the company, and by custom and usage the relation of employer and employee was in force for that time. This is the most limited period that can be claimed for their term of service under the evidence before me."

Now, Mr. Lennon had left the service of the company without having completed the run. Therefore the learned judge was not inconsistent, and he did not fail, as asserted, to emphasize the contractual character of the obligation which the court had enforced.

III.

12. The right of Association; its limits. Functions of the State with regard to Associations.

The right of association is a natural right, no less than the freedom of contract. "Particular societies, although they exist within the State, and are each a part of the State, nevertheless cannot be prohibited by the State absolutely and as such. For to enter into a society of this kind is the natural right of man; and the State must protect natural rights, not destroy them." These are the words of Leo XIII. in the encyclical which has been already quoted. Of course this does not imply the right to enter societies whose ends are unjust, or which use unjust means to compass their ends. "There are times, no doubt, when it is right that the law should interfere to prevent association; as when men join together for purposes which are evidently bad, unjust, or dangerous to the State." * Nothing of the kind is asserted of the Brotherhood of Engineers, or that of firemen; such are their purposes, according to Judge Taft:

"The purpose of the Brotherhood is declared in its constitution to be 'more effectually to combine the interests of locomotive engineers, to elevate their standing as such and their character as men.' These ends are sought to be obtained by requiring that every member shall be a

---

* Ibid.

man of good, moral character, of temperate habits, and a locomotive engineer in actual service, with a year's experience; and by imposing the penalty of expulsion upon any member guilty of disgraceful conduct or drunkenness, of neglect of duty, of injury to the property of the employer, or of endangering the lives of persons."

Everything in this public platform is legitimate. Moreover, it is admitted that these brotherhoods are "generally law-abiding." When the ends are legitimate and the means usually lawful, associations have certainly a right to the protection of the State.

13. Rule XII.— Why it was objectionable. It is true that there was in their rules an article not generally known, and legally objectionable. The court ordered its production, and had a perfect right to do so; for the law can neither maintain nor restrain what is sheltered from the view by a dark lantern. Grand-Master Arthur, as a good and law-abiding citizen, produced the document. Here it is:

RULE XII.

"Twelfth.—That hereafter, when an issue has been sustained by the Grand-Chief and carried into effect by the Brotherhood of Locomotive Engineers, it shall be recognized as a violation of obligation for a member of the Brotherhood of Locomotive Engineers' Association who may be employed on a railroad running in connection with, or adjacent to, said road to handle the property belonging to said railroad or system in any way that may benefit said company in which the Brotherhood of Locomotive Engineers is at issue, until the grievance or issue of whatever nature or kind has been amicably settled."

This Rule XII. is certainly objectionable from an ethical, as well as from a legal point of view; but it may easily be modified or repealed, and it is not, even now, universally acknowledged by the order. It must be considered as an accidental and secondary feature of the association, and, from a mere ethical standpoint, it does not justify the opinion that " the existence and enforcement of Rule XII., under these organized laws, make *the whole Brotherhood a criminal conspiracy against the laws of their country.*"

The court, however, was administering common law, and common law is sometimes less liberal than ethics.

IV.

14. Strikes and Boycotts. It is said, and, we think, justly, that Rule XII. is objectionable, because it makes of boycotts regular and allowable weapons in the war against capital; but what is a boycott, and how does a boycott differ morally from a strike? The definitions are not uniform, and legislation itself has varied;* hence we shall place ourselves on the ethical plane, and leave to jurists the question of legality. In the contemplation of ethics, a strike consists in *an agreement among workmen, owing to which they cease to work for an employer, in order to compel that employer to redress a grievance.* Provided that the grievance be real and of a serious character, there is nothing morally wrong in the strike: in fact, it is almost the only weapon in the hands of the workingman. True, it is a double-edged sword, which cuts the hand that

---

* Vide The Law of Criminal Conspiracies, p. 144 et seq.

wields it, but it is better to be wounded than to be starved to death, and when a strike is wisely undertaken and conducted in an orderly manner, it is a painful, but sometimes necessary means to obtain justice.

The word "boycott" has at least two different significations. Sometimes it means *a cessation of economic intercourse with a particular firm on account of a real or supposed wrong, together with an effort to induce other persons to cease also to deal with the offenders.* This is a comparatively harmless kind of boycott. If the wrong which is complained of be real, and no coercion, no misrepresentation be used, it cannot be said to be *unjust,* and may be excused as a means to obtain redress. When resorted to as a means of revenge it is unchristian, but it is not necessarily against commutative justice; for others as well as ourselves are perfectly free to deal with whatever firm they please. But boycott often means a far more objectionable device; it is *an attempt to compel, by coercion or by moral pressure,* other persons *not concerned in the quarrel to give up their business relations with the supposed offenders,* irrespective of the moral or *legal obligations existing between the parties on whom the pressure is exercised.* This kind of boycott is radically wrong for two reasons: 1st. It is an abuse of our liberty to check or abridge that of persons who have done us no wrong, an abuse which usually inflicts great damages on unoffending persons. 2d. It is an attempt to compel others to disregard their own contracts or the behests of the law.

Unfortunately, this seems to be the kind of boycott advocated in Rule XII. Sound morals will not allow a man to do evil in order that good may follow. If workingmen are not secure enough in the enjoyment of their rights, let their legal defences be improved and strengthened, but in the meantime let the majesty of the law be respected. To think that socialism could cure all the ills attendant on the present economic system would be a fatal illusion. Were the State, or, to speak more truly, the men who run the Government, to hold in their hands all the instruments of production, the workingmen would be wronged, as they are now, probably more than they are now, and they would have no redress. They can in many cases bring to terms the most powerful combinations of capital; could they contend against Leviathan?

TWELFTH LECTURE.

Legal Ethics.*

1. In order that Justice may rule, Laws must be equitable, and they must be enforced impartially. Legislative, Executive, and Judicial functions are interdependent.

If justice ceased to rule nations, might would take the place of right, civilization would recede, and there would be an end of social well-being. Justice is the very foundation of the social fabric. But in order that justice may reign in the commonwealth, two conditions are indispensable: the laws themselves must be equitable, and they must be enforced firmly and impartially. To legislators belongs the framing of laws: to the executive power the duty to carry them out; to the judiciary that of applying them to individual cases, and deciding the questions of right and wrong which arise from the conduct of citizens and the conflict of interests. In theory, the making of the law and the administration of it belong to distinct provinces of the civil power; in prac-

---

* In the preparation of this paper, the excellent work of **Judge Sharswood**, on the same subject, has been drawn upon freely.

tice, men who belong to the one have often to cross the boundaries of the other. Legislators appointed by the people are commonly taken from the ranks of the jurists, and the people are fully justified in their preference; for jurists, knowing well what a law should be, are abler to frame laws that will endure criticism and remain on the statute-book. Moreover, in a country where precedents may gradually become laws, the magistrate that originates or follows such a precedent indirectly becomes a lawgiver. Hence, in order that our remarks may be more useful, we shall apply the data of Ethics, first, to the legislators; secondly, to the judges; thirdly, to those who judge the questions of fact, *i.e.*, to jurymen; fourthly, to lawyers and attorneys. It is a general rule, applicable to all professions, that nobody can undertake with safe conscience the performance of a duty which he is not competent to discharge. If a man knowingly attempt to do what he is not qualified to accomplish, he becomes responsible for all the damages caused by his culpable ignorance.

Let us speak first of lawmakers.

SEC. I. LEGISLATORS.

2. Knowledge required of the Legislator. It may be said that in a democracy every citizen is something of a lawmaker, but when we speak of legislators we speak of the men who are intrusted by the people with the special duty of framing laws for the community. Hence the term as we understand it comprises chiefly senators and congressmen. It applies also, though not in so strict a sense, to the magistrates who have such a right to interpret existing laws that their decisions practically determine what was indefinite in preceding legislation. Lastly, the President, when making use of the veto power, and the people, when using their right to approve or amend constitutions, may be said, in a broad sense, to legislate.

It is needless to say that all those who are called by special duties to help in framing laws or in carrying them out must have a fair amount of mental training, and more than an average education. *The blissful times of David Crockett have gone by forever.* A man who should now attempt to deal with the highly complex organism of the commonwealth, though conscious of having but a half-trained and half-educated mind, would be guilty both against God and against Society. Among other branches, the lawgiver must be well acquainted with sociology and political economy, besides Natural Law, Constitutional Law, International Law, and Statute Law. He need not be *a specialist* in any of these branches, but he must have mastered the principles sufficiently to be aware of his deficiency, whenever his acquired knowledge is at fault, and to know where to go for more complete information.

A legislator must have made a conscientious study of history, especially of the history of his own people. General history will make him acquainted with human nature at large, and with the forces that determine the rise and fall of nations; the history of his own people will show the distinctive characteristics of the nation for which he will have to legislate.

He must know thoroughly the resources of his country, both in time of peace and in time of war; he must also be conversant with the wealth and strength of other nations with whom his own country may make treaties or come into conflict. It is true that excellent statistics and statistical abstracts are at his disposal, but he must at least be able to avail himself of those sources of information, and resort to them whenever the occasion requires.

A man who does not know these things, and yet coolly asks the people to make him a senator or a congressman, is deceiving his constituents, and getting public money under false pretences.

3. In the framing of Laws, both Justice and Expediency must be taken into account.

In the framing of laws the first standard to be held in view is natural equity, for any law evidently unjust is by the very fact null and void; it is not a law, but an act of legislative tyranny.

Next to justice, expediency must be considered, for many measures are just and good in theory, but prove impossible in practice, either because they are too burdensome to the community, or because they do more harm than good by provoking too many conflicts. Thus a law ordering a revision of all the title-deeds would not be against justice, but it would be the reverse of expedient; for it would bring about an immense amount of litigation and make property insecure. Let us bear in mind that legislators are not called upon to do all the good they can think of, or to prevent all the evils which may exist in a community, but that they must wield their power for the greatest good of all; not the greatest *ideal* good, but the greatest *practical* good. As a rule, a law which is not in accordance with enlightened public opinion should not be enacted. We say *enlightened* public opinion, because the whims and fads which become for a time popular cannot serve as guides of legislative action.

4. Beware of laws which cannot be enforced, or which must be often modified. Legislators must beware of enacting laws which cannot be enforced. Whenever a law becomes a dead letter, especially when this happens a short time after it has been promulgated, the majesty of law is impaired, and the supreme civil power receives a check. No doubt, customs introduced *bona fide*, without protestation from the civil power, and with the implied consent of the people, can abrogate pre-existing legislation, and it were absurd as well as inexpedient to revive obsolete legislation, which the people at large had discarded; but if such cases occur frequently, authors of those discarded laws must have been unwise, and their want of foresight may prove seriously injurious to social order. Let the line of Horace which describes the caution of old age be borne in mind by every law-maker: *Commisisse cavet, quod mox mutare laboret.** Only men of ripe years and wide experience ought to try their hands at law-making. The same thing must be said of judges who have to

---

* "He shall be wary of doing what he soon may labor to undo."

give a new interpretation of existing laws, swerve from the precedents on record, or who themselves originate a precedent.

This brings us to say that laws must not be changed often, even under the pretence of improvement, reform, progress, and what not. We do not mean to say that they should *never be changed,* for it is evident that they must be adapted to the wants of the people, but we deplore the mania of changing for the sake of a change. We moreover aver that a slight improvement, especially if conjectural, is no compensation for the loss of stability caused by tinkering with existing laws. Let a State, for instance, adopt hanging as a way to dispose of criminals, then prefer death by electricity, afterward choose the knife as more certain, later determine on chloroform or morphia as more humane, to come back at last to the rope as more appropriate. Would not such a legislation be a round of horrors? In legislating, beware of fads!

5. Laws must not be multiplied without necessity. Beware of retrospective Laws.
If it is not expedient to alter laws too often, much less is it advisable to multiply laws without necessity. We have already mentioned elsewhere that the multiplicity of laws was considered by Cicero as a token of national decline. Many statesmen have endorsed this opinion. One thing is certain: every law restrains liberty, and if we wish to prevent by legislation every possible evil, we shall at the same time prevent every individual good. We completely endorse the following declaration of Rutherford, as quoted by Sharswood:

"Civil legislative power is not, in the strict sense of the word, an absolute power of restraining or altering the rights of the subjects; it is limited in its own nature to its proper objects, to those rights only in which the common good of society or of its several parts requires some restraint or alteration. So that whenever we call the civil legislative power, either of society in general or of a particular legislative body within any society, an absolute legislative power, we can only mean that it has no external check upon it in fact; for all civil legislative power is in its own nature under an internal check of right: it is a power of restraining or altering the rights of the subjects for the purpose of advancing or securing the general good, and not of restraining or altering them for any purpose whatever, and much less for no purpose at all."*

The modern tendency is to have recourse to legislation to cure all the evils of the body politic. It is as wise as binding a man hand and foot to prevent him from making a false step. It is an abuse that each incoming congressman should deem himself bound to have some law of his own passed by Congress, in order that his constituents may see that he earns his money.

Never enact retrospective laws, much less retrospective statutes; for, as Bacon says: *Non placet janus in legibus*— the double-faced God has no attraction in law. Of course this must not apply to retrospective laws which have for their object the *relief of some person or persons,* which

---

* Professional Ethics, Introduction, p. xiv.; Rutherford, Inst. of Nat. Law, Book II., Chap. VI.

relief may be due, but to *restraining* or *penal laws,* for such, when retroactive, are essentially unjust. A man is bound to obey the law as it stands when he is yet free to act, not as it may stand when the act shall have been already consummated.

To sum up in a few words: laws must be both just and equitable; expedient, that is, practically useful; capable of being enforced; framed with prudence and foresight; not easily changed; not multiplied without necessity; not retroactive.

Let us now devote our attention to those who have the principal share in upholding the majesty of the law.

SEC. II. JUDGES.

6. High dignity of Judgeship. We have mentioned the saying of Aristotle, that a judge must stand before the people as the *impersonation of justice.* He wields one of the essential powers of the State, and that power has its fountain-head in God Himself. The reason is evident. By nature men are equal and independent; no man or collection of men has, in virtue of nature alone, jurisdiction over any other man or set of men. Hence, when we find jurisdiction among men, it must be traced ultimately to one who is the ruler of men and the Lord of the whole nature. This power, originally divine, the Author of nature delegates to the supreme civil power, and the supreme civil power appoints the judges and gives them a sub-delegated jurisdiction. Hence, the judge, when occupying the bench, is the representative of the supreme civil power, and, indirectly, of the Author of commonwealths, as well as of individuals,—we mean the Supreme Ruler of the universe. Hence the respect which surrounds, or ought to surround, the judge when he fulfils his official duties; hence the exalted moral character which he is bound to maintain, and the profound science which is required of him. It is my duty here to state that, as a body, the judges in this country are up to the high standard that their profession requires, and in civil society no profession is more justly honored than that of the men who dispense justice; not only because their exalted functions claim the respect of all, but also because their science and their virtues make this respect a willing tribute cheerfully paid by their fellow-citizens.

7. A judge must know Equity Jurisprudence as well as Positive Law.
A judge must know equity as well as mere legality. He may not have to try equity cases, but he will certainly have to interpret municipal law, and, in interpreting it, it becomes sometimes indispensable to refer to a standard of right anterior and superior to positive law. For the same reason, he must be thoroughly acquainted with constitutional law, for whenever some particular interpretation brings an act of legislature into conflict with the Constitution, the conflicting interpretation must be given up, or the act itself must be repealed. "It is emphatically the province and duty of the judicial department"—we quote Judge Marshall,—"to say what the law is. Those who apply the rule to particular cases must, of necessity, expound and interpret that

rule. If two laws conflict with each other the courts must decide on the operation of each. So, if a law be in opposition to the Constitution; if both the law and the Constitution apply to a particular case, so that the court must either decide that case conformably to the law, disregarding the Constitution, or conformably to the Constitution, disregarding the law, the court must determine which of these conflicting rules governs the case. This is of the very essence of judicial duty. If, then, the courts are to regard the Constitution, and the Constitution is superior to any act of legislature, the Constitution, and not such ordinary act, must govern the case to which they both apply." * It is true that we must not easily suppose that a particular legislative act does conflict either with natural law or constitutional law, but the case may sometimes occur, and the judge must decide according to the higher standard or refer the case to the Supreme Court.

We must observe, *en passant*, that the history of a legal enactment often throws a flood of light on its true import, and that a reference to the Roman origin of a point of common law will sometimes leave no doubt with regard to the intent of the legislator. Some knowledge of the "Institutes" and Pandects, will prove most serviceable in important cases which involve natural law.

It seems hardly necessary to say, that a judge who stands as *the impersonation of justice* must carefully avoid partiality. If in presiding over the debate, hearing the witnesses, admitting or ruling out exceptions, charging the

---

* Marshall, as quoted by Sharswood, XXII.

jury, etc., etc., he inclines the scales either way, as much as a hair's breadth, he is guilty of malfeasance in office, whether the trespass can be proved or cannot be proved against him. Impartiality is for him a bounden duty; should he have swerved from it *wilfully,* he is bound in conscience to make up for the losses caused by his delinquency. Should he be the personal friend of one of the parties, or for any other reason feel that his judgment may easily be biased, it is his duty to call another to the judgment-seat, or to *grant a change of venue.* The latter is often necessary when the court observes that prejudice or passion warp the judgment of jurymen. If the judge is conscious of having been biased, or of having committed an error, although without deliberation or malice, he must allow a new trial, suggest an appeal, or resort to any other legal remedy that the law may have provided.

8. Bribes, if received, must be refunded. It is a grievous offence, both against natural law and common law, to receive bribes of any kind, and should such bribes have been taken, it is a strict duty to refund the ill-gotten gain, whether the decision be just or not. If the decision be just, then the judge had no right to be paid for a thing which he was already bound to do, and the money must be returned to the giver; if the decision be unjust, then he owes a compensation for the damage inflicted on the party that was a victim of his partiality. What, then, shall we say of a man who takes bribes from both parties and gives for excuse (like Lord Bacon) that he did decide the case according to its merits? We shall let a contemporary witness, Hugh Latimer, answer the question. I must confess that his oratory is intemperate, especially when we bear in mind that his scathing denunciation was uttered from the pulpit:

"I am sure this is *scala inferni* (hell's own ladder), the right way to hell, to be covetous, to take bribes, and pervert justice. If a judge should ask me the way to hell, I would show him this way. First let him be a covetous man; let his heart be poisoned with covetousness. Then let him go a little farther and take bribes; and lastly, pervert judgment. Lo, there is another, and the daughter, and the daughter's daughter. Avarice is the mother; she brings forth bribe-taking, and bribe-taking perverting of judgment. There lacks a fourth thing to make up the mess, which, so help me God, if I were a judge, should be *hangum tuum*, a Tyburn tippet to take with him; an it were the judge of the King's Bench himself, my Lord Chief Justice of England, yea, an it were my Lord Chancellor, to *Tyburn with him*. He that took the silver basin and ewer for a bribe, thinketh that it will never come out. But he may know that I know it, and there be more beside me who know that I know it. O briber and bribery! He was never a good man that will so take bribes. It will never be merry England till we have the skins of such." *

It is evidently as wrong to receive presents from the parties during the trial or even to take a hint that presents will be forthcoming. But is it criminal to accept a present when the case has been already decided, provided no im-

---

* Lord Campbell, Chancellors of England, Vol. II., p. 398.

plied agreement has preceded, and the present is a mere gratuity? It would be difficult to prove that such a conduct is positively criminal, but it is highly unbecoming and contrary to professional ethics. We may say the same things of those trifles which can hardly be called bribes, but yet may unconsciously incline the mind of the judge to favor one party. We speak of sweetmeats, fruits, and other trifles of the kind. No judge who has a respect for professional ethics and for the stainless purity of the ermine will accept such gifts from persons with whom he is likely to act in a judicial capacity. Of old bribes were often concealed under sugar-plums, hence the word *douceur*, i. e., *sweetmeat*. The pill was sugar-coated. At the present time, a judge who would accept any kind of present from either of the contending parties would at once lose caste *forever*.

9. Patience necessary. Doubt, in civil cases and in criminal cases. Patience is another virtue which is often severely taxed in a judge. To listen to all that is said on either side is often a fearful ordeal; the judge may of course prevent lawyers from talking idly and aimlessly, but he must not hinder them from saying anything relevant and useful to their cause. The poor overtaxed magistrate must try not to sleep, but be ready to catch any point of law, any fact which may be submitted to his consideration. This is a severe duty, but on this point ethics is inexorable. Moreover, the judge must preserve his temper, even when harassed by disrespectful counsellors. This does not mean that he should not punish impertinence, but, in order to do so judiciously, it is necessary that he should preserve perfect self-control.

Let us suppose that the judge has done all he can to arrive at the truth, and to master the intricacies of the case, but that, owing to a conflict of laws, or a conflict of testimony, he cannot make up his mind. What then? If the case be a criminal one, the decision must be in favor of the defendant; in point of fact, the axiom *nemo malus nisi probetur* holds good everywhere in criminal jurisprudence. But in civil cases, the judge cannot decide in favor of the defendant without inflicting a loss on the plaintiff; he must, therefore, carefully weigh the probabilities, and decide according to the axioms of jurisprudence, which are found both in civil and in canon law; such, for instance, as *stat presumptio pro possidente,* the presumption stands *for the actual possessor.* The magistrate must find out on which side rests the burden of the proof, and if the proof is not satisfactory, the one in possession must be maintained in possession. Thus, if some one claims that, although the legal time has elapsed, the statute of limitation does not prescribe against a note of hand, the claimant must show cause why the statute should have remained inoperative. He will have to prove, for instance, that partial payments have been made, or the note has been renewed, etc., etc. Until the proof is made, the signer of the note cannot be obliged to pay. The statute of limitation and the lapse of time are facts; the alleged bar to the statute is a mere assertion. When you are in possession of a certain fact, a proof is required before the significance of this fact can be neglected. The judge can never follow an opinion which is *less probable* as long as a *more probable* conclusion can be reached. It is for him a professional necessity to make up his mind according to the evidence.

10. A judge must not act according to a mere subjective standard; he must avoid delays, and beware of crowding the docket.
A judge must take the law as it is, and not substitute for it his own notions of right and wrong. The following case will illustrate the mischief that may be done by following a merely subjective standard: A young man was condemned to the penitentiary for obtaining money under false pretences. The accusation had not been supported by sufficient evidence, but during the trial it appeared that previously the same young fellow had forged the name of another man to a note. This of course would have fully justified the sentence, had the defendant been prosecuted for it, but he was not; he was condemned for a crime which he had not committed, on account of a crime for which he was not prosecuted. He should have either been set free, or prosecuted for forgery and condemned on that count.

When we have added that a judge must avoid unnecessary delays; avoid, if possible, crowding the docket, and take each case in its turn, without showing favor to those who may have been recommended to him, we have completed our short synopsis of his duties, as deduced from natural law. Rules of conduct which are based only on agreement, or long-prevailing customs, must be observed, but they do not belong directly to natural ethics.

SEC. III. JURORS.

11. Jurors must remain within their own sphere, keep free from undue influence, avoid intercourse with the parties.

A part of the judicial power devolves on jurymen; they are not supposed to be acquainted with the legal science, but to be judicious and strictly upright. The respective spheres of the court and of the jury are seemingly well defined: *Ad questiones juris respondeant judices, ad questiones facti juratores.* Such is the old and received axiom of common law. But there is a tendency, in some States, to extend the *attributions* of jurymen at the expense of those of judges; to give them, for instance, the right to impose damages which are punitive in their character, and which really ought to be considered as *fines.* We doubt very much the wisdom of this extension. But if the State gives them such a power, they have to exercise *distributive justice,* the most difficult part of judicial functions. There is, however, no help for it, and where such is the law, jurymen are bound in conscience to determine the award according to strict equity—a matter which cannot fail to perplex conscientious men.

But jurymen do not always remain within their sphere; they forget that they are not the judges of law; they set up for themselves a subjective standard of right and wrong, and abide by it, whatever the judge may say. It is a dangerous undertaking for a lawyer to make them thus encroach on the judicial province; if the judge is wrong, the remedy is an appeal by writ of error or any other way of bringing the case before an appellate court; but verdicts rendered against the charges of the magistrate ought always to be set aside, for they involve the usurpation of an authority which does not belong to the jury.

The great difficulty of jurors is to free themselves from undue influences. They generally reflect the prejudices and passions of the class of citizens from which they are taken. For instance, they will return a verdict against a corporation, on the ground that a corporation can bear a loss better than a poor man—a consideration that has nothing to do with the justice of the case. The popularity or unpopularity of the plaintiff has a great deal to do with the verdict. If they believe that the penalty attending the violation of the law is too severe, they will return a verdict of *not guilty,* notwithstanding an overwhelming evidence to the contrary. Lawyers are well aware of the tempers of juries, and when a member of the bar happens to be both cunning and unscrupulous, he can often warp the vision of jurymen, or at least of one of them. It need not be told that such practices are against natural law, tend to weaken the authority of tribunals, and sometimes lead to a criminal resort to lynch law.

When jurymen, through their own fault, render a verdict contrary to the evidence, they are guilty of a grievous wrong against justice. Moreover, when, through a want of attention to the evidence, or through conscious prejudice, they have caused some damage to a citizen, all those who have contributed to the wrong verdict are bound collectively and severally, or (to use the technical word) *in solido,* to repair the damage inflicted, but few, we apprehend, are aware of the obligations which are entailed by the returning of a wrong verdict.

Immediately before or during the progress of the trial, no member of the jury should hold intercourse with the parties, their agents or their lawyers. Even though they should talk of matters which are apparently unconnected with the lawsuit, there would be some suspicion of connivance, and that suspicion would cause some scandal. During a suit against a railroad, a juryman who visits the company's office lays himself open to suspicion. We remember a case in which some extra-judicial words of a lawyer, utterly harmless in appearance, and said in an undertone to one of the jurors, caused the returning of a wrong verdict. Such communications should never be tolerated by the presiding judge.

These remarks of ours will certainly not reach the jurors, but remember that any man who wilfully causes another to do wrong is himself the principal author of the wrong, and responsible for all the consequences which flow from it.

SEC. IV. LAWYERS.

12. A lawyer need not know everything, but must be conscious of his own limitations. In the term *lawyers* I comprehend *counsellors, attorneys, sergeants and pleaders,* for these distinctions have no real existence in the United States.

According to Cicero and to Warren,* a lawyer would have to be omniscient. This, of course, is an impossibility, but what is absolutely required is to have a broad and accurate fund of information, and in special cases to go to specialists and spare no trouble or expense to become thoroughly posted. Otherwise the lawyer is at the mercy of so-called experts, who sometimes happen to be frauds. For instance, in a case of poisoning, the help of a first-class organic chemist is indispensable; in a case of forgery, you need the help of a good microscopist; the rhythm of the arterial throbbing is betrayed by the points and lines which make up writing, and it is sometimes easy to identify before a jury, by projecting on a screen the special features of the penmanship, the true author of a written document, for no man can mimic the arterial beat or the nervous motion of another man.

A good general education, a conscientious study of law, great care in preparing the case, untiring diligence in securing the special knowledge which each case may require —such are the means to obtain the knowledge which is necessary to conduct a case to a successful termination.

---

* Law Studies, Chap. VI.

13. A lawyer must be truthful, respectful to the court, obliging and peaceable. Before all, it is necessary for a lawyer to have a high standing as a man of integrity, of honor, of strict adherence to truth, and the best way to obtain this high reputation is to deserve it. Every young lawyer begins his career with the intention of imitating in this respect the father of his country; but the temptations to *prevaricate* (this is the term commonly used) are both strong and subtle. Many a hoary lawyer will state that he has found it extremely difficult to avoid every kind of prevarication, yet all agree that if a man has pluck enough to remain perfectly truthful under the most trying circumstances, he will be amply rewarded for his moral fortitude. Let us now consider briefly the duties of the lawyer to the court, to his brethren of the Bar, and to his clients.

To the court, the practitioner must always be respectful. Opposition may at times be necessary, but it must always take a modest and polite form. "An exception to the opinion of the Bench," observes Sharswood, "may be noted as easily in an agreeable and polite as in a contemptuous and insulting manner." To be respectful to the court is the plain duty of the lawyer, and it is also sound policy. It is often better to acquiesce in a ruling of the court to which exception might be taken, than to object too repeatedly, especially if the objections be presented in a petulant and angry manner.

Above all, the lawyer must not only abstain from trying to exert on the judge a *personal* influence, but he must screen the court from such attempts on the part of his client. Such efforts to bias the court are both criminal and extremely dangerous.

With regard to his brethren of the Bar, a lawyer must always be courteous, kind, accommodating. He must avoid carefully anything like deceit, sharp practice, trap or surprises; that is, if the point can be made good otherwise than by being sprung suddenly on the opposite party. Quoting wrongly, so as to make the author say what he really did not mean, or suppressing a text which qualifies what the author did say, or ignoring subsequent reversals and repeals, constitute as many kinds of prevarication, which are morally wrong, and which make the tricky practitioner an object of distrust and aversion.

Avoid personal difficulties with great care; they lead to serious trespasses against the divine precepts and against professional ethics. Try by all means to win the good opinion and the good will of the Bar; it is more valuable to you than monetary popularity or success, purchased at the cost of integrity.

14. Duties of the lawyer toward his client. Difference between civil cases and criminal cases. With regard to his client, the lawyer is bound to use the diligence which is necessary to make the best of the case; gross neglect makes the practitioner liable to restitution, according to moral law, and actionable according to civil law. He is, moreover, to a certain extent, the keeper of his client's conscience; that is to say, he must dissuade him from any course contrary to morality. He is also bound to let him know when the case is hopeless; he must not cause him useless expenses.

But what must the lawyer do if his client is not honest? Here we must, in the first place, distinguish between civil and criminal cases.

A lawyer may accept a retainer, although the case may at first sight appear unjust; for upon more serious examination it may be found to be just; but as soon as it is evident to him that he cannot win *justly,* he must get out of the case. However, with regard to the obliquity of the client, his lips are sealed by the professional secret.

In criminal cases, an attorney cannot continue to prosecute a person whom he has found to be innocent, but the defendant's counsel must continue to do his best for him, even when he knows for certain that the defendant is guilty. The reason is, that even a guilty party is entitled to be protected as long as he is not convicted: *Nemo malus nisi probetur*—this is an axiom of civil and canon law. But the lawyer must be careful, first, not to stake his own personal veracity on the innocence of his client; secondly, not to throw the suspicion on innocent persons; thirdly, not to use prevarication or any other immoral act as a means of defence. Observe that the plea *not guilty* is not a lie, because the phrase " not guilty," even when the client is guilty, has a definite legal meaning, which every one understands.

The lawyer has also some duties toward the adverse party. He must not deprive them of their rights, or keep them out of their honest dues, by trickery or sharp practice. He must treat them with proper decorum, and observe the usual rules of charity. He must abstain from browbeating and confusing the witnesses so that they may be driven to commit lying or perjury, almost without being conscious of it. But there is this substantial difference between his obligations to his client and his duties toward the opposite party, that the former are based on *commutative justice,* and the latter on *legal justice.* Hence, he is bound to compensation when he has caused a loss to his client by gross neglect or culpable ignorance; with regard to the opposite party, he is only accountable for *positive injustice,* or calumny. He has made no contract with them.

But the absence of contractual obligations does not free the lawyer from the universal law of charity. The practice of intimidating witnesses until they do not know what they say, or are driven to commit perjury; or of trying to weaken their testimony by innuendoes, which they have no means of refuting, and which may destroy their reputation forever—that practice is morally wrong, and ought to be checked and reproved by the court.

Much more might be said, and perhaps ought to be said, with regard to the ethics of the profession, but I know that I can rely fully on the keen sense of honor which is the common inheritance of American jurists. Not only will it guide you surely under ordinary circumstances, but it will also enable you to decide moral questions which are not contained in Horner, Hoffman, or Warren. These authors condemn any kind of champerty, or buying of causes, but in none of them can be found the condemnation of a modern practice, that of paying a lawyer for not accepting a retainer, lest he should wring from the jurors by his eloquence a verdict of acquittal.

For the correct solution of this and other questions which may arise in the future, I appeal confidently to the keen sense of honor of the American Bar, which is always guided by the highest principles of religion and morality.

APPENDIX.

RULES FOR THE GUIDANCE OF A LAWYER'S PROFESSIONAL CONDUCT.*

1. In all cases and under all circumstances a lawyer should be a gentleman, and should never permit professional zeal to carry him beyond the limits of propriety.

2. A lawyer should always be respectful to the judges in court, inasmuch as they are then the impersonation of the law; and this should be entirely regardless of their personal character, and likewise of any indignities that may be offered by them, which should be met only with temperate, but firm assertions of professional right and duty.

3. A lawyer should ever be courteous with his professional brethren, even with those who are professionally dishonest, although with these latter he should hold no more than the most formal intercourse.

4. To the officers of court a lawyer should be studiously respectful and considerate.

5. A lawyer should never consent to be employed in a

---

* These rules have been drawn by a magistrate of great experience and of national reputation, who prefers that his name should not be mentioned.

case to the exclusion of previously employed counsel, or even in connection with such counsel, except at the special instance of such counsel and with the consent of the client. There are exceptions to this rule; but they should be exceedingly rare.

6. A lawyer who has severed his connection with a case should never appear afterward on the opposite side of it.

7. A promise made to opposing counsel should be strictly observed, unless it has been made in error, through inadvertence, or in ignorance of the rights of one's client. And if opposing counsel will not release one from the promise, and the rights of the client would be materially impaired by adherence to it, the duty of counsel is to withdraw from the case.

8. A lawyer should not permit himself to be used by a client to prosecute a cause which he knows to be unjust, or to interpose frivolous, vexatious, or unjust defences for him. A lawyer is not justified in attempting to prove as a fact that which he knows to be untrue, and to prove as untrue that which he knows to be a fact. Nor is he justified in advancing as a proposition of law that which he knows to be unfounded in the law. This, however, does not preclude him from maintaining a plausible opinion, when perhaps a contrary opinion is better supported in reason and by authority.

9. A lawyer should never interject his own personality into a cause, either by a statement of his own individual

views in regard to facts, or by the artifices of a meretricious eloquence to elicit undue sympathy or to work upon the prejudices of juries. There are usually two sides anyhow to most cases that come before the courts, contrary to what is generally supposed; and the true and great lawyer will always content himself with the forcible presentation of his own side, without misrepresentation of the other. This serves to give him more force, weight, and influence both with courts and juries.

10. A lawyer should never undertake a cause to subserve an ulterior purpose having no proper connection with the cause.

11. In criminal causes the duty of a lawyer is limited to that which the client may do for himself. If the client is innocent, or so believed by counsel to be, the fact may be shown by all proper and available testimony. But if the client is guilty, the duty of counsel is generally of a negative character. He may, if possible, disprove the testimony of the prosecution or throw doubt upon it; and he may introduce testimony on his own side tending to show the client's innocence, but always within the limits of the truth. He is not permitted under any circumstances, either by statement, by introduction of testimony, or otherwise, to attempt to maintain the truth of that which he knows to be untrue.

12. In view of the great difficulties involved in the management of criminal causes with reference to the crime of perjury, it always behooves a lawyer to be exceedingly

careful and circumspect, both in the assumption of such cases and in the conduct of them. Unprofessional and dishonorable conduct most frequently happens in the conduct of such cases; and the lawyer who takes them should take the utmost care not to be drawn into any impropriety.

13. A just cause should not be refused because the client has no money wherewith to compensate professional services.

14. Compensation for services should be reasonable, and in accordance with usage, and should be firmly insisted on where the client is able to pay; and usually there should be no commutation or compromise or scaling of fees, nor should there be in any case an underbidding of other lawyers.

15. It is unprofessional and ungentlemanly to stir up litigation, or specially to solicit employment in cases of personal injury.

16. It is iniquitous for a lawyer to purchase a client's cause or any interest in it. But this does not forbid arrangements for the payment of contingent fees—that is, fees contingent on success. Such arrangements, however, must be made before counsel enters upon the cause, and must be reasonable under all the circumstances.

17. A retaining fee is, and generally should be, required before one enters upon a case, and it is paid in consideration of contemplated services. If, through no fault or failure of the client, those services are not rendered, it is the duty of the lawyer to return the retainer.

18. Funds collected for a client should be immediately turned over to him; and delay in so doing, when without justification, is dishonest.

19. Upon the conclusion of a cause and the determination of the relation of counsel and client, all papers of the client should be carefully returned to him.

20. All opinions, whether oral or written, given by counsel to a client, should be honest expositions of the law, as counsel understands it, and should not be moulded to gratify the interest or the predilections of the client, and least of all to incite litigation from which the counsel may profit.

21. A lawyer should be modest in the assertion of his opinions, for law is a large science.

22. A lawyer, unless in very exceptional cases, and possibly for mere formal matters in other cases, should not appear as a witness where he is counsel. If his testimony is necessary to his client, he should withdraw as counsel.

23. Letters should be promptly answered. It is both rude and unprofessional unduly to delay an answer to a business letter. And courtesy is even more essential in the matter of correspondence than in personal intercourse. Promptness and courtesy in correspondence make and retain many friends, and contribute greatly to professional success.

24. In the examination of witnesses, courtesy and gentlemanly conduct are more potent with courts and juries,

as well as with witnesses themselves in eliciting the truth, than is the rudeness, scarcely to be distinguished from ruffianism, in which too many lawyers indulge. By such rudeness lawyers make enemies for themselves and accomplish no good result. With reference to cross-examination, in which such rudeness usually occurs, it has sometimes been said that the first rule governing the subject is not to cross-examine at all.

25. Counsel should not confer with opposing parties who have counsel, except in the presence and with the consent of the adverse counsel.

26. Counsel should be faithful to the interests of their clients, should carefully guard their disclosures to them, and should not neglect or improperly postpone the management of their business. Neglect of the interests of clients is dishonesty.

27. A lawyer should never forget that he is an officer and minister of the law, as much so in his sphere as is the judge in his judicial position; and it should always be his paramount purpose to subserve the interests of justice. Judicious advice by which litigation is avoided is therefore even more his duty than is the proper and judicious conduct of litigation intrusted to him.

28. Professional dishonesty sometimes meets with a measure of success, as does dishonesty in other pursuits. The opportunities for it are great in the legal profession. But true success in the profession is dependent upon zeal, earnestness, honesty, and integrity.

STANDARD CATHOLIC BOOKS

PUBLISHED BY

BENZIGER BROTHERS,

CINCINNATI: NEW YORK: CHICAGO:
343 Main St. 36 & 38 BARCLAY ST. 178 Monroe St

ABANDONMENT; or, Absolute Surrender of Self to Divine Providence. By Rev. J. P. CAUSSADE, S.J. 32mo, *net*, 0 40
ALTAR BOY'S MANUAL, LITTLE. Illustrated. 32mo, 0 25
ANALYSIS OF THE GOSPELS of the Sundays of the Year. By Rev. L. A. LAMBERT, LL.D. 12mo. *net*. 1 25
ART OF PROFITING BY OUR FAULTS, according to St. Francis de Sales. By Rev. J. TISSOT. 32mo, *net*. 0 40
BIBLE, THE HOLY. With Annotations, References, and an Historical and Chronological Index. 12mo, cloth, 1 25
BIRTHDAY SOUVENIR, OR DIARY. With a Subject of Meditation for Every Day. By Mrs. A. E. BUCHANAN. 32mo, 0 50
BLESSED ONES OF 1888. 16mo, illustrated, 0 50
BLIND FRIEND OF THE POOR: Reminiscences of the Life and Works of Mgr. DE SEGUR. 16mo, 0 50
BLISSYLVANIA POST-OFFICE, THE. By MARION AMES TAGGART. 16mo, 0 50
BONE RULES; or, Skeleton of English Grammar. By Rev. J. B. Tabb. 16mo, *net*, 0 35
BOYS' AND GIRLS' MISSION BOOK. By the Redemptorist Fathers. 48mo, 0 35
BOYS' AND GIRLS' ANNUAL. 0 05
BROWNSON, ORESTES A., Literary, Scientific, and Political Views of. Selected from his works. 12mo, *net*, 1 25
BUGG, LELIA HARDIN. Correct Thing for Catholics. 16mo, 0 75
—— A Lady. Manners and Social Usages. 16mo, 1 00
BY BRANSCOME RIVER. By M. A. Taggart. 16mo, 0 50
CANTATA CATHOLICA. Containing a large collection of Masses, etc. HELLEBUSCH. Oblong 4to, *net*, 2 00
CATECHISM OF FAMILIAR THINGS. Their History and the Events which led to their Discovery. 12mo, illustrated, 1 00
CATHOLIC BELIEF; or, a Short and Simple Exposition of Catholic Doctrine. By the Very Rev. JOSEPH FAÀ DI BRUNO, D.D. 200th Thousand. 16mo.
Paper, 0.25; 25 copies, 4.25; 50 copies, 7.50; 100 copies, 12 50
Cloth, 0.50; 25 copies, 8.50; 50 copies, 15.00; 100 copies, 25 00
"The amount of good accomplished by it can never be told."—*Catholic Union and Times.*

1

CATHOLIC CEREMONIES and Explanation of the Ecclesiastical Year. By the Abbé Durand. With 96 illustrations. 24mo.

Paper, 0.25; 25 cop., 4.25; 50 cop., 7.50; 100 cop.,   12 50

Cloth, 0.50; 25 cop., 8.50; 50 cop., 15.00; 100 cop.,   25 00

A practical, handy volume for the people at a low price. It has been highly recommended by Cardinals, Archbishops, and Bishops.

CATHOLIC FAMILY LIBRARY. Composed of "The Christian Father," "The Christian Mother," "Sure Way to a Happy Marriage," "Instructions on the Commandments and Sacraments," and "Stories for First Communicants." 5 volumes in box,   2 00

CATHOLIC HOME ANNUAL.   0 25

CATHOLIC HOME LIBRARY. 10 volumes. 12mo, each,   0 45
Per Set,   3 00

CATHOLIC WORSHIP. The Sacraments, Ceremonies, and Festivals of the Church Explained. Brennan. Paper, 0.15; per 100, 9.00. Cloth, 0.25; per 100,   15 00

CATHOLIC YOUNG MAN OF THE PRESENT DAY. By Right Rev. Augustine Egger, D.D. 32mo, cloth, 0.25; per 100,   15 00

CHARITY THE ORIGIN OF EVERY BLESSING. 16mo, 0 75

CHILD OF MARY. A complete Prayer-Book for Children of Mary. 32mo,   0 60

CHRIST IN TYPE AND PROPHECY. By Rev. A. J. Maas, S.J. 2 vols., 12mo,   *net*, 4 00

CHRISTIAN ANTHROPOLOGY. By Rev. J. Thein. 8vo, *net*, 2 50

CHRISTIAN FATHER, THE: What he Should be, and What he Should Do. Paper, 0.25; per 100, 12.50. Cloth, 0.35; per 100,   21 00

CHRISTIAN MOTHER, THE: the Education of her Children and her Prayer. Paper, 0.25; per 100, 12.50. Cloth, 0.35; per 100,   21 00

CIRCUS-RIDER'S DAUGHTER, THE. A novel. By F. v. Brackel. 12mo,   1 25

CLARKE, REV. RICHARD F., S.J. The Devout Year. Short Meditations. 24mo,   *net*, 0 60

COBBETT, W. History of the Protestant Reformation. New Edition with Notes and Preface, by Very Rev. F. A. Gasquet, D.D., O.S.B., 12mo, cloth,   *net*, 0 50

COMEDY OF ENGLISH PROTESTANTISM, THE. Edited by A. F. Marshall, B.A. Oxon. 12mo,   *net*, 0 50

COMPENDIUM SACRAE LITURGIAE Juxta Ritum Romanum una cum Appendice De Jure Ecclesiastico Particulari in America Foederata Sept. vigente scripsit P. Wapelhorst, O.S.F. 8vo,   *net*, 2 50

CONFESSIONAL, THE. By Right Rev. A. Roegel, D.D. Translated by Rev. Augustine Wirth, O.S.B. 12mo,   *net*, 1 00

CONNOR D'ARCY'S STRUGGLES. A novel. By Mrs. W. M. BERTHOLDS 12mo, 1 25
COUNSELS OF A CATHOLIC MOTHER to Her Daughter. 16mo, 0 50
CROWN OF MARY. THE. A Complete Manual of Devotion for Clients of the Blessed Virgin. 32mo, 0 60
CROWN OF THORNS, THE; or, The Little Breviary of the Holy Face. 32mo, 0 50
DATA OF MODERN ETHICS EXAMINED, THE. By Rev. JOHN J. MING, S.J. 12mo, net, 2 00
DE GOESBRIAND, RIGHT REV. L. Christ on the Altar. 4to, richly illustrated, gilt edges, 6 00
—— Jesus the Good Shepherd. 16mo, net, 0 75
—— The Labors of the Apostles. 12mo, net, 1 00
DEVOTIONS AND PRAYERS BY ST. ALPHONSUS. A Complete Prayer-Book. 16mo, 1 00
EGAN, MAURICE F. The Vocation of Edward Conway. A novel. 12mo, 1 25
—— Flower of the Flock, and Badgers of Belmont. 12mo, 1 00
—— How They Worked Their Way, and Other Stories, 1 00
—— The Boys in the Block. 24mo, leatherette, 0 25
—— A Gentleman. 16mo, 0 75
ENGLISH READER. By Rev. EDWARD CONNOLLY, S.J. 12mo, 1 25
EPISTLES AND GOSPELS. 32mo, 0 25
EUCHARISTIC CHRIST, THE. Reflections and Considerations on the Blessed Sacrament. By Rev. A. TESNIÈRE. 12mo, net, 1 00
EUCHARISTIC GEMS. A Thought about the Most Blessed Sacrament for Every Day. By Rev. L. C. COELENBIER. 16mo, 0 75
EXAMINATION OF CONSCIENCE for the use of Priests who are Making a Retreat. By GADUEL. 32mo, net, 0 30
EXPLANATION OF THE BALTIMORE CATECHISM of Christian Doctrine. By Rev. THOMAS L. KINKEAD. 12mo, net, 1 00
EXPLANATION OF THE COMMANDMENTS, ILLUSTRATED. By Rev. H. ROLFUS, D.D. With a Practice and Reflection on each Commandment, by Very Rev. F. GIRARDEY, C.SS.R. 16mo, 0 75
This is a very interesting and instructive explanation of the Commandments of God and of the Church, with numerous examples, anecdotes, Scripture passages, etc.
EXPLANATION OF THE GOSPELS, and Explanation of Catholic Worship. 24mo, illustrated.
Paper, 0.25; 25 copies, 4.25; 50 copies, 7.50; 100 copies, 12 50
Cloth, 0.50; 25 copies, 8 50; 50 copies, 15.00; 100 copies, 25 00
EXPLANATION OF THE MASS. By Father VON COCHEM. Preface by Bishop MAES. 12mo, 1 25
EXPLANATION OF THE OUR FATHER AND THE HAIL MARY. Adapted by Rev. RICHARD BRENNAN, LL.D. 16mo, 0 75
EXPLANATION OF THE SALVE REGINA. By St. ALPHONSUS LIGUORI. 16mo, 0 75

EXPLANATION OF THE PRAYERS AND CEREMONIES OF THE MASS, ILLUSTRATED. By Rev. I. D. LANSLOTS, O.S.B. With 22 full page illustrations. 12mo, 1 25
    Clearly explains the meaning of the altar, of its ornaments, of the vestments, of the prayers, and of the ceremonies performed by the celebrant and his ministers.

EXTREME UNCTION. Paper, 10 cents;   per 100, 5 00
    The same in German at the same prices.

FABIOLA; or, The Church of the Catacombs. By CARDINAL WISEMAN. Illustrated Edition. 12mo, 1 25
    Edition de luxe, 6 00

FATAL DIAMONDS, THE. By ELEANOR C. DONNELLY. 24mo, fancy leatherette binding, 0 25

FINN, REV. FRANCIS J., S.J. Percy Wynn; or, Making a Boy of Him. 12mo, 0 85
——— Tom Playfair; or, Making a Start. 12mo, 0 85
——— Harry Dee; or, Working it Out. 12mo, 0 85
——— Claude Lightfoot; or, How the Problem was Solved. 12mo, 0 85
——— Ethelred Preston, or, The Adventures of a Newcomer. 12mo, 0 85
——— That Football Game, and What Came of It. 12mo, 0 85
——— Mostly Boys. 16mo, 0 85
——— My Strange Friend. 24mo, leatherette, 0 25

FIRST COMMUNICANT'S MANUAL. Small 32mo, 0 50

FIVE O'CLOCK STORIES; or, The Old Tales Told Again. 16mo, 0 75

FLOWERS OF THE PASSION. Thoughts of St. Paul of the Cross. By Rev. LOUIS TH. DE JÉSUS-AGONISANT. 32mo, 0 50

FOLLOWING OF CHRIST, THE. By THOMAS À KEMPIS.
    With reflections. Small 32mo, cloth, 0 50
    Without reflections. Small 32mo, cloth, 0 45
    Edition de luxe. Illustrated. From 1 50 up.

FRANCIS DE SALES, ST. Guide for Confession and Communion. Translated by Mrs. BENNETT-GLADSTONE. 32mo, 0 60
——— Maxims and Counsels for Every Day. 32mo, 0 50
——— New Year Greetings. 32mo, flexible cloth, 15 cents; per 100, 10 00

GENERAL PRINCIPLES OF THE RELIGIOUS LIFE. By Very Rev. BONIFACE F. VERHEYEN, O.S.B. 32mo, *net*, 0 30

GLORIES OF DIVINE GRACE. From the German of Dr. M. JOS. SCHEEBEN, by a BENEDICTINE MONK. 12mo, *net*, 1 50

GLORIES OF MARY. By St. Alphonsus. 2 vols. 12mo, *net*, 2 50

GOD KNOWABLE AND KNOWN. RONAYNE. 12mo, *net*, 1 25

GOFFINE'S DEVOUT INSTRUCTIONS. Illustrated Edition. Preface by His Eminence Cardinal GIBBONS. 8vo, cloth, 1.00; 10 copies, 7.50; 25 copies, 17.50; 50 copies, 33 50
    This is the best, the cheapest, and the most popular illustrated edition of Goffine's Instructions.

"GOLDEN SANDS," Books by the Author of:
  Golden Sands. Little Counsels for the Sanctification and Happiness of Daily Life. Third, Fourth, Fifth Series. 32mo, each,   0 60
  Book of the Professed. 32mo.
    Vol. I. ⎫   ⎧ *net*, 0 75
    Vol. II. ⎬ Each with a steel-plate Frontispiece. ⎨ *net*, 0 60
    Vol. III. ⎭   ⎩ *net*, 0 60
  Prayer. 32mo,   *net*, 0 40
  The Little Book of Superiors. 32mo,   *net*, 0 60
  Spiritual Direction. 32mo,   *net*, 0 60
  Little Month of May. 32mo, flexible cloth,   0 25
  Little Month of the Poor Souls. 32mo, flexible cloth,   0 25
  Hints on Letter-Writing. 16mo,   0 60

GROU, REV. J., S.J. The Characteristics of True Devotion. A new edition, by Rev. SAMUEL H. FRISBEE, S.J. 16mo, *net*, 0 75

―――― The Interior of Jesus and Mary. Edited by Rev. SAMUEL H. FRISBEE, S.J. 16mo, 2 vols.,   *net*, 2 00

HANDBOOK FOR ALTAR SOCIETIES, and Guide for Sacristans and others having charge of the Altar and Sanctuary. 16mo.   *net*, 0 75

HANDBOOK OF THE CHRISTIAN RELIGION. By Rev. W. WILMERS, S.J. From the German. Edited by Rev. JAMES CONWAY, S.J. 12mo,   *net*, 1 50

HAPPY YEAR, A; or, The Year Sanctified by Meditating on the Maxims and Sayings of the Saints. By ABBÉ LASAUSSE. 12mo,   *net*, 1 00

HEART, THE, OF ST. JANE FRANCES DE CHANTAL. Thoughts and Prayers. 32mo,   *net*, 0 40

HEIR OF DREAMS, AN. By SALLIE MARGARET O'MALLEY. 16mo,   0 50

HELP FOR THE POOR SOULS IN PURGATORY. Sm. 32mo,   0 50

HIDDEN TREASURE; or, The Value and Excellence of the Holy Mass. By ST. LEONARD OF PORT-MAURICE. 32mo,   0 50

HISTORY OF THE CATHOLIC CHURCH. By Dr. H. BRUECK. 2 vols., 8vo,   *net*, 3 00

HISTORY OF THE CATHOLIC CHURCH. Adapted by Rev. RICHARD BRENNAN, LL.D. With 90 Illustrations. 8vo,   1 50

HISTORY OF THE MASS and its Ceremonies in the Eastern and Western Church. By Rev. JOHN O'BRIEN, A.M. 12mo, *net*, 1 25

HOLY FACE OF JESUS, THE. A Series of Meditations on the Litany of the Holy Face. 32mo,   0 50

HOURS BEFORE THE ALTAR; or, Meditations on the Holy Eucharist. By Mgr. DE LA BOUILLERIE. 32mo,   0 50

HOW TO GET ON. By Rev. BERNARD FEENEY. 12mo,   1 00

HOW TO MAKE THE MISSION. By a Dominican Father. 16mo, paper, 10 cents; per 100,   5 00

HUNOLT'S SERMONS. *Complete Unabridged Edition.* Translated from the original German edition of Cologne, 1740, by the Rev. J. ALLEN, D.D. 12 vols., 8vo, 30 00
  Vols. 1, 2. The Christian State of Life.
  Vols. 3, 4. The Bad Christian.
  Vols. 5, 6. The Penitent Christian.
  Vols. 7, 8. The Good Christian.
  Vols. 9, 10. The Christian's Last End.
  Vols. 11, 12. The Christian's Model.
  His Eminence Cardinal Gibbons, Archbishop of Baltimore: "... Contain a fund of solid doctrine, presented in a clear and forcible style. These sermons should find a place in the library of every priest. ..."

HUNOLT'S SHORT SERMONS. *Abridged Edition.* Arranged for all the Sundays of the year. 8vo, 5 vols., *net*, 10 00

IDOLS; or, The Secret of the Rue Chaussée d'Antin. A novel. By RAOUL DE NAVERY. 12mo, 1 25

ILLUSTRATED PRAYER-BOOK FOR CHILDREN. 32mo, 0 35

IMITATION OF THE BLESSED VIRGIN MARY. After the Model of the Imitation of Christ. Translated by Mrs. A. R. BENNETT GLADSTONE. Small 32mo, 0 50
Edition de luxe, with fine illustrations. 32mo, from 1 50 up.

INSTRUCTIONS ON THE COMMANDMENTS and the Sacraments. By ST. LIGUORI. 32mo. Paper, 0.25; per 100, 12 50
Cloth, 0.35; per 100, 21 00

KONINGS, THEOLOGIA MORALIS. Novissimi Ecclesiæ Doctoris S. Alphonsi. Editio septima, auctior, et novis curis expolitior, curante HENRICO KUPER, C.SS.R. Two vols. in one, half morocco, *net*, 4 00

—— Commentarium in Facultates Apostolicas. New, greatly enlarged edition. 12mo, *net*, 2 25

—— General Confession Made Easy. 32mo, flex., 0 15

LAMP OF THE SANCTUARY. A tale. Wiseman. 48mo, 0 25

LEGENDS AND STORIES OF THE HOLY CHILD JESUS from Many Lands. Collected by A. FOWLER LUTZ. 16mo, 0 75

LEPER QUEEN, THE. A Story of the Thirteenth Century. 16mo, 0 50

LETTERS OF ST. ALPHONSUS LIGUORI. Centenary Edition. 5 vols., 12mo. Each, *net*, 1 25

LIBRARY OF THE RELIGIOUS LIFE. Composed of "Book of the Professed," by the author of "Golden Sands," 3 vols.; "Spiritual Direction," by the author of "Golden Sands"; and "Souvenir of the Novitiate." 5 vols., 32mo, in case, 3 25

LIFE AND ACTS OF LEO XIII. By Rev. JOSEPH E. KELLER, S.J. Fully and beautifully illustrated. 8vo, 2 00

LIFE OF ST. ALOYSIUS GONZAGA. Edited by Rev. F. GOLDIE, S.J. Edition de luxe, richly illustrated. 8vo, *net*, 2 50

LIFE OF THE BLESSED VIRGIN, ILLUSTRATED. Adapted by Rev. RICHARD BRENNAN, LL.D. With fine half-tone illustrations. 12mo, 1 25

LIFE OF CHRIST, ILLUSTRATED. By Father M. v. COCHEM. Adapted by Rev. B. HAMMER, O.S.F. With fine half-tone illustrations. 12mo, 1 25

LIFE OF FATHER CHARLES SIRE. By his brother, Rev. VITAL SIRE. 12mo, *net*, 1 00

LIFE OF ST. CLARE OF MONTEFALCO. By Rev. JOSEPH A. LOCKE, O.S.A. 12mo, *net*, 0 75

LIFE OF THE VEN. MARY CRESCENTIA HÖSS. 12mo, *net*, 1 25

LIFE OF ST. FRANCIS SOLANUS. 16mo, *net*, 0 50

LIFE OF ST. GERMAINE COUSIN. 16mo, 0 50

LIFE OF ST. CHANTAL. See under St. CHANTAL. *net*, 4 00

(LIFE OF) MOST REV. JOHN HUGHES, First Archbishop of New York. By Rev. H. A. BRANN, D.D. 12mo, *net*, 0 75

LIFE OF FATHER JOGUES. By Father FELIX MARTIN, S.J. From the French by JOHN GILMARY SHEA. 12mo, *net*, 0 75

LIFE OF MLLE. LE GRAS. 12mo, *net*, 1 25

LIFE OF MARY FOR CHILDREN. By ANNE R. BENNETT, née GLADSTONE. 24mo, illustrated, *net*, 0 50

LIFE OF RIGHT REV. JOHN N. NEUMANN, D.D. By Rev. E. GRIMM, C.SS.R. 12mo, *net*, 1 25

LIFE OF FR. FRANCIS POILVACHE. 32mo, paper, *net*, 0 20

LIFE OF OUR LORD AND SAVIOUR JESUS CHRIST and of His Blessed Mother. Adapted by Rev. RICHARD BRENNAN, LL.D. With nearly 600 illustrations. No. 1. cloth, *net*, 5 00
No. 3. Morocco back and corners, gilt edges, *net*, 7 00
No. 4. Full morocco, richly gilt back, gilt-edges, *net*, 9 00
No. 5. Full morocco, block-panelled sides, gilt edges, *net*, 10 00

LIFE, POPULAR, OF ST. TERESA OF JESUS. By L'ABBÉ MARIE-JOSEPH. 12mo, *net*, 0 75

LIGUORI, ST. ALPHONSUS DE. Complete Ascetical Works of. Centenary Edition Edited by Rev. EUGENE GRIMM, C.SS.R. Price, per volume, *net*, 1 25

Each book is complete in itself, and any volume will be sold separately.

Preparation for Death.
Way of Salvation and of Perfection.
Great Means of Salvation and Perfection.
Incarnation, Birth, and Infancy of Christ.
The Passion and Death of Christ
The Holy Eucharist.
The Glories of Mary, 2 vols.
Victories of the Martyrs.

True Spouse of Christ, 2 vols.
Dignity and Duties of the Priest.
The Holy Mass.
The Divine Office.
Preaching.
Abridged Sermons for all the Sundays.
Miscellany.
Letters, 4 vols.
Letters and General Index.

LINKED LIVES. A novel. By Lady DOUGLAS. 8vo, 1 50

LITTLE CHILD OF MARY. Large 48mo, 0 25
LITTLE MANUAL OF ST. ANTHONY. Illustrated. 32mo, cloth, 0 60
LITTLE OFFICE OF THE IMMACULATE CONCEPTION. 32mo, paper, 3 cents; per 100, 2 00
LITTLE PICTORIAL LIVES OF THE SAINTS. With Reflections for Every Day in the Year. Edited by JOHN GILMARY SHEA, LL.D. With nearly 400 illustrations. 12mo, cloth, ink and gold side, 1 00
10 copies, 6.25; 25 copies, 15.00; 50 copies, 27.50; 100 copies, 50 00
This book has received the approbation of 30 Archbishops and Bishops.
LITTLE PRAYER-BOOK OF THE SACRED HEART. Prayers and Practices of Blessed Margaret Mary. Sm. 32mo, cloth, 0 40
LITTLE SAINT OF NINE YEARS. From the French of Mgr. DE SEGUR, by MARY McMAHON. 16mo, 0 50
LOURDES. Its Inhabitants, Its Pilgrims, Its Miracles. By R. F. CLARKE, S.J. 16mo, illustrated, 0 75
LUTHER'S OWN STATEMENTS concerning his Teachings and its Results. By HENRY O'CONNOR, S.J. 12mo, paper, 0 15
MANIFESTATION OF CONSCIENCE. Confessions and Communions in Religious Communities. By Rev. PIE DE LANGOGNE, O.M.Cap. 32mo, *net*, 0 50
MANUAL OF THE HOLY EUCHARIST. Conferences and Pious Practices, with Devotions for Mass, etc. Prepared by Rev. F. X. Lasance, Director of the Tabernacle Society of Cincinnati. Oblong 24mo, 0 75
MANUAL OF THE HOLY FAMILY. Prayers and Instructions for Catholic Parents. 32mo, cloth, 0 60
MANUAL OF INDULGENCED PRAYERS. A Complete Prayer-Book. Arranged and disposed for daily use. Small 32mo, 0 40
MARCELLA GRACE. A novel. By ROSA MULHOLLAND. With illustrations after original drawings. 12mo, 1 25
MARRIAGE. By Very Rev. PÈRE MONSABRÉ, O.P. From the French, by M. HOPPER. 12mo, *net*, 1 00
MAY DEVOTIONS, NEW. Reflections on the Invocations of the Litany of Loretto. 12mo, *net*, 1 00
McCALLEN, REV. JAMES A., S.S. Sanctuary Boy's Illustrated Manual. 12mo, *net*, 0 50
——— Office of Tenebræ. 12mo, *net*, 1 00
——— Appendix. Containing Harmonizations of the Lamentations. 12mo, *net*, 0 75
MEANS OF GRACE, THE. A Complete Exposition of the Seven Sacraments, of the Sacramentals, and of Prayer, with a Comprehensive Explanation of the "Lord's Prayer" and the "Hail Mary." By Rev. RICHARD BRENNAN, LL.D. With 180 full-page and other illustrations. 8vo, cloth, 2.50; gilt edges, 3.00; Library edition, half levant, 3 50
MEDITATIONS (BAXTER) for Every Day in the Year. By Rev. ROGER BAXTER, S.J. Small 12mo, *net*, 1 25

MEDITATIONS (CHAIGNON, S.J.) FOR THE USE OF THE SECULAR CLERGY. By Father CHAIGNON, S.J. From the French, by Rt. Rev. L. DE GOESBRIAND, D.D. 2 vols., 8vo, *net*, 4 00

MEDITATIONS (HAMON'S) FOR ALL THE DAYS OF THE YEAR. For the use of Priests, Religious, and the Laity. By Rev. M. HAMON, SS., Pastor of St. Sulpice, Paris. From the French, by Mrs. ANNE R. BENNETT-GLADSTONE. With Alphabetic Index. 5 vols., 16mo, cloth, gilt top, each with a Steel Engraving. *net*, 5 00

"Hamon's doctrine is the unadulterated word of God, presented with unction, exquisite taste, and freed from that exaggerated and sickly sentimentalism which disgusts when it does not mislead."—MOST REV. P. L. CHAPELLE, D.D.

MEDITATIONS (PERINALDO) on the Sufferings of Jesus Christ. From the Italian of Rev. FRANCIS DA PERINALDO, O.S.F. 12mo, *net*, 0 75

MEDITATIONS (VERCRUYSSE), for Every Day in the Year, on the Life of Our Lord Jesus Christ. By the Rev. Father BRUNO VERCRUYSSE, S.J. 2 vols., *net*, 2 75

MEDITATIONS ON THE PASSION OF OUR LORD. By a PASSIONIST FATHER. 32mo, 0 40

MISSION BOOK of the Redemptorist Fathers. 32mo, cloth, 0 50

MISSION BOOK FOR THE MARRIED. By Very Rev. F. GIRARDEY, C.SS.R. 32mo, 0 50

MISSION BOOK FOR THE SINGLE. By Very Rev. F. GIRARDEY, C.SS.R. 32mo, 0 50

MISTRESS OF NOVICES, The, Instructed in her Duties. From the French of the ABBÉ LEGUAY, by Rev. IGNATIUS SISK. 12mo, cloth, *net*, 0 75

MOMENTS BEFORE THE TABERNACLE. By Rev. MATTHEW RUSSELL, S.J. 24mo, *net*, 0 40

MONK'S PARDON. A Historical Romance of the Time of Philip IV. of Spain. By RAOUL DE NAVERY. 12mo, 1 25

MONTH OF THE DEAD. 32mo, 0 75

MONTH OF MAY. From the French of Father DEBUSSI, S J., by ELLA MCMAHON. 32mo, 0 50

MONTH OF THE SACRED HEART. HUGUET. 0 75

MONTH, NEW, OF MARY, St. Francis de Sales. 32mo, 0 40

MONTH, NEW, OF THE SACRED HEART, St. Francis de Sales. 32mo, 0 40

MONTH, NEW, OF ST. JOSEPH, St. Francis de Sales. 32mo, 0 40

MONTH, NEW, OF THE HOLY ANGELS, St. Francis de Sales. 32mo, 0 40

MOOTED QUESTIONS OF HISTORY. By H. DESMOND. 16mo, 0 75

MR. BILLY BUTTONS. A novel. By WALTER LECKY. 12mo, 1 25

MY FIRST COMMUNION: The Happiest Day of My Life. BRENNAN. 16mo, illustrated, 0 75

MÜLLER, REV. MICHAEL, C.SS.R. God the Teacher of Mankind. A plain, comprehensive Explanation of Christian Doctrine. 9 vols, crown 8vo. Per set, *net*, 9 50
    The Church and Her Enemies. *net*, 1 10
    The Apostles' Creed. *net*, 1 10
    The First and Greatest Commandment. *net*, 1 40
    Explanation of the Commandments, continued. Precepts of the Church. *net*, 1 10
    Dignity, Authority, and Duties of Parents, Ecclesiastical and Civil Powers. Their Enemies. *net*, 1 40
    Grace and the Sacraments. *net*, 1 25
    Holy Mass. *net*, 1 25
    Eucharist and Penance. *net*, 1 10
    Sacramentals—Prayer, etc. *net*, 1 00

—— Familiar Explanation of Catholic Doctrine. 12mo, 1 00

—— The Prodigal Son; or, The Sinner's Return to God. 8vo, *net*, 1 00

—— The Devotion of the Holy Rosary and the Five Scapulars. 8vo, *net*, 0 75

—— The Catholic Priesthood. 2 vols., 8vo, *net*, 3 00

NAMES THAT LIVE IN CATHOLIC HEARTS. By ANNA T. SADLIER. 12mo, 1 00

NEW TESTAMENT, THE. Illustrated Edition. With 100 fine full page illustrations. Printed in two colors. 16mo, *net*, 0 60
    The advantages of this edition over others consist in its beautiful illustrations, its convenient size, its clear, open type, and substantial and attractive binding. It is the best adapted for general use on account of its compactness and low price.

OFFICE, COMPLETE, OF HOLY WEEK, in Latin and English. 24mo, cloth, 0.50; cloth, limp, gilt edges, 1 00
    Also in finer bindings.

O'GRADY, ELEANOR. Aids to Correct and Effective Elocution. 12mo, 1 25

—— Select Recitations for Schools and Academies. 12mo, 1 00

—— Readings and Recitations for Juniors. 16mo, *net*, 0 50

—— Elocution Class. 16mo, *net*, 0 50

ON CHRISTIAN ART. By EDITH HEALY. 16mo, 0 50

ON THE ROAD TO ROME, and How Two Brothers Got There. By WILLIAM RICHARDS. 16mo, 0 50

ONE AND THIRTY DAYS WITH BLESSED MARGARET MARY. 32mo, flexible cloth, 0 25

ONE ANGEL MORE IN HEAVEN. With Letters of Condolence by St. Francis de Sales and others. White mor., 0 50

OUR BIRTHDAY BOUQUET. Culled from the Shrines of Saints and the Gardens of Poets. By E. C. DONNELLY. 16mo, 1 00

OUR FAVORITE DEVOTIONS. By Very Rev. Dean A. A. LINGS. 24mo, 0 60
    While there are many excellent books of devotion, there is none made on the plans of this one, giving ALL the devotions in general use among the faithful. It will be found a very serviceable book.

OUR FAVORITE NOVENAS. By the Very Rev. Dean A. A.
LINGS. 24mo, 0 60
Gives forms of prayer for all the novenas for the feasts of Our Lord, the Blessed Virgin, and the Saints which pious custom has established.

OUR LADY OF GOOD COUNSEL IN GENAZZANO. By
ANNE R. BENNETT, née GLADSTONE. 32mo, 0 75

OUR OWN WILL, and How to Detect it in our Actions. By Rev.
JOHN ALLEN, D.D. 16mo, *net*, 0 75

OUR YOUNG FOLKS' LIBRARY. 10 volumes. 12mo. Each,
0 45; per set, 3 00

OUTLAW OF CAMARGUE, THE. A novel. By A. DE LAMOTHE,
12mo, 1 25

OUTLINES OF DOGMATIC THEOLOGY. By Rev. SYLVESTER
J. HUNTER, S.J. 3 vols, 12mo, *net*, 4 50

PARADISE ON EARTH OPENED TO ALL; or, A Religious
Vocation the Surest Way in Life. 32mo, *net*, 0 40

PASSING SHADOWS. A novel. By ANTHONY YORKE. 12mo, 1 25

PEARLS FROM FABER. Selected and arranged by MARION J.
BRUNOWE. 32mo, 0 50

PETRONILLA, and other Stories. By E. C. DONNELLY. 12mo, 1 00

PHILOSOPHY, ENGLISH MANUALS OF CATHOLIC.
    Logic. By RICHARD F. CLARKE, S.J. 12mo, *net*, 1 25
    First Principles of Knowledge. By JOHN RICKABY. S J.
    12mo, *net*, 1 25
    Moral Philosophy (Ethics and Natural Law). By JOSEPH
    RICKABY, S.J. 12mo, *net*, 1 25
    Natural Theology. By BERNARD BOEDDER, S.J. 12mo. *net*, 1 50
    Psychology. By MICHAEL MAHER, S.J. 12mo, *net*, 1 50
    General Metaphysics. By JOHN RICKABY. S.J. 12mo, *net*, 1 25
    Manual of Political Economy. By C. S. DEVAS. 12mo, *net*, 1 50

PEW-RENT RECEIPT BOOK. 800 receipts, *net*, 1 00

PICTORIAL LIVES OF THE SAINTS. With Reflections for
Every Day in the Year. 50th Thousand. 8vo, 2 00
5 copies, 6.65; 10 copies, 12.50; 25 copies, 27.50; 50 copies, 50 00

POPULAR INSTRUCTIONS ON MARRIAGE. By Very Rev.
F. GIRARDEY, C.SS.R. 32mo. Paper, 0.25; per 100, 12 50
Cloth, 0.35; per 100, 21 00

POPULAR INSTRUCTIONS TO PARENTS on the Bringing Up
of Children. By Very Rev. F. GIRARDEY, C.SS.R. 32mo.
Paper, 0 25; per 100, 12.50. Cloth, 0.35; per 100, 21 00

PRAYER. The Great Means of Obtaining Salvation. LIGUORI.
32mo, 0 50

PRAYER-BOOK FOR LENT. Meditations and Prayers for Lent.
32mo, cloth, 0 50

PRAXIS SYNODALIS. Manuale Synodi Diocesanæ ac Provincialis Celebrandæ. 12mo, *net*, 0 60

PRIEST IN THE PULPIT, THE. A Manual of Homiletics and
Catechetics. SCHUECH-LUEBBERMANN. 8vo, *net*, 1 50

PRIMER FOR CONVERTS, A. By Rev. J. T. DURWARD. 32mo,
flexible cloth, 0 25

PRINCIPLES OF ANTHROPOLOGY AND BIOLOGY. By Rev THOMAS HUGHES, S.J 16mo, *net*, 0 75

REASONABLENESS OF CATHOLIC CEREMONIES AND PRACTICES. By Rev. J. J. BURKE. 12mo, flexible cloth, 0 35

READING AND THE MIND, WITH SOMETHING TO READ. O'CONOR, S J. 12mo, *net*, 0 50

REGISTRUM BAPTISMORUM 3,200 registers. 11 x 16 inches, *net*, 3 50

REGISTRUM MATRIMONIORUM. 3,200 registers. 11 x 16 inches, *net*, 3 50

RELIGIOUS STATE, THE. With a Short Treatise on Vocation to the Priesthood. By ST. ALPHONSUS LIGUORI. 32mo, 0 50

REMINISCENCES OF RT. REV. EDGAR P. WADHAMS, D.D., By Rev. C. A. WALWORTH. 12mo, illustrated, *net*, 1 00

RIGHTS OF OUR LITTLE ONES; or, First Principles of Education in Catechetical Form. By Rev. JAMES CONWAY, S.J 32mo, paper, 0.15; per 100. 9.00; cloth, 0.25; per 100, 15 00

ROSARY, THE MOST HOLY, in Thirty-one Meditations, Prayers, and Examples. By Rev. EUGENE GRIMM, C.SS.R. 32mo, 0 50

ROUND TABLE, A, of the Representative *American* Catholic Novelists, containing the best stories by the best writers. With half-tone portraits, printed in colors, biographical sketches, etc. 12mo, 1 50

ROUND TABLE, A, of the Representative *Irish and English* Catholic Novelists, containing the best stories by the best writers. With half-tone portraits, printed in colors, biographical sketches, etc. 12mo, 1 50

RUSSO, N., S.J.—De Philosophia Morali Prælectiones in Collegio Georgiopolitano Soc. Jes. Anno 1889-1890 Habitæ, a Patre NICOLAO RUSSO. Editio altera. 8vo, half leather, *net*, 2 00

SACRAMENT OF PENANCE, THE. Lenten Sermons. Paper, *net*, 0 25

SACRIFICE OF THE MASS WORTHILY CELEBRATED, THE. By the Rev. Father CHAIGNON, S.J. Translated by Rt. Rev. L. DE GOESBRIAND, D.D. 8vo, *net*, 1 50

SACRISTY RITUAL. Rituale Compendiosum, seu Ordo Administrandi quædam Sacramenta et alia officia Ecclesiastica Rite peragendi ex Rituali Romano novissime edito desumptas. 16mo. flexible, *net*, 0 75

ST. CHANTAL AND THE FOUNDATION OF THE VISITATION. By Monseigneur BOUGAUD. 2 vols., 8vo, *net*, 4 00

ST. JOSEPH OUR ADVOCATE. From the French of Rev. Father HUGUET, 24mo, 1 00

SACRAMENTALS OF THE HOLY CATHOLIC CHURCH, THE. By Rev. A. A. LAMBING, LL.D. Illustrated edition. 24mo.

Paper, 0.25; 25 copies, 4.25; 50 copies, 7.50; 100 copies, 12 50
Cloth, 0.50; 25 copies, 8.50; 50 copies, 15.00; 100 copies, 25 00

SACRED HEART, BOOKS ON THE.
 Child's Prayer-Book of the Sacred Heart. Small 32mo,   0 25
 Devotions to the Sacred Heart for the First Friday. 32mo, 0 40
 Imitation of the Sacred Heart of Jesus. By Rev. F. ARNOUDT, S.J. From the Latin by Rev. J. M. FASTRÉ, S.J. 16mo, cloth, 1 25
 Little Prayer-Book of the Sacred Heart. Small 32mo,   0 40
 Month of the Sacred Heart of Jesus. HUGUET. 32mo,   0 75
 Month of the Sacred Heart for the Young Christian. By BROTHER PHILIPPE. 32mo,   0 50
 New Month of the Sacred Heart, St. Francis de Sales. 32mo, 0 40
 One and Thirty Days with Blessed Margaret Mary. 32mo, 0 25
 Pearls from the Casket of the Sacred Heart of Jesus. 32mo, 0 50
 Revelations of the Sacred Heart to Blessed Margaret Mary; and the History of her Life. BOUGAUD. 8vo,   *net*, 1 50
 Sacred Heart Studied in the Sacred Scriptures. By Rev. H. SAINTRAIN, C.SS.R. 8vo,   *net*, 2 00
 Six Sermons on Devotion to the Sacred Heart of Jesus. BIERBAUM. 16mo,   *net*, 0 60
 Year of the Sacred Heart. Drawn from the works of PÈRE DE LA COLOMBIÈRE, of Margaret Mary, and of others. 32mo, 0 50

SACRED RHETORIC. 12mo,   *net*, 0 75

SECRET OF SANCTITY, THE. According to ST. FRANCIS DE SALES and Father CRASSET, S.J. 12mo,   *net*, 1 00

SERAPHIC GUIDE. A Manual for the Members of the Third Order of St. Francis.   0 60
 Roan, red edges,   0 75
 The same in German at the same prices.

SERMONS. See also "Sacrament of Penance," "Seven Last Words," "Two-Edged Sword," and "Hunolt."

SERMONS. EIGHT SHORT PRACTICAL, ON MIXED MARRIAGES. By Rev. A. A. LAMBING, LL.D. Paper, *net*, 0 25

SERMONS, OLD AND NEW. 8 vols., 8vo,   *net*, 16 00

SERMONS, LENTEN. Large 8vo,   *net*, 2 00

SERMONS, FUNERAL. 2 vols.,   *net*, 2 00

SERMONS ON THE CHRISTIAN VIRTUES. By the Rev. F. HUNOLT, S.J. Translated by Rev. J. ALLEN, D.D. 2 vols., 8vo,   *net*, 5 00

SERMONS ON THE DIFFERENT STATES OF LIFE. By Rev. F. HUNOLT, S.J. Translated by Rev. J. ALLEN, D.D. 2 vols., 8vo,   *net*, 5 00

SERMONS ON THE SEVEN DEADLY SINS. By Rev. F. HUNOLT, S.J. Translated by Rev. J. ALLEN, D.D. 2 vols., 8vo.,   *net*, 5 00

SERMONS ON PENANCE. By Rev. F. HUNOLT, S.J. Translated by Rev. J. ALLEN, D.D. 2 vols., 8vo,   *net*, 5 00

SERMONS ON OUR LORD, THE BLESSED VIRGIN, AND THE SAINTS. By Rev. F. HUNOLT, S.J. Translated by Rev. J. ALLEN, D.D. 2 vols., 8vo, *net*, 5 00
SERMONS ON THE BLESSED VIRGIN. By Very Rev. D. I. McDERMOTT. 16mo, *net*, 0 75
SERMONS, abridged, for all the Sundays and Holydays. By ST. ALPHONSUS LIGUORI. 12mo, *net*, 1 25
SERMONS for the Sundays and Chief Festivals of the Ecclesiastical Year. With Two Courses of Lenten Sermons and a Triduum for the Forty Hours. By Rev. JULIUS POTTGEISSER, S.J. From the German by Rev. JAMES CONWAY, S.J. 2 vols., 8vo, *net*, 2 50
SERMONS ON THE MOST HOLY ROSARY. By Rev. M. J. FRINGS. 12mo, *net*, 1 00
SERMONS, SHORT, FOR LOW MASSES. A complete, brief course of instruction on Christian Doctrine. By Rev. F. X. SCHOUPPE, S.J. 12mo, *net*, 1 25
SERMONS, SIX, on Devotion to the Sacred Heart of Jesus. From the German of Rev. Dr. E. BIERBAUM, by ELLA McMAHON, 16mo, *net*, 0 60
SEVEN LAST WORDS ON THE CROSS. Sermons. Paper, *net*, 0 25
SHORT CONFERENCES ON THE LITTLE OFFICE OF THE IMMACULATE CONCEPTION. By Very Rev. JOSEPH RAINER. With Prayers. 32mo, 0 50
SHORT STORIES ON CHRISTIAN DOCTRINE: A Collection of Examples Illustrating the Catechism. From the French by MARY McMAHON. 12mo, illustrated, *net*, 0 75
SMITH, Rev. S. B., D.D. Elements of Ecclesiastical Law.
    Vol. I. Ecclesiastical Persons. 8vo, *net*, 2 50
    Vol. II. Ecclesiastical Trials. 8vo, *net*, 2 50
    Vol. III. Ecclesiastical Punishments. 8vo, *net*, 2 50
—— Compendium Juris Canonici, ad Usum Cleri et Seminariorum hujus regionis accommodatum. 8vo, *net*, 2 00
—— The Marriage Process in the United States. 8vo, *net*, 2 50
SODALISTS VADE MECUM. A Manual, Prayer-Book, and Hymnal. 32mo, cloth, 0 50
SOUVENIR OF THE NOVITIATE. From the French by Rev. EDWARD I. TAYLOR. 32mo, *net*, 0 60
SPIRITUAL CRUMBS FOR HUNGRY LITTLE SOULS. To which are added Stories from the Bible. RICHARDSON. 16mo, 0 50
STANG, Rev. WILLIAM, D.D. Pastoral Theology. New enlarged edition. 8vo, *net*, 1 50
—— Eve of the Reformation. 12mo, paper, *net*, 0 50
STORIES FOR FIRST COMMUNICANTS, for the Time before and after First Communion. By Rev. J. A. KELLER, D.D. 32mo, 0 50
SUMMER AT WOODVILLE, A. By ANNA T. SADLIER. 16mo 0 50

SURE WAY TO A HAPPY MARRIAGE. A Book of Instructions for those Betrothed and for Married People. From the German by Rev. EDWARD I. TAYLOR. Paper, 0.25; per 100, 12.50; cloth, 0.35; per 100, 21 00

TALES AND LEGENDS OF THE MIDDLE AGES. From the Spanish of F. DE P. CAPELLA. By HENRY WILSON. 16mo, 0 75

TAMING OF POLLY, THE. By ELLA LORAINE DORSEY. 12mo, 0 85

TANQUEREY, Rev. Ad., S.S. Synopsis Theologiæ Fundamentalis 8vo, *net*, 1 50

—— Synopsis Theologia Dogmatica Specialis. 2 vols., 8vo, *net*, 3 00

THINK WELL ON'T; or, Reflections on the Great Truths of the Christian Religion. By the Right Rev. R. CHALLONER, D.D. 32mo, flexible cloth, 0 20

THOUGHT FROM ST. ALPHONSUS, for Every Day of the Year. 32mo, 0 50

THOUGHT FROM BENEDICTINE SAINTS. 32mo, 0 50

THOUGHT FROM DOMINICAN SAINTS. 32mo, 0 50

THOUGHT FROM ST. FRANCIS ASSISI and his Saints. 32mo, 0 50

THOUGHT FROM ST. IGNATIUS. 32mo, 0 50

THOUGHT FROM ST. TERESA. 32mo, 0 50

THOUGHT FROM ST. VINCENT DE PAUL. 32mo, 0 50

THOUGHTS AND COUNSELS FOR THE CONSIDERATION OF CATHOLIC YOUNG MEN. By Rev. P. A. VON DOSS, S.J. 12mo, *net*, 1 25

THREE GIRLS AND ESPECIALLY ONE. By MARION AMES TAGGART. 16mo, 0 50

TRUE POLITENESS. Addressed to Religious. By Rev. FRANCIS DEMARE. 16mo, *net*, 0 60

TRUE SPOUSE OF CHRIST. By ST. ALPHONSUS LIGUORI. 2 vols., 12mo, *net*, 2.50; 1 vol., 12mo, 1 50

TWELVE VIRTUES, THE, of a Good Teacher. For Mothers, Instructors, etc. By Rev. H. POTTIER, S J. 32mo, *net*, 0 30

TWO-EDGED SWORD, THE. Lenten Sermons. Paper. *net*, 0 25

TWO RETREATS FOR SISTERS. By Rev. E. ZOLLNER. 12mo, *net*, 1 00

VADE MECUM SACERDOTUM. Continens Preces ante et post Missam modum providendi Infirmos nec non multas Benedictionum Formulas. 48mo, cloth, *net*, 0.25; morocco, flexible, *net*, 0 50

VISIT TO EUROPE AND THE HOLY LAND. By Rev. H. F. FAIRBANKS. 12mo, illustrated, 1 50

VISITS TO THE MOST HOLY SACRAMENT and to the Blessed Virgin Mary. For Every Day of the Month. By ST. ALPHONSUS DE LIGUORI. Edited by Rev. EUGENE GRIMM. 32mo, 0 50

VOCATIONS EXPLAINED: Matrimony, Virginity, the Religious State, and the Priesthood. By a Vincentian Father. 16mo, flexible, 10 cents; per 100, 5 00
WARD, REV. THOS. F. Fifty-two Instructions on the Principal Truths of Our Holy Religion. 12mo, *net*, 0 75
—— Thirty-two Instructions for the Month of May and for the Feasts of the Blessed Virgin. 12mo, *net*, 0 75
—— Month of May at Mary's Altar. 12mo, *net*, 0 75
—— Short Instructions for all the Sundays and Holydays. 12mo, *net*, 1 25
WAY OF INTERIOR PEACE. By Rev. Father DE LEHEN, S.J. From the German Version of Rev. J. BRUCKER, S.J. 12mo, *net*, 1 25
WAY OF THE CROSS. Illustrated. Paper, 5 cents; per 100, 3 00
WHAT CATHOLICS HAVE DONE FOR SCIENCE, with Sketches of the Great Catholic Scientists. By Rev. MARTIN S. BRENNAN. 12mo, 1 00
WOMAN OF FORTUNE, A. A novel. By CHRISTIAN REID. 12mo, 1 25
WOMEN OF CATHOLICITY: Margaret O'Carroll—Isabella of Castile—Margaret Roper—Marie de l'Incarnation—Margaret Bourgeoys—Ethan Allen's Daughter. By ANNA T. SADLIER. 12mo, 1 00
WORDS OF JESUS CHRIST DURING HIS PASSION, Explained in their Literal and Moral Sense. By Rev. F. X. SCHOUPPE, S.J. Flexible cloth, 0 25
WORDS OF WISDOM. A Concordance of the Sapiential Books. 12mo, *net*, 1 25
WUEST, REV. JOSEPH, C.SS.R. DEVOTIO QUADRAGINTA HORARUM. 32mo, *net*, 0 25
YOUNG GIRL'S BOOK OF PIETY. 16mo, 1 00
ZEAL IN THE WORK OF THE MINISTRY; or, The Means by which every Priest may render his Ministry Honorable and Fruitful. From the French of L'ABBÉ DUBOIS. 8vo, *net*, 1 50

AN AMERICAN INDUSTRY. A full description of the Silversmith's Art and Ecclesiastical Metalwork as carried on in Benziger Brothers' Factory of Church Goods, De Kalb Avenue and Rockwell Place, Brooklyn, N. Y. Small quarto, 48 pp., with 75 illustrations, printed in two colors. Mailed gratis on application.

This interesting book gives a full description of the various arts employed in the manufacture of Church goods, from the designing and modelling, through the different branches of casting, spinning, chasing, buffing, gilding, and burnishing. The numerous beautiful half-tone illustrations show the machinery and tools used, as well as rich specimens of the work turned out.

www.ingramcontent.com/pod-product-compliance
Lightning Source LLC
Chambersburg PA
CBHW020241240426
43672CB00006B/603